BUILDING STRONG NATIONS

Building Strong Nations
Improving Governability and Public Management

ERAN VIGODA-GADOT
University of Haifa, Israel

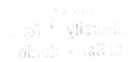
ASHGATE

Published by
Ashgate Publishing Limited
Wey Court East
Union Road
Farnham
Surrey, GU9 7PT
England

Ashgate Publishing Company
Suite 420
101 Cherry Street
Burlington
VT 05401-4405
USA

www.ashgate.com

British Library Cataloguing in Publication Data
Vigoda-Gadot, Eran, 1966-
    Building strong nations : improving governability and
    public management
    1. Political stability 2. Legitimacy of governments
    3. Public administration 4. Democracy
    I. Title
    320'.011

Library of Congress Cataloging-in-Publication Data
Vigoda-Gadot, Eran, 1966-
    Building strong nations : improving governability and public management / by Eran
Vigoda-Gadot.
        p. cm.
    Includes bibliographical references and index.
    ISBN 978-0-7546-7546-4 (hardcover) 1. Bureaucracy. 2. Democracy. I.
Title.

    JF1501.V54 2008
    351--dc22

                                                                2008029509

ISBN 978 0 7546 7546 4

Mixed Sources
Product group from well-managed
forests and other controlled sources
www.fsc.org Cert no. SA-COC-1565
© 1996 Forest Stewardship Council
FSC

Printed and bound in Great Britain by
MPG Books Ltd, Bodmin, Cornwall.

Contents

List of Figures   *vii*
List of Tables   *ix*
Preface   *xi*
Acknowledgements   *xiii*
Framework of the Book   *xvii*
Target Readers   *xxi*

Introduction
   Strong Nations, Weak Nations, and the Enigma
   of Effective Governability   1

PART I   The State of Modern Nations and the Rebirth of an Old Paradox   5

1   Theoretical Approaches to Nation Building   7

2   Dilemmas of Governability Under Democratic
   and Bureaucratic Constraints   29

PART II   Caught Between Democracy and Bureaucracy: An Anthology
   of Empirical Examinations   45

3   The Power of Bureaucracy: Managerial Quality and Performance   47

4   The Charm of Democracy: Building on Democratic Values
   and Good Citizenship   67

5   Empirical Evidence: A Longitudinal National Study of Bureaucracy
   and Democracy in Israel   93

PART III   Strong Nations and Reconciliation of the
   Democratic–Bureaucratic Paradox: Several Alternatives   149

6   Strong Nations and Collaboration in Public Administration:
   A Myth or Necessity?   151

7   Strong Nations and Innovation in the Public Sector   165

8   Strong Nations and Global Reforms in Public Administration:
       A New, Borderless Public Policy   187

9   Building Strong Nations by Effective Governability
       in a Democratic Cosmos   195

Appendix – The Questionnaire   *211*
Bibliography   *225*
Index   *249*

List of Figures

1.1   Theoretical approaches to nation building   8
1.2   Trust in American governmental institutions
      (support by percentage)   15
1.3   Trust in the European civil service (support by percentage)   16
1.4   Trust in the civil service, World Values Study, OECD
      countries, percentage showing a great deal or quite a lot
      of confidence in the civil service (1995–2000)   17
2.1   World economic growth: A historical view of gross
      global product per capita (GGP) portrait   34
2.2   World economic growth in the second half of the
      twentieth century   36
2.3   Expected world per capita global gross product (GGP) until 2050   36
2.4   The pyramidal paradox of democracy and bureaucracy   43
4.1   Good citizenship behavior: Dimensionality and level of analysis   77
5.1   The relationship between trust and public sector performance   97
5.2   Research model   107
5.3   Three proposed models of bureaucracy–democracy
      interaction portrait   122
5.4   Aftermaths to organizational politics and ethics in public
      administration: A citizens' perspective of satisfaction,
      trust, and voice orientations   137
5.5   A revised model: Path coefficients (β) and effect size (ES)
      (in parentheses)   143
5.6   The change in the research variables during the years of the study   144
7.1   Basic system-approach to innovation   170
7.2   Innovation in classic public administration   171
7.3   Innovation in the modern business arena   172
7.4   Innovation in New Public Management   175
7.5   Innovation in a global post-managerial public administration   177
9.1   Building strong nations by reconciliation of the
      democratic–bureaucratic paradox   195
9.2   Collaboration and citizenship for strong nations   202

List of Tables

2.1	A simple typology of instrument types	32
2.2	A simple typology of governance types	33
5.1	Psychometric characteristics of the variables over time	95
5.2	Descriptive statistics and inter-correlations for the study variables (reliabilities in parentheses)	100
5.3	Goodness of fit summary for the research models	101
5.4	Path coefficients and explained variance (R2) for the models	102
5.5	Psychometric characteristics of the variables in each of the yearly samples (2001–2005)	111
5.6	Correlation matrix (pairwise deletion) for the research variables (reliabilities in parentheses)	112
5.7	Multiple regression analysis (standardized coefficients) for the effect of the independent variables on perceived managerial quality of the public sector (MQ) and on perceived public sector performance (PSP)	113
5.8	Multiple hierarchical regression analysis (standardized coefficients) for the relationship between the independent variables, trust in administrative agencies, and democratic participatory behavior	114
5.9	Descriptive statistics and inter-correlations matrix (reliabilities in parentheses) for the public personnel sample	125
5.10	Descriptive statistics and inter-correlations matrix (reliabilities in parentheses) for the citizens sample	126
5.11	Goodness of fit indices	126
5.12	Path coefficients and explained variance	127
5.13	Correlation matrix among the research variables for the combined sample (2001–2005)	141
5.14	Multiple regression analysis for the direct effect of Organizational Politics (OP) and Ethics (ET) on Satisfaction with Services (SWS), Trust in government (TRS), Political Efficacy (PE), and Political Participation (PP) (standardized coefficients; t-test in parentheses)	142
5.15	Hierarchical regression analysis for the effect of Organizational Politics (OP) and Ethics Perceptions on Political Efficacy (PE) and Political Participation (PP) (standardized coefficients; t-test in parentheses)	143

7.1   An evolutionary analysis of innovation in public
        administration: Towards building strong nations   178
8.1   Policy transfer and diffusion perspectives on policy change   190
9.1   Building strong nations with two types of citizenship profiles
        and possible interrelationships   203

Preface

We live in an era of dramatic political, economic, and social changes with strong global effects in almost every segment of our life. New nations are born, and old nations disintegrate. The world order is shifting from bi-polar to uni-polar to multi-polar and perhaps back again. World security is being threatened by non-conventional risks of global terror, political extremism, and violence of a kind we have never witnessed before. The economy is prospering in some parts of the globe, with too little positive spillover onto other parts that remain underdeveloped and in despair. Rapid changes in technology, communication, knowledge creation and dissemination, transition of capital, and environmental quality will obviously have long-term effects on our future lives and our quality of life. Moreover, the modern world is comprised of a growing number of independent states but none of them can function independently in the global village. Global trends in finance, trade, commerce, employment, and manufacturing lead to positive changes, but also bring challenges such as worldwide social pandemics and environmental problems that humanity has never before confronted. While modernity has brought prosperity to various parts of the world, in many other parts, indeed, in too many other parts, it has had little positive impact. Our children will probably have to grapple with the results of these trends that reflect shortsighted governmental policies, locally, nationally, and internationally. Undoubtedly, all these transformations affect humankind regardless of geography, nationality, citizenship, and socio-political status. Their meaning and aftermaths will remain with us for many years to come.

In the face of these challenges and changes, some may even say because of them, one major dilemma looms large for citizens and leaders worldwide. How can we ensure that our countries address these challenges successfully? How do we create effective mechanisms that have the potential of overcoming the instability and uncertainty to which the rapid transformation of values, beliefs, and priorities in our world often gives birth? And who is responsible for instituting and managing these necessary changes and reforms for the public? Putting it another way, what path we must follow in order to build strong nations that ensure our safety and wealth for generations? The search for answers to these questions was the main impetus for writing this book. And, as I will argue and attempt to demonstrate, the answer can be found in a better match between the nature of modern bureaucracy and the spirit of modern democracy, as well as by improving methods and ideas for "cleaver governance" and better governability. The book will therefore try to suggest potential directions for improving governability and public management against the backdrop of the tension between bureaucracy and democracy that has given rise to increasing mistrust of and lack of confidence in public institutions.

For several years, I have been interested in the mechanisms and processes of rebuilding trust in government by improving the performance of public administration agencies. This process requires the integration of theory, knowledge, experience, and practices of various social disciplines. The main goal of this book is therefore to suggest several possible answers to the paradox of building strong nations in a weakening international system, particularly by enacting enlightened public sector reforms, leveraging globalization, and increasing collaboration among partners in modern nations. The book tries to point to potential mechanisms that may support long-range positive reforms in state management and by so doing, also promote new and creative avenues for building strong and stable nations in our chaotic world.

Obviously, complicated and ambitious questions like these call for equally complicated and creative answers. These answers are driven by two major engines of change – the *power of bureaucracy* and the *spirit and rule of democracy,* both of which lead to the book's central thesis: *Building strong nations is very much about the reconciliation of the bureaucratic–democratic paradox.* Furthermore, the best possible way to create such a reconciliation is by promoting innovation, creativity, and global reforms in public administration (Vigoda-Gadot et al., 2005b; Levi-Faur and Vigoda-Gadot, 2004a, 2004b, 2006), and by increasing collaboration among social, political, and business partners (Vigoda-Gadot, 2002b, 2003a). Finally, the book advances the idea that the major partners, and perhaps even initiators and facilitators of these reforms are our communities, supported by the rising power of civic society. Thus, genuine participation in decision-making, especially by individual citizens, independently or in an organized manner through social groups, interest groups, social movements, charities, and other social platforms, becomes essential and crucial. The above mechanisms are an important vehicle for regaining citizens' trust in government on one hand and ensuring governments' belief in and empowerment of citizens on the other. Both governments and citizens, as partners, are the essence and the target of the modernization and advancement of a prosperous democratic society. Hence, this book hopes to enrich the discussion about moving modern nations forward despite major problems such as the clash of ideologies, the overburdening of and expectations from public administration, and the growing instability in world economics and international relations. I believe that such a discourse is useful and essential for meeting future policy challenges that will confront modern nations in the third millennium.

Acknowledgements

The genesis of this work began with numerous of articles that I published, alone and with several other colleagues over the past decade. During this period, I spent time in American and European universities and met a number of people who had a strong influence on my thinking and understanding of the twilight zone between democracy and bureaucracy. The journey began in 1999, soon after I completed my doctorate at the University of Haifa, under the supervision of Professor Aaron Cohen. I owe a great debt to Aaron for being the first to open the doors of research to me in the very first years of my exploration of academic work. My dissertation dealt with the elusive phenomenon of organizational politics in public administration systems and its relevancy for the Israeli public sector. With time, the issue of organizational politics, ethics, and effective management, especially in the public sector arena, became one of my major fields of interests. As evident from this book, it continues to be a core facet of my explorations of the nature of bureaucracy. Moreover, several papers resulted from my work on organizational politics and served as core ideas in my thinking about political behavior, good citizenship behavior, and the nexus between them. For this initial mentoring, I am grateful to Aaron, who is today my closest friend and colleague in the Division of Public Administration and Policy at the University of Haifa.

As a postdoctoral fellow at the University of Georgia, I spent many hours with Professor Robert T. Golembiewski who encouraged me to further explore questions of citizenship, performance, and innovation in the public sector. The first fruits of our discussions were published under the title "Citizenship Behavior and the spirit of New Managerialsim: A Theoretical Framework and Challenge for Governance" in the *American Review of Public Administration* (2001), vol. 31, 273–95. A few years later, I published a second essay, developing our original views, under the title, "Rethinking Citizenship in Public Administration: One More Look in a Series" in *Current Topics in Management* (2005), vol. 10, 241–61. Both of these essays serve as cornerstones of my discussion about citizenship and citizenship behavior as a central apparatus for resolving the bureaucratic–democratic paradox.

Another source that influenced my thinking was the intense interest I have had over the years in the meaning of good citizenship behavior and in the relationship between the citizenry, governance, and the business sector. I published several essays on this topic, some of which I wrote alone, but many of which I co-authored with my colleague, Shlomo Mizrahi, from Ben-Gurion University of the Negev. Among them are "Are You Being Served? The Responsiveness of Public Administration to Citizens' Demands: An Empirical Examination in Israel." *Public*

Administration (2000), 78, 1, 165–91; "From Responsiveness to Collaboration: Governance, Citizens, and the Next Generation of Public Administration." *Public Administration Review* (2002), 62, 5, 515–28; "Managerial Quality, Administrative Performance, and Trust in Government: Can We Point to Causality?" *Australian Journal of Public Administration* (2003), 62, 3, 12–25; "Managerial Quality, Administrative Performance, and Trust in Government Revisited: A Follow-up Study of Causality." *International Journal of Public Sector Management* (2003), 16, 7, 502–22; "The State of Bureaucracy: Public Opinion about the Performance of Government Agencies in Israel and the Role of Socioeconomic and Demographic Variables." *International Journal of Public Opinion Research* (2004), 16, 1, 63–80; "Public Sector Innovation for the Managerial and the Post-managerial Era: Promises and Realities in a Globalizing Public Administration." *International Public Management Journal* (2005), 8, 1, 57–81; "Citizens' Perceptions of Organizational Politics and Ethics in Public Administration: A Five-year Study of their Relationship to Satisfaction with Services, Trust in Government, and Voice Orientations." *Journal of Public Administration Research and Theory* (2007), 17, 285–305; "Public Sector Management and the Democratic Ethos: A Longitudinal Study of Key Relationships in Israel." *Journal of Public Administration Research and Theory* (2007). I am therefore grateful to Shlomo, who was originally supposed to be the co-author of this book, but whose prior commitments precluded him from participating. Still, his talent, wisdom, and close friendship has inspired me throughout this journey and hopefully will continue to do so in the years to come.

Several books and symposium presentations also came out of these studies. First, *Managing Collaboration in Public Administration: Governance, Businesses, and Citizens in the Service of Modern Society* (2003) was published by Praeger-Greenwood Press. An edited volume entitled *Citizenship and Management in Public Administration: Integrating Behavioral Theories and Managerial Thinking* (2004), co-authored with Aaron Cohen, was published a year later by Edward Elgar Press. In the same year, another volume that I edited with David Levi-Faur, entitled *International Public Policy and Management: Policy Learning Beyond Regional, Cultural and Political Boundaries* was published by Marcel Dekker/Taylor and Francis Press. In addition, I edited a symposium entitled "Bridging performance and democratic values in the public sector" for the *International Journal of Public Administration* (vol. 26, 8–9) and joined forces again with David Levi-Faur in editing another symposium for the same journal (vol. 29, 4–6) entitled "Policy learning and management in a global world." These works have left their mark on this book as well. Many ideas and analytical models described here in a more developed form were first formulated and presented in these earlier works. Thus, I want to thank Aaron and David for their help and cooperation in walking me through the processes necessary to having these books and symposia discussions published. Clearly, I have benefited from their informed input and insightful contributions.

Furthermore, I also feel deeply indebted to those persons who worked behind the scenes on these projects and supported them from the beginning including the late Professor Jack Rabin, an outstanding designer of unique projects in the field of public administration, who gave me, and many others, a solid basis for developing and presenting our research projects. Jack was one of those giants whose contributions will be recognized even more over the years as his inspiration spreads globally like the seeds of the sunflower. I am also deeply grateful to Nic Philipson, senior editor of business and economics at Praeger Press; Catherine Ott from Taylor and Francis; Francine O'Sullivan, Suzanne Mursell, Nap Athwal, Caroline Cornish, and Alexandra Minton at Edward Elgar Press. I would also like to thank Aviv Shoham, Ayalla Ruvio, Nitza Schwabski, Itai Beeri, and Taly Birman-Shemes for working with me on a large-scale, three-year, cross-European project about innovation in the public sector. This study was supported by the 5FP of the European Commission, which allocated 1.3 million Euro for the study. Only a portion of whose results is presented in the later chapters of this book. In addition, I want to thank other colleagues who have read this manuscript and made useful comments and those who have shared their knowledge and good ideas with me throughout the years: Professor Yael Yishai, Professor Arie Halachmi, Professor Amos Drory, Professor Ayala Malach-Pines, Professor Aaron Kfir, Professor Gerald Caiden, Professor Naomi Caiden, Dr. Yair Zalmanivich, Dr. Pieter Van-Housse, Dr. Dana Vashdi, and Dr. Itai Beeri. They deserve my deepest gratitude and sincere appreciation.

Finally, and above all, I am grateful to my family, who suffered with me as I struggled between my desire to complete (another) scientific piece and my love for each one of them that pulled me toward spending time with them. They are certainly deserving of that time, and over the years, I have wished I could offer more of it to them. I am grateful to you all.

Eran Vigoda-Gadot
Haifa, 2008

Framework of the Book

The book is divided into three parts and nine chapters. Each part of the book is built around a different theoretical, empirical, or analytical framework. First, I set the stage for the core arguments by identifying the major questions, dilemmas, and paradoxes of democracies and public service under stress. Hence, the first part deals with the state of modern nations and the emergence of the bureaucratic–democratic paradox from the perspective of public administration; it includes two chapters. Chapter 1 presents a trinity of theoretical approaches to what I define as Nation Building. I use this provocative terminology to illustrate the complexity of the task. Building strong nations is much more than doing good or even promoting effective politics. It calls for many more skills and sources of knowledge from the fields of sociology, economics, law, communication, management, business, and other disciplines. As I try to explain, the eclectic "science of nation building" is the tool and vision necessary for building effective governability and modern public management. This discussion follows an interdisciplinary approach to the core argument that modern democracies are under increasing stress.

Several major explanations, based on previous writing in political science, policy studies, sociology, and economics are suggested and evaluated. A trilogy of ideas and alternative models to understanding the (declining) state of modern nations is suggested. They deal with nations as socio-political structures, nations as organizations, and nations as a marketplace. Examining the current condition of modern democracies through a socio-political lens reveals a conflicting duality in which the ethos of political liberalism is facing stronger demands from the public for welfare nets that support the needs of the citizens. Next, the institutionalized and organizational theory analyzes nations as systems of organized order. According to this view, I suggest that modern nations are at an administrative and managerial crossroads. The dilemmas related to this perspective put New Public Management (NPM) values in the forefront, highlighting an urgent call for professionalism, goal-setting approaches, and effective managerial and administrative values to improve the running of nations and their administrative branches. Finally, an alternative model, stemming mainly from the economic point of view, relies on the metaphor of states as a marketplace. This view advocates the view that nations are comparable to a business organization in which finance, budgeting, and the "cost" of the service and product dominate the socio-political debate. In my view, the integrated socio-political, organizational/institutional, and economic considerations establish the groundwork for the other parts of the book by framing the problem for both bureaucracy and democracy of managing modern nations in the face of threats, demands, and increasing challenges.

Chapter 2 presents the problem of effective governability under the various democratic and bureaucratic constraints pointed out earlier. I will argue that running modern nations effectively becomes a very complicated task not only because of the growing fragmentation of the international world order, but also because of the clash between democratic and bureaucratic ideologies. I present the clash of ideologies and explore a pyramidal paradox – the coexistence of democracy and bureaucracy – as well as their "black box" of interface. Modern nations are often weakened by the contradictory impulses to defend democracy on one hand and strengthen bureaucracy on the other. This conflict of ideas is evident when threats to essential values are expressed and voiced by external and internal stakeholders. No doubt, in many modern nations there has been an exponential increase in the curve of calls and demands for reforming the political order, reforming the public sector, and perhaps even a hidden agenda of reforming culture by manipulating the citizens' voice and their values. Two types of governability under stress are therefore suggested: top-down and bottom-up.

The second part elevates the theoretical discussion into an empirically-oriented one. In Chapter 3, I focus on the power of bureaucracy and its core elements: managerial quality and performance measurement. Whereas the former is an expression of inputs into the administrative state, the latter assesses the output of such efforts. Similarly, Chapter 4 explores the meaning and variations of democracy. While much literature has been published on the models of democracy and its meaning for our times, my goal is different. I want to highlight both the epistemological aspects of the meaning of citizenship in modern democracies and the resulting attitudinal and behavioral aftermaths of such an ideology. Thus, this chapter discusses the meaning of citizenship, loyalty and identity, trust in government and in public administration, stakeholders' participation in decision-making, political efficacy, perceived representation and discrimination, and actual behaviors such as political participation and community involvement. Chapter 5 presents empirical evidence about the relationships between the democratic and the bureaucratic realms. I rely on a longitudinal seven-year national study in Israel to demonstrate a number of possible relationships between constructs of the democratic system and those of the bureaucratic system. Four sections of empirical examination are presented. For each one, I develop a rationale and provide findings that try to shed light on the "black box" of the democratic–bureaucratic interface.

The goal of the third part is to offer several alternatives that may reconcile the democratic–bureaucratic paradox. Based on the theoretical framework presented earlier and on the empirical findings cited in the later portion of the book, I believe that there are several promising paths nations can follow in order to strengthen themselves. In this section, I deal with mechanisms that can increase the involvement of citizens in governmental decision-making, reduce governmental red tape, promote creativity and innovation in public administration, and use information systems and technology to bridge the gap between democracy and bureaucracy. They all fall into the category of the "black box" interfaces suggested in the opening chapters. Hence, this closing section builds on the four previous chapters. Chapter 6 suggests a strategy of cross-sectoral collaboration as a necessity for building strong nations. This strategy is perhaps the most powerful but also the most complicated task and challenge facing modern democracies. Bringing all three sectors of society into a process of recognizing, understanding, planning, and implementing a useful collaborative process based on their mutual interests may seem like a fantasy. However, a handful of successful cases attest to the fact that it is possible. Thus, I advocate collaboration as one promising vehicle for resolving the paradox of bureaucracy and democracy. Next, Chapter 7 offers innovation and creativity in the public sector as another promising mechanism for reconciling the democratic–bureaucratic paradox because it increases the tools available to public servants and builds a larger pool of resources for state leaders and the executive branches in public administration. Chapter 8 develops a third idea that global reforms in public administration are needed, beyond merely those that suit one nation or one region. It advocates the search for a new, borderless public policy that is much more global, transferable, and flexible than current reforms. It suggests that global reforms have much to do with the process of building strong nations, worldwide. Finally, in Chapter 9, I offer a synthesis, a summary, and an epilogue. This closing chapter presents the notion that building strong nations must combine two conflicting visions: safeguarding democracy and strengthening bureaucracy. Safeguarding democracy requires us to find creative ways to regain the trust of citizens. Citizens' trust in democracy and building confidence in government are necessary core elements in the building of strong nations. I trace the problem of distrust that was suggested in the previous chapter as a major obstacle to building strong nations and offer several ideas about ameliorating it. Empirical findings are presented on the risk of mistrust and on how to restore trust in government. Nonetheless, increasing trust is just one essential task of the modern nations. I further argue that a supplementary essential process must be strengthening bureaucracy through improved governability. I suggest that strong nations should not undermine the need to control and monitor public policies and hence effective bureaucracy must evolve alongside with grass-root democracy. The summary highlights the core argument presented in this book that building strong nations requires a much wider process of collaboration, innovation, and coordinated global reforms in public administration, processes that put citizens at the center of governmental interest but also position the democratic state at the forefront of citizens' actions. The synthesis of the book brings together theories and ideas about citizens' empowerment, managerial knowledge and expertise, and a global vision of international policy development, emulation, and dissemination. In my view, only these elements can ensure a peaceful resolution of the bureaucratic–democratic paradox.

Target Readers

Building Strong Nations is primarily a theoretical dialogue between advocates of a strong democracy and those who favor a strong bureaucracy. While some may find these concepts largely contradictory, there are many common denominators and paths for integrating one into the other. My major goal is to suggest a different perspective on this paradox, a perspective based on managerial, administrative, and empirical considerations. My ultimate goal is to expand our knowledge about the linkage between the realms of bureaucracy and democracy and the potential mutual contribution of one to the other. While this paradox has been the focus of several books and essays, the discussion developed here aims at different targets and a wider audience. The book is primarily targeted at scholars, academics, and students in the fields of political science, public administration, management, sociology and behavioral sciences, business administration, and international studies. This audience is in an continuous search for answers about how to safeguard nation states while promoting social achievements and encouraging economic expansion, growth, and quality of life in a liberal society.

Still, to advance the idea of effective governability as a key concept in building strong nations, this book must reach beyond this audience. In my view, it must win the minds and hearts of various other types of readers, such as the leaders of modern societies, be they politicians, public administrators, social leaders, or CEOs of the business sector. Such individuals, who constitute the elite of our society, also bear the responsibility for building strong nations, not merely speaking or writing about them. They must find the ways to reconcile democracy and bureaucracy and make governments more effective, trustworthy, and responsive to citizens. However, there is no doubt that citizens themselves may also find the book enlightening, and its ideas may contribute to the formation of strong communities. Accordingly, readers may come from various social venues, ranging from the business sector to the public sector and to the third sector, as they are all major partners in the process of nation building and reformation.

Introduction

Strong Nations, Weak Nations, and the Enigma of Effective Governability

If one were asked to divide the world into strong nations and weak nations, there is little doubt what the resulting list would be. Most probably, a majority of the respondents would put the developed world of wealthy, Western states and some of the richest Asian countries in the column of strong nations, while the poorest countries in the developing world would be defined as weak nations. There would probably be little debate about the political, economic, and military power of each state. Still, one wonders what makes some nations strong, regardless of their military power, natural resources, capital, and geo-political situation, and other nations weak, even when they hold several assets of the kind mentioned above. It is puzzling that nations with few resources are viewed both by public opinion and according to objective measures as "stronger" or "weaker." What is the secret of building strong nations, and how can we penetrate this enigma to help governments build stronger nations?

This book offers a somewhat different answer than the conventional ones suggested above. I will argue that, from the perspective of managing the state, reconciliation of what is defined as "the bureaucratic–democratic paradox" is at the heart of building strong nations. This reconciliation is crucial for the formation of a public administration that works, and thus restores citizens' trust and confidence in state authority and authorities.

The paradox between bureaucracy and democracy has been a fascinating field of study for many scholars from various social disciplines over the years. Sociologists, political scientists, scholars of organizational studies and management have focused on this topic, which has received growing public attention especially in the face of political crises, policy weakness, and a decline in public sector organizations. A long list of scientific books and essays have dealt with this issue, among them, a number that I have used extensively in this book: W.D. Richardson (1997), *Democracy, Bureaucracy, and Character*; E. Etzioni-Halevi (1983), *Bureaucracy and Democracy: A Political Dilemma*; R.C. Box (1998), *Citizen Governance: Leading American Communities into the 21st Century*; C.T. Goodsell (1983), *The Case for Bureaucracy: A Public Administration Polemic*; L.C. Gawthrop (1996), *Democracy, Bureaucracy, and Hypocrisy Redux*; C. King and C. Stivers (1998), *Government is Us: Public Administration in an Anti-Government Era*; F. Mosher (1982), *Democracy and the Public Service*; W.N. Niskanen (1994), *Bureaucracy and Public Economics*; G. Peters (2001), *The Politics of Bureaucracy* and many others. Most of these works have discussed the ideological or political conflict between democracy and bureaucracy, with some of them defining it as a paradoxical relationship. Most of these studies conclude that democracy and bureaucracy are two separate structures living together under the framework of the nation state and the liberal society. However, even though they are separate, they are also related in many ways.

Therefore, one may ask, what has changed? Is there anything new in this debate about bureaucracy and democracy and can this book offer a different perspective and other insights? I feel the answer to both of these questions is positive. Yes, there are many changes and new directions in our modern world that justify reconsideration of the paradox, this time from a more policy-oriented and public management-oriented perspective. There are changes in the nature of modern bureaucracy and in the nature of democracy in our times that are worthy of reconsideration in light of the classic clash between democracy and bureaucracy. And yes, this book is trying to deal with the paradox from a different angle, one that appeals to public administration and policy studies theoreticians and practitioners, rather than to merely political scientists or political philosophers, or even to organizational sociologists. Too few of the above studies have focused on the managerial and administrative analysis of this paradoxical relationship and, as far as I could find, none has based its theoretical arguments on solid empirical evidence derived from a systematic collection of data over time.

In our changing world, being economically wealthy, militarily strong and powerful, or socially responsive and compassionate still leaves us with many disagreements and conflicts in national life. A mechanism for reconciliation between the political order of democracies and the administrative order of bureaucracies must be constructed if citizens and leaders wish to build a stronger society and a stronger nation. In my view, the path to national strength or weakness is guided by effective mechanisms of governability. Using this criterion, a strong nation is not the one with merely economic superiority, military dominance, or high levels of education, but the one that, through the consensus of its population, has found a way to bring together the conflicting ideas and imperatives of democracy and bureaucracy peacefully. Perhaps this is not the only recipe for building a strong nation, but it is undoubtedly a rather underdeveloped idea worthy of consideration and empirical examination.

Given that this book focuses on democracy, bureaucracy, and mechanisms that can bridge them, it must deal comprehensively with the meaning of governability. Building strong nations essentially calls for strong governments and a strong administrative order that implements the government's decisions in the best possible way. Recent studies have called this phenomenon the rise of the "administrative state." In this context, governments and the branches that implement their decisions are a bridge between thematic ideologies and actual policy-making. Governments and their social proxies are the glue that makes society a coherent institution of mutual power, goals and vision. To achieve this goal, governments must be granted legitimacy and power, but at the same time, they must be prevented from misusing this power, mishandling resources, or making faulty judgments and decisions that could jeopardize the public interest. Governability is therefore the potential power of governments to rule and lawfully implement public policy for citizens, and with them.

Historically, governability is a concept developed in the 1970s in the United States and Europe to express the difficulties of ruling. It reflects the problems facing states wherever and whenever they respond to the demands of different sectors of society and the impossibility of formulating policies based on those demands. However, the concept of governability has changed over the years. Governments across the globe are playing less of a role in the national economic and social sphere due to the increasing involvement of other sectors and players in these areas. At the same time, governments are buckling under growing demands from the public, international risks, and calls for the expansion of the welfare state to meet the new values of justice, equity, and the equitable distribution of wealth. This process is accompanied by a substantial decline in citizens' trust and confidence in governments and in their ability to meet new challenges. Skeptics looking at this criticism of the existing political and social order may conclude that we have reached a dead end.

Thus, governability today has at least two faces: the ability of governments to respond efficiently and legitimately to the interests of various segments of the society, and the adaptation to a process where civil society has self-organizing capabilities that improve its cohesion and become a counter-power to governments. Governability involves new forms of political, economic, and social organization that allow the state to respond to the challenges of modernization, changing individual and collective values, and the presence of new social demands and expectations that exceed the limits of traditional institutions.

PART I

The State of Modern Nations and the Rebirth of an Old Paradox

The state of modern nations serves as a good starting point for a book seeking explanations on how to encourage governability and build strong nations in the modern era. It is also not surprising that this idea is of prime interest to an author from Israel, a state whose "strength" and vigor had been put to the test so many times, and perhaps will continue to be questioned in the years to come. From one perspective, the state of our nations today (mostly democracies, new and old) is much better than it used to be in previous years. This statement obviously holds in the developed world, in most of Europe and North America, but is also true in many countries in South America, Asia, the Far East, and Australia. It holds, but to a lesser degree, in other continents such as those in Africa, Eastern Europe, and the Middle East. However, even in these latter countries much has been achieved in recent years that has improved the quality of life and increased the longevity and overall prosperity of many people in numbers and scales that could only be dreamt of in previous centuries.

This observation by no means contradicts the fact that too many nations are in a deep crisis resulting from poor management or poor political order that prevents modernization, progress, and the advancement of much of the world's population. Even in those countries that are going through rapid positive change in their social and political order, such as Eastern European countries or several Asian nations, the problem of governability still exists. How do we reconcile a liberal and democratic political order with "hands on" public policies that help nations progress and promote growth and prosperity? Obviously, this cannot be done by merely talking about freedom of choice or about free market orientations that leave many, too many, of the disadvantaged and weaker sectors of society behind.

This section deals with the state of modern nations, but this time from a slightly different angle. Most studies of this topic have been written from a single perspective, usually that of political science, sociology, economics, or administration. It is our goal to suggest a multi-focal view that integrates several disciplines and offers a different look at the democratic–bureaucratic paradox. I suggest a specific concept for this purpose – *nation building*. This chapter will defend this multidimensional and interdisciplinary position and demonstrate its usefulness, both theoretically and empirically, for the purpose of building strong nations. Public administration still features at the center of this argument. I will argue in this section that the most pressing need in today's struggle between nations, leaders, and people is the need to resolve the dilemma of governability within the context of the conflict between democracy and bureaucracy. This is, in my view, the essence of the democratic–bureaucratic paradox that the book aims to discuss and clarify.

Chapter 1
Theoretical Approaches to Nation Building

The term *nation building* draws substance from many perspectives. However, to the best of my knowledge, it has not been used extensively elsewhere in any of the relevant administrative sciences dealing with public policy, public management or governance. Whereas we are quite familiar with political sciences, policy studies, or research on government and governance, we tend to be much less open to new terminology such as this one. Nonetheless, I felt that using this concept that builds on the integration of knowledge from socio-political sciences, administrative sciences, and economics is a good start for a book that deals with multidisciplinary aspects of how to run modern nations. Hopefully, this term will help us illuminate one of the leading challenges of modern times: How do we explain the appearance and disappearance of nations worldwide, and how do we build strong nations that are robust and secure locally, regionally, and internationally? There are many answers to these ambitious questions – and what I suggest here aims to explore my view as a rather positivistic academician from the public management side of the court.

Indeed, from an academic point of view, the use of the term *nation building* may, at first glance, seem historically oriented. After all, nation building may be seen as the territory of historians who try to explain, retrospectively, the processes and elements contributing to the emergence or decline of states and political entities. Furthermore, the concept may draw heavy fire from multiple sources. I expect this fire to come and to some extent even welcome it in the hope that it will encourage a dialogue with critics because the questions at hand are too important to ignore. I expect this heavy fire even though this is not entirely a new concept in political sciences or in public administration/policy studies. For example, Hood (1998) hinted at the term indirectly when he spoke about the "art of the state." Justifying the existence of a "science" (or art) of the state is indeed an ambitious task. Today knowledge about states or nations is customary gathered together under umbrella terms such as "politics," "political sciences," "policy studies," or "governance." However, political sciences or policy studies do not tell us the whole story about what is needed for running a modern national machinery, nor do administrative sciences or economics. Each one contributes to a better understanding of some aspects of the big picture but the glue that holds the pieces together is rather weak. The knowledge about building strong nations is therefore distributed among many players, disciplines, and actors who are, at best, not always familiar with each other. At worst, they conflict and disagree and sometimes build borders instead of bridges between islands of knowledge. Sometimes, even when familiarity with the various disciplines is greater, we face a lack of willingness to cooperate or collaborate and share experience and knowledge in order to make our modern societies a better place in which to live, and an easier place for governments to rule.

I therefore decided to use this terminology of *nation building* for two main reasons. First, I believe that the grey areas between the above fields offer much material for study and often do not receive enough attention specifically within and independently of one another. Second, in my view, the term *nation building*, and even more so *building strong nations*, points not only to a neglected academic arena, but also to one with much future potential for interdisciplinary thinking and practical actions. It reflects the desire to create an added value by harvesting the best (and finest) of all (scientific and practical) worlds. In its totality, *nation building* is the knowledge of how to effectively run our communities, countries, states, and nations, building on unbiased, interdisciplinary experiences with democratic mechanisms and bureaucratic systems – together and alone.

Similarly, there are at least three major theories that can help to explain what I define as *nation building*. First is the traditional socio-political discipline that highlights class, domination, values and political processes in the process of running the state and building a nation. Several names and studies should be discussed under this approach, including the views of Marx, Mosca, Michels, Weber, Dahl

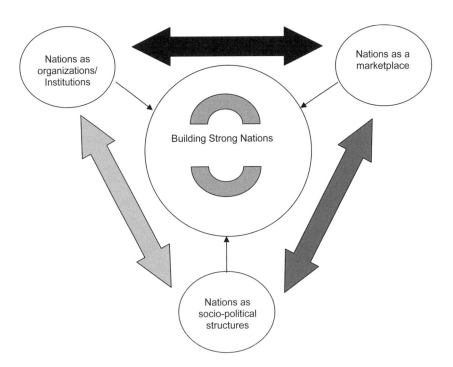

Figure 1.1   Theoretical approaches to nation building

and others. Second is the managerial and administrative discipline with its notion of institutional dominance as expressed by Osborne and Gaebler, Pollitt, Lynn, and others. Third is the economic discipline, which analyzes states and nations as marketplaces and financial centers. Advocates of this position include Niskanen, Mises, and others. The next sections review the general rationality behind each approach and the contribution each makes to a better explanation of current problems in building strong nations.

Nations as socio-political structures: Class, domination, and citizens' mistrust

The natural habitat of nation building is the socio-political arena. What could be more natural than drawing on the arsenal of political and social ideas, ideologies, and practices for a better understanding of how to build strong nations? Indeed, nations are, first and foremost, socio-political entities run by politicians, arguably for the collective benefit of all citizens. Nations and states are created to allow national aspirations and to express the common good of people with similar values and heritage. They are built to protect the interests of these people and allow them to run their lives as they choose. However, according to many theoreticians and ideologists, powerful groups of organized elites in society dominate these people. These upper classes have much more power and resources than the masses and thus direct the nation according to their self-interests, which often contradict the collective interest. Similarly, the most powerful and dominant jargon for dealing with nation building would be the political and social one that derives from the political sciences, sociology, and cultural studies of the state.

Etzioni-Halevy (1983) suggests a socio-political analysis of the relationship between bureaucracy and democracy in modernizing states. According to her view there are at least two historical phases for this analysis: (1) classical theories of Marx, Michels, Mosca, and Weber; and (2) modern theories of pluralism, technocracy, and corporatism.

Classical theories

Among the most influential theoreticians who struggled with the idea of bureaucracy, democracy, and their interchange are Karl Marx (1818–1883), Gaetano Mosca (1858–1941), Robert Michels (1878–1936), and Max Weber (1864–1920). Let us briefly review their ideas.

Marx suggested that, in accordance with Hegel's ideas, bureaucracy mediates between the state and other players such as citizenry groups in the civil society and private corporations and the free market. However, Marx believed that bureaucracy is an inherent part of the state itself and has immense power that manipulates the world and its own members. Thus, the state and its bureaucracy seem very similar to any other organization with the goal of guaranteeing the property and interests of the ruling class. Marx was also rather pessimistic about democracy and viewed it as a developed form of bourgeois rule. According to Etzioni-Halevy (1983: 13), Marx meant that with the evolvement of democracy across Europe and the Americas, bureaucracy and the state in general would gradually lose their coercive and exploitative character. Over time, society would absorb their functions and roles as citizens became more involved in running the state. Citizens will therefore be administrated and administrators at the same time.

The ideas of Mosca were somewhat different from those of Marx. In his view, bureaucracy deserves independent attention, as it represents a distinct order of political organizations. Mosca believed that bureaucracy is part of a theory about a politically dominant class, whereas Marx saw it as part of the economically dominated class (Etzioni-Halevy, 1983: 14). According to Mosca's view, any society can be divided into a small ruling class that holds a monopoly on power and authority, and a much larger ruled class. The ruling class is organized, whereas the ruled class remains unorganized. The hold of the ruling class remains intact over time because one leader transfers his power to another to prevent losing it to the masses. Mosca explains developments in history where struggles over power were always among the ruling minorities and explains how a bureaucracy was created to safeguard the advantages of the politically ruling class. Mosca believed that in either a monarchy, a feudal state, or a representative national system the politically organized ruling minority imposes its will on the disorganized majority, and the power of bureaucracy is thus much stronger than the power of democracy. Even in what seems to be a democratic, representative system, the only candidates who have any chance of winning an election must come from the organized minorities or at least have strong contacts with them.

Following the ideas of Marx and Mosca, the German sociologist, Robert Michels (1915) suggested the "iron rule of oligarchy." According to this rule, democratic institutions, organizations, and bodies tend to suffer from an inherent pandemic of reformation towards oligarchy. According to Michels, bureaucracy is an inherent part of the modern state and enables its proper functioning. It is through strong bureaucracy and administrative bodies that the ruling parties and classes secure their domination in the society. At the same time, the lower classes suffer from this domination because their aspirations for security and welfare are denied and suppressed. Etzioni-Halevy summarizes this argument by noting that for Michels, "the bureaucracy is thus a source of power for the politically dominant class, a source of security for the large part of the middle class, but a source of oppression for the rest of the society" (p. 19). Michels was most interested in the structure of political parties and trade unions, and his observations led him to conclude that in these institutions, as in many other organizations, democracy in its pure essence cannot work properly. According to his analysis of the reality of his time, even organizations whose principles were democratic in time turned towards an oligarchic structure because they could not function effectively any other way. This is the "iron rule of oligarchy" that turns any democratic structure into a hierarchical one dominated by a minority, despite aspirations for equity and freedom of choice. The major limitations to sustaining a democratic system are therefore the size of organizations, their complexity, the need for quick decisions, the need for experience, mass information and technology, improved political and leadership skills of those in power, the need for continuity, the apathy of most citizens, and the vested interest in power that allows an oligarchy to grow and prosper.

Finally, the Weberian legacy of the German sociologist Max Weber is of the most fundamental for the study of classic bureaucracy and democracy. Weber was perhaps the first to analyze bureaucracy in its modern structure and its relevancy for large-scale organizations. He based many of his observations on the Prussian and British bureaucracies and their armies, eventually formulating the "ideal type of bureaucracy" for the modern society. Weber also dealt with the meaning of power, hierarchy, and authority and how they are divided in organizations. Weber mentioned three types of authority: traditional, charismatic, and legal-rational. The last type of authority, the legal-rational, is the one that forms the basis for bureaucracy. The ideal type of bureaucracy, according to Weber, encompasses several features that all contradict the democratic ethos of any social structure: clear duties for members, units organized by order of hierarchy, authority that is restricted to official duties, officials who hold office by appointment, selection for office by objective qualifications, offices that are held for life, officials who are separated from the means of administration, activities anchored in strict formal rules, impersonality of actions, and a bureaucracy that frequently has a non-bureaucratic head (Etzioni-Halevy, 1983: 28). Therefore bureaucracy seems like a highly rational machinery that may contradict the irrationality and affective characteristics of democracy. Weber also noted that this ideal type of bureaucracy may yield "specialists without spirit, sensualists without heart" (Weber, 1958: 182). Moreover, while bureaucracy and democracy may develop together, when one promotes the evolvement of the other, the two may be pitted against one another. Democracy opposes bureaucracy because officials are removed from the people by formal tools of expertise, tenure, and impersonality. Democracy also strives to shorten the term of office by elections, which goes against the stability of formal rules and hierarchy of a bureaucracy. Thus, according to Etzioni-Halevy (1983: 34), Weber understood that "bureaucracy is rather suspect in its implications for both democracy and equality. But it would be fruitless to try and eliminate it."

Modern theories

Etzioni-Halevy (1983: 41–73) suggests that modern theories of bureaucracy and democracy emphasize several views such as the pluralistic perspective, the overload on government, the technocratic view, and the corporatist view. She also includes the Marxist view in this category, but in my opinion the theory's roots in classical approaches more appropriately classifies it in earlier thinking.

According to the pluralistic view that became popular in the middle of the twentieth century, bureaucracy and democracy in times of modernization are affected by the fragmentation of the political order and the political system in many nations. This view treats the political system as an arena where many conflicting interests of individuals and groups are mixed and balanced to produce public policy. This policy is a democratic outcome of a bureaucratic input. Whereas no group has a monopoly on the results of the process, they all seem to have an unequal ability to reshape government decisions to act or withhold actions. In such a system, where authority is divided among many independent bureaucrats (Dahl, 1967) there is opportunity for democratic views to be expressed, but also for many obstacles to proper governability and efficient policies to flourish. Thus, the pluralistic view acknowledges the voices of societies' stakeholders but at the same time, puts up barriers on the road to efficiency and the maximum performance of governments, states and nations. A similar perspective is expressed by pluralists about the nature of bureaucracy. In this vein, bureaucrats seem unable to rule alone because they need the input and legitimacy of street-level citizens and groups in the civic society, as well as other partners in society (that is, religious groups, the private and business sector, and so on). Nonetheless, no one else can rule without bureaucrats who hold the key to the proper codes of management in government (Rourke, 1976). In sum, bureaucracy and democracy both rely on vast support from a fragmented society, which in itself is a cause of many delays and restraints in the making of public policy. According to the pluralistic view, a paradoxical result of the clash between bureaucracy and democracy may be that in the name of pluralism and high-level democracy, many of the citizens' essential interests and needs cannot be fulfilled even at a minimal level.

According to Etzioni-Halevy (1983), the pluralistic view may also suggest that the government is overloaded. This overload is a type of pluralism because many groups of citizens and new players from the private sector become involved in what seemed to be in the past to be the sole responsibility of the state. Alternatively, they put stronger pressures on states and governments to meet new needs and fulfill new demands (i.e., Bell, 1975; Crozier et al., 1975; King, 1975). The overload on governments may clearly result in problems of governability that will be discussed in the later chapters of this book.

In contrast with the previous modern approaches, the technocratic view suggests that democracy is ruled by an elite group of powerful technocrats. This view, mainly drawing substance from the French heritage, argues for the domination of a leading elite of administrators who are the most influential in the state economy (i.e., Dye and Zeigler, 1975; Mills, 1959). The power of these technocrats is growing at the expense of elected political bodies and thus expresses the superiority of bureaucracy over much of the democratic system. According to the technocratic view, politicians as elected individuals do have the power to execute decisions but such actions often clash with the views of administrators, resulting in a waste of time and energy that the politicians cannot afford or are unwilling to risk. Thus, they tend to focus on crucial issues that deserve their attention and effort. Etzioni-Halevy (1983: 57–8) suggests several explanations for the growing power of technocrats: increasing government intervention, greater complexity of governments' tasks, the high value placed on expertise in modern societies, the immense growth of the information society, the growing size of the bureaucratic machinery and the time dedicated to its proper functioning, the minimal interest of politicians in many public issues that do not seem important, the decline of parliamentary power, and ministerial turnover. In terms of the relationship with democracy the technocrat view posits a threat in which the power of the appointed bureaucrat is much more effective and influential than the power of the elected politician who is expected to voice the citizens' needs and demands. This situation may increase citizens' dissatisfaction with the democratic process and lead to mistrust in government. Another problem in relation to the democratic–bureaucratic nexus is the tendency of the technocrat to hoard information and knowledge and not share it with the public. As in any elite system, the bureaucrats maintain their advantage by concentrating power and never delegating it to external bodies, thereby safeguarding their role and the need for their services in the future. In fact, the technocratic view contrasts sharply with the pluralistic view and gains credence by the growing citizens' mistrust of the democratic political system.

The corporatist view of bureaucracy and democracy may be seen as one sub-model of the technocratic view. Corporatism is defined as the "institutional arrangement whereby public policy is worked out through an interaction between top state elites and the leadership of a limited number of corporate organizations (mainly business and industrial corporations on the one hand and the labor unions on the other)" (Etzioni-Halevy, 1983: 63). This perspective defends the ideology of elitism by noting that there is a small group (or a collection of groups) that holds power in society and is dominant in a nation or a state. Whereas the technocratic view posits a somewhat similar line, they argue that this elite group is made up of officers of the bureaucracy and of technocrats, whereas according to the corporatists, these groups represent the political system of decision makers as well as other social leaders of the civic society (which is somewhat similar to the beliefs of the pluralists). While the leaders should represent the followers' views, this is not always the case in practice (Schmitter, 1979). Corporatism also has several sub-divisions ranging from state corporatism to more liberal corporatism. Nevertheless, all types of corporatism see the bureaucracy as another way for elite groups to dominate the lower classes and the ordinary people, be it in organizations or in the society as a whole. This ideology largely reflects practical democratic processes in modern nations where parliaments and governments have superior power over other bodies in the society. At the same time there is much room to argue that an inherent principle of democracy is damaged when ordinary people do not have actual and equal influence over their lives due to the extensive power granted to other elites. Corporatism also implies that bureaucracy is not really needed because it is within the power of the politicians and the stronger leaders of society to decide and implement their decisions as they see fit. Corporatism also works through quasi-governmental organizations, which make public administration quite redundant. Therefore, and as noted by Etzioni-Halevy (1983: 71), with regard to the linkage between democracy and bureaucracy, the corporatist view is at the opposite end of the continuum with pluralism. The corporatist view is less liberal in giving many segments of the society an opportunity to have input into the political system and at the same time calls for a stronger bureaucracy, based on the immense power granted to politicians over the administrative state. Thus, the corporatist view suggests that, at least to a certain degree, elite groups of the socio-political system stand above not only some democratic principles, but also some traditional technocratic–bureaucratic principles.

The state of modern nations: Mistrust in governments

What are the essential ingredients for building strong, stable, and healthy democracies? There are many answers to this question but when studying the link between democracy and bureaucracy, we can identify at least three such ingredients. First, public institutions need to fulfill their core duty of providing services to the people. In order to do this they need to develop and maintain professional staffs, methods, and tools that increase their responsiveness to their citizens. Second, citizens must indicate that they are satisfied with these institutions and public sector services, as this satisfaction is the prime indicator of a bureaucracy that is functioning effectively. Third, and most important, such performance and satisfaction need to be in line with peoples' political attitudes towards governance, especially their level of trust in the government (Miller and Listhaug, 1998).

Moreover, as customers of public services, citizens tend to generalize their attitudes towards decision makers and public institutions as well as toward any specific person whom they encounter in such agencies. Yet most surprisingly, in many modern democracies the public expresses a great deal of dissatisfaction with public administration. Studies conducted in different countries, using various means and methods, repeatedly conclude that in general, the public trust in government and its administrative branches is low (Pharr, 1997), that people are usually dissatisfied with public services (Nye et al., 1997: 1–18), and that many times the level of government responsiveness is poor (Vigoda, 2000a). Modern public administration thus encourages the use of satisfaction measures as part of performance evaluations both inside public agencies and around them (e.g., Poister and Henry, 1994; Swindell and Kelly, 2000). It should also be noted that this strategy has been adopted despite some limitations it has and some criticism it needs to address (Stipak, 1979, 1980).

The relationship between political trust and economic indicators of performance and citizens–clients' satisfaction is also elusive. King and Stivers describe it as the "anti-government era" and state clearly, in the introduction to their book, that: "Over 200 years American citizens have tended to tolerate government rather than to support it with enthusiasm. Yet, in recent decades, distaste for government seems to have deepened" (1998; p. 3). For example, Americans' trust in their government dropped in the late 1960s (Nye et al., 1997) despite the economic stability during that time period. Many American scholars are similarly worried about the declining trend in Americans' trust in public institutions that had been briefly renewed during the 1990s (Citrin and Luks, 2001). Neither stability in foreign affairs (the end of the Cold War) nor economic strength were enough to shore up Americans' trust in governmental institutions (Hibbing and Theiss-Morse, 2001).

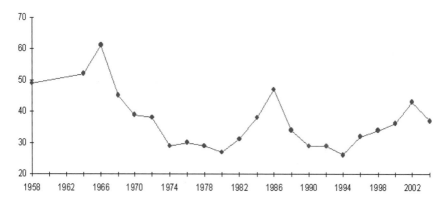

Figure 1.2   Trust in American governmental institutions (support by percentage)

Source: The American National Election Studies.

Nevertheless, there have been some fluctuations in public trust, such as during the period after the terror attack of September 11th, which dramatically increased the level of trust in the government (Hibbing and Theiss-Morse, 2002). Overall, however, the perception of government and the bureaucratic system in America is becoming negative over time and expresses a sense of mistrust or even paranoia about government (King and Stivers, 1998: 5).

The American people are not alone in this trend. Findings from Eastern European countries show a very similar picture. A comparative study from Norway, Sweden, and the United States between 1964 and 1986 found that all three countries suffered from a decline in public trust in government (Miller and Listhaug, 1990), yet satisfaction with public services was usually high. The same evidence has been found in Britain, Italy, Belgium, Spain, The Netherlands, and Ireland (Nye, 1997). Canadian political institutions as well suffer from this tendency to mistrust the government (Adams and Lennon, 1992), and Pharr (1997) describes the deep crises of trust that plague the government and public administration in Japan. This level of mistrust is particularly noteworthy, as both Canada and Japan maintain highly successful economies offering modern services to their citizens. This phenomenon has not left the post-communist countries in Europe untouched (Mishler and Rose, 1997) nor has it spared other countries such as Israel (Vigoda and Yuval, 2003a, 2003b, 2004).

In the context of ruling and being ruled in return, Citrin (1974) suggested that "political elites produce policies; in exchange, they receive trust from citizens satisfied with these policies and cynicism from those who are disappointed" (p. 973). However, the exact interrelationship between the outcomes of bureaucracy and the outcomes of democracy is still vague. It seems that there is a linkage between policies and their economic outputs and other political indicators of trust and faith in government (i.e., Citrin, 1974; King, 1997; Lane, 1965). The exact nature of that relationship and its causality, however, remain unclear.

	1981	1990	1999	90 vs. 81	99 vs. 90	99 vs. 81
France	52.1	49	45.9	-3.1	-3.1	-6.2
UK	47	44	45.9	-3	1.9	-1.1
Germany	32.3	39	38.7	6.7	-0.3	6.4
Italy	26.8	27	33.2	0.2	6.2	6.4
Spain	39.1	37	40.5	-2.1	3.5	1.4
Portugal		32	53.6		21.6	
Belgium	46.3	46	46.1	-0.3	0.1	-0.2
Netherlands	44.4	46	37.5	1.6	-8.5	-6.9
Denmark	46.9	51	54.9	4.1	3.9	8
Sweden	46	44	48.8	-2	4.8	2.8
Finland	53		40.9	-53		-12.1
Iceland	48		55.9	-48		7.9
Ireland	54.4	59	59.3	4.6	0.3	4.9

Figure 1.3   Trust in the European civil service (support by percentage)

Source: European Values Survey.

In light of the historical overview of socio-political ideologies for nation building, it is rather obvious why most modern nations face a crisis of mistrust in government. In this regard, the problems and dilemmas facing most of today's developed countries are related to sharp transformations of values and the emergence of citizens' mistrust in governments. Public opinion data about Americans' view of government at the state and federal level attests to the fact that trust is in sharp decline (see Figure 1.2). Similar data from Europe are not much different (see Figure 1.3). Moreover, as Figure 1.4 illustrates, mistrust in government is a worldwide pandemic. In most of the Western world, be it in established or less established democracies, the level of trust in government wavers around 50 percent or even much lower. Is this a problem that modern democracies must live with and get used to? Can we foresee any stable and steady development in democracies, both economically and politically, under such a massive decline in public trust? Or perhaps this is a chronic illness stemming from the weakness of the democratic system?

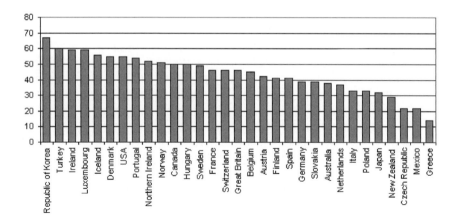

Figure 1.4 **Trust in the civil service, World Values Study, OECD countries, percentage showing a great deal or quite a lot of confidence in the civil service (1995–2000)**

Nations as organizations: An administrative and (new) managerial crossroads

A conventional theoretical approach to the study of the "state of the nations" is based on the idea that running a state or a nation shares much in common with managing an organization or any other social or even political institution. The conservative cornerstones of modern nations are territory, people, and a monopoly on power by the leadership. However, states and nations are much more than just that, and looking at modern nations may suggest that their responsibilities have been extended to many other territories. One may view the core structures of modern nations as a collection, an integration, or even a collage of bodies, ideas, missions, institutions, technologies, and resources that join together under the same goals, aspirations, and vision of life.

The approach of dealing with nations as organizations or institutions is strongly rooted in the administrative and managerial sciences. For example, Fox and Miller (1996) suggest that institutionalism and constitutionalism focus attention on institutional categories as power of the presidency, where tax bills originate, who makes war, who confirms treaties, whether or not a president (or any other state leader) can fire a … cabinet officer, etc. Similarly, Giddens (1984) suggests the structuration theory that allows one to assess the behavior-channeling practices that make up what are called institutions and to focus on social aspects of institutional-like practices. Furthermore, much of the public administration discourse of recent decades is about effectively running the state or the nation based on the "good practices" learned from the business sector (Osborne and Gaebler, 1992).

The New Public Management (NPM) doctrine that evolved in the United States and in Europe beginning in the late 1980s has been the most influential proponent of the metaphor of running the state like a business. NPM represents *an approach in public administration that employs knowledge and experiences acquired in business management and other disciplines to improve efficiency, effectiveness, and general performance of public services in modern bureaucracies.* Despite contradictory views about the meaning and implications of this doctrine, there is no doubt that it has become extremely influential in public administration theory and practice since the 1980s.

In the last decade, we have witnessed an ongoing debate among scholars and practitioners of public administration about the best way to revitalize and renew old style bureaucracies. Since the early 1980s, much work has been conducted in public administration theory and practice that claimed to go beyond the conservative approach in the field. Modern public administration has been urged to innovate and reform itself in a style better suited to the twenty-first century and the growing demands for better efficiency and effectiveness. Drawing on the experience of the business/industrialized/private sector, scholars have suggested taking a more "demanding" attitude towards the dynamics, activity and productivity of public organizations. Similarly, a significant conceptual change has transformed the "old" style of public administration into the "new" approach of public management. This "liberalization" of public administration is recognized today as the New Public Management (NPM) doctrine.

What is the meaning of NPM? What are its roots and in what way is it actually a *new* arena in the study of the public sector? Has it achieved enough success in recent years to justify further inquiry into its principles and promises? These questions, as well as many others, have received considerable attention during recent years and in fact, a large number of varying opinions have emerged. Proponents of this approach have provided detailed explanations and a variety of examples that demonstrate the enormous positive impact of the approach. Those who critique NPM counter with the argument that it has nothing new or notable to contribute to the field. They thus tend to treat it as a seasonal fashion that will eventually fade in the face of other "new" doctrines. Therefore, advocates of NPM constantly confront critics who are unconvinced as to the merits of NPM as an administrative philosophy.

Theoretical foundations

To better resolve these conceptual and practical conflicts regarding the contribution of NPM to public administration, one must become familiar with several fundamental concepts. The first, and probably the most basic premise of NPM, emerges from the distinction between two proximate terms or fields of research – *administration* and *management*. Since the late 1880s, the monopoly on the term "administration" has been in the hands of political scientists. Scholars like Goodnow and Wilson perceived public administration as a separate and unique discipline that should consist of independent theory, practical skills, and methods. In contrast, the term "management" refers to a more general arena, used by all social scientists and mainly by those who practice and advance theories in organizational psychology and business studies. Consequently, conservative administration science tends to analyze the operation of large bureaucratic systems as well as other governmental processes aimed at policy implementation. Management, on the other hand, refers to the general practice of empowering people and groups in various social environments and the handling of manifold organizational resources to maximize efficiency and effectiveness in the process of producing goods or services.

A second premise of NPM derives from the nature and values of democratic nations. By voting, citizens of modern democracies delegate power to politicians and administrators to do what is best for people and societies. However, representative democracy leaves its fingerprints on the actions and operation of bureaucracies. For many years, bureaucracies worked in a manner far removed from citizens and with a lack of sensitivity to the growing needs and demands of heterogeneous populations. As suggested by Rainey (1990), the 1960s and the 1970s were characterized by the initiation of unsuccessful public policies in Europe and in America. At least some of these unsuccessful experiences were due to the lack of reliable analyses about the needs and demands of the public, while other failures were caused by incorrect assessments regarding the power of bureaucracies. Over the years, efforts by governments to create extensive changes in education, welfare systems, health programs, internal security, and crime control were widely criticized for being ineffective and unproductive and for misusing public funds. Responsiveness to the real needs and demands of citizens was paltry. The crisis in practical public policy implementation, together with the increased cynicism of citizens toward government and public administration systems, generated rich scholarly activity aimed at creating useful alternatives for improved policy in various social fields as well as in the administrative processes in general. Voters expressed their dissatisfaction with elected officials and hand in hand with the academic community called for extensive reforms in government. This call produced a large number of working papers, articles, and books that proposed extensive administrative changes. One of the most inspiring works, Osborne and Gaebler's *Reinventing Government* (1992), is frequently mentioned as the unofficial starting point of such reforms, later known as NPM.

As time went on, a growing number of political scientists perceived public administration as an *old* and declining discipline. It was unable to provide the public with adequate practical answers to its demands and moreover, left the theoreticians with epidemic social dilemmas awaiting study. Evidence for this shift in attitude appears in the transformation of many schools of public administration into schools of public management that took place during the 1980s and 1990s. Looking for alternative ideas, management theory was proposed as a source for a new and refreshing perspective. It was suggested that public management instead of public administration could contribute to a new understanding of how to run the government more efficiently and thereby overcome some of its pandemic problems.

Core definitions of NPM

Based on the growing alienation of citizens, the ineffective performance of bureaucracy, and the growing demands for a real change in public policy and activity, NPM flourished. But what is the essence of NPM and the best way to define it? During the last two decades many definitions have been suggested. In the early 1980s, Garson and Overman (1983) defined it as *an interdisciplinary study of the generic aspects of administration ... a blend of the planning, organizing, and controlling functions of management with the management of human, financial, physical, information and political resources* (p. 278).

Hood (1991) identified seven doctrinal components of NPM: (1) "hands on" professional management in the public sector, (2) explicit standards and measures of performance that were later defined as PIs (Performance Indicators), (3) greater emphasis on output control, (4) a shift to the disaggregation of the unit, (5) a shift to greater competition, (6) a stress on private sector styles of management practice, (7) a stress on greater discipline and parsimony in resource use. This definition implies that NPM relies heavily on the theory of the marketplace and on a businesslike culture in public organizations. Other definitions were suggested in the 1990s and drew on the extensive writing in the field. For example, Hays and Kearney (1997) found that most of the studies on NPM had mentioned five core principles of NPM and thus concluded that they represent the most important aspects of the discipline: (1) downsizing – reducing the size and scope of government, (2) managerialism – using business protocols in government, (3) decentralization – moving decision-making closer to the service recipients, (4) debureaucratization – restructuring government to emphasize results rather than processes, and (5) privatization – directing the allocation of governmental goods and services to outside firms (Weikert, 2001). All of these principles are mutually related, relying heavily on the theory of the private sector and on business philosophy, but aimed at minimizing the size and scope of governmental activities. Integrated with ideas rooted in political economy, they have now been applied to public sector institutions.

Hence, governments that are far from being simple businesses have been encouraged to manage and run themselves like businesses. An integrative definition for NPM that relies on the previous works would thus argue that NPM represents *"an approach in public administration that employs knowledge and experiences acquired in business management and other disciplines to improve the efficiency, effectiveness, and general performance of public services in modern bureaucracies."*

What makes New Public Management new?

NPM is growing in popularity in North America and across the world, and many governments have adopted of its ideas and recommendations that have proven beneficial, thereby arguing for the continued implementation of this strategy. A consensus exists today that NPM has become extremely popular in theory and in practice in public arenas. Relying on an extensive survey of public management research in America, Garson and Overman (1983: 275) argue that this increasing popularity is due to the more aggressive connotation of the term "management" as compared with "administration."

Yet, is NPM really a new doctrine in public administration or just another variation on old concepts and ideas? There is no doubt that the increased impact of new ideas and methods from the field of public management into that of administrative science is essential and natural. It reflects a special focus of modern public administration that must not be ignored. It may also be viewed as a major segment of the broader field of public administration because it focuses on the profession and on public managers as practitioners of that profession. Thus, public management does indeed contain some new elements of vital and innovative thinking. Furthermore, it emphasizes well-accepted managerial tools, techniques, knowledge, and skills that can be used to turn ideas and policy into successful programs of action.

Other scholars (e.g., Lynn, 1996: 38–9) delineate six differences between public administration and public management that transform the latter into a new field of study and practice: (1) the inclusion of general management functions such as planning, organizing, control, and evaluation in lieu of simple discussion about social values and the conflicts of bureaucracy and democracy; (2) an instrumental orientation favoring the use of the criteria of economy and efficiency in lieu of equity, responsiveness, or political salience; (3) a pragmatic focus on mid-level managers in lieu of the perspective of political or policy elites; (4) a tendency to consider management as generic, aimed at minimizing the differences between the public and private sectors in lieu of accentuating them; (5) a singular focus on the organization where external relations are treated in the same rational manner as internal operations in lieu of a focus on laws, institutions, and political bureaucratic processes; (6) a strong philosophical link with the scientific management tradition in lieu of close ties to political science or sociology.

While the emergence of NPM is frequently related to the increasing impact of positivist behavioral science on the study of politics and government (e.g., Lynn, 1996: 5–6), the practical aspect of this process should also be considered. Practical public managers, as well as political scientists, refer to the difficulties in policy making and policy implementation that faced many Western societies in Europe, America, and elsewhere during the 1970s. These practical difficulties are viewed today as an important trigger for the development of NPM. Reviewing two recent books on NPM (Aucoin, 1995; Boston, Martin, Pallot, and Walsh, 1996), Khademian (1998: 269) argues that American and British advocates of the field find common ground in explaining why such reforms were necessary. The problem of an inflexible bureaucracy that often could not respond efficiently and promptly to the public needs contradicted basic democratic principles and values in these countries. Elegantly, Peter Aucoin summarizes a "trinity" of broadly based challenges with which Western democracies have coped and with which they will probably continue to struggle in the future, partly through management reform: (1) growing demands for restraint in public sector spending, (2) increasing cynicism regarding government bureaucracies' responsiveness to citizens' concerns and political authority and dissatisfaction with program effectiveness, and (3) a growing international, market driven economy that does not defer to domestic policy efforts. It seems that these challenges have led many Western governments in America, Britain, New Zealand, Canada and elsewhere to the recognition that firm reforms and changes in public service should be made.

Critique of NPM

Certainly, the NPM approach suggests a different type of interaction between citizens and rulers in democracies. However, the roots of such interactions can be found a century ago. For example, Weikert (2001) asserted that "the ideas behind NPM are not new" and that "NPM builds on a long history of using business practices in government and reflects a resurgence of old ideas about the form and functions of government" (p. 362). During the first years of the twentieth century, reformers and business leaders demanded greater accountability in local government, and many politicians as well as public officials turned to business principles to improve governmental activities, invigorate performance, and reduce corruption. However, the vision of NPM is also far different from the old business-guided governance in that it looks to reduce government size and minimize its involvement in citizens' lives. As is evident from the above principles, NPM advocates that governments and public administrative bodies view citizens as clients/customers of the public sector, while governments and the public sector are perceived as managers of large bureaucracies. According to this view (Aucoin, 1995; Garson and Overman, 1983; Pollitt and Bouckaert, 2000), the state and its bureaucratic subsystems are equivalent to a large private organization operating in an economic environment of supply and demand. In this spirit, a major goal of government is to satisfy the needs or demands of citizens, namely to show greater responsiveness to the public as clients. In line with this approach, it is obvious that modern nations must rely more on private and third sector institutions and less on government to satisfy the societal needs of heterogeneous populations. The goal of satisfying the needs of citizens became central to the NPM philosophy.

Nevertheless, NPM may be criticized for not doing enough to encourage and incorporate the idea of collaboration or partnership between citizens and the public sector and for failing to apply these themes to modern managerial thinking (Vigoda and Golembiewski, 2001). Unlike traditional public administration, the NPM movement focuses on citizens as sophisticated clients in complex environments. The principles of NPM are compatible with theories of political economy such as regulative policy by governments or the policy of transferring responsibilities from the public sector to the private and third sectors. These ideas, and the governmental policies deriving from them, frequently challenge various social democratic principles, norms and values in Britain, America, and many other

Western democracies. Public authorities are urged to treat the public well, not only because of their presumed administrative responsibility for quality in action but also because of their obligation to marketplace rules and to economic demands, and above all because of their fear of losing clients in an increasingly competitive businesslike arena. In fact, while NPM is an improvement over more classic views of public administration that saw citizens as subjects or voters, it does not go far enough in fostering the idea of vital collaboration between citizens, governments and the public sector, which is the essence of democratic civil society (Vigoda, 2002b).

In line with this, "Neo-Managerialism" (Terry, 1998) notes an additional obstacle to productive partnership that must also be recognized and surmounted. According to Terry, neo-managerialism supports the idea that administrative leaders should assume the role of public entrepreneurs. However, "public entrepreneurs of the neo-managerialist persuasion are oblivious to other values highly prized in the US constitutional democracy. Values such as fairness, justice, representation, or participation are not on the radar screen (and) this is indeed, troublesome" (p. 200). In many respects neo/new managerialism and NPM encourage passivity among the citizenry. They offer citizens the power of *exit* (which indeed was virtually unavailable in the past), but at the same time they discourage use of the original power of *voice* by citizens who may have much to contribute to their communities (Vigoda and Golembiewski, 2001). Exit is an economic choice, while voice is more of a political action by individuals in and around organizational systems. Exit is also classified as a generally destructive behavior, while voice is a productive one. According to this argument, NPM restricts and discourages the productive political voices of the people.

Hence, recent developments in the study of NPM have focused on the responsibilities of governments and public agencies in their interaction with citizens, but similarly have paid far less attention to the active roles of citizens and to their obligations to the community. Most of the current NPM literature favors massive socialization of business management practices in the public sector to provide governments with better tools for policy implementation. But on the other hand, these orientations and practices have not yet been integrated with another core-construct of healthy democracies – genuine collaboration and partnership with citizens based on equal opportunities for participation and massive involvement in running public life more effectively. This lack of emphasis on the idea of partnership and collaboration in favor of good responsive management may be deemed a flaw in contemporary NPM theory.

The ongoing pursuit of "new" and "newer" initiatives in public administration

Scholars today agree that at least some of the accumulated wisdom of the private sector in developed countries is transferable to the public sector. Some even say that this export of ideas can contribute to the reconciliation of bureaucracy and democracy as more freedom is infused into old style public organizations and greater efficiency is encouraged in democratic systems. Anyhow, in an attempt to "liberate" the public sector from its old conservative image and moribund practice, NPM was advanced as a relevant and promising alternative. Thus, NPM literature has tried to recognize and define new criteria that may help in determining the extent to which public agencies succeed in meeting the growing needs of the public. NPM has continuously advocated the implementation of specific Performance Indicators (PIs) used in private organizations to create a performance-based culture with matching compensatory strategies. It has recommended that these indicators be applied in the public sector because they can function as milestones by which to better gauge the efficiency and effectiveness of public agencies.

Moreover, citizens' awareness of the performance of public services was suggested as a core element of NPM because it can increase the political pressure placed on elected and appointed public servants, thereby enhancing both managerial and financial efficiency in the public sector. Scholars who advocate NPM compare this process of public accountability to stakeholders/citizens to the role adopted by financial reporting in the private/corporate sector. As in the private sector, increasing external outcomes can have a meaningful impact on internal control mechanisms, as managers and public servants become more sensitive to their duties and more committed to serving citizens as customers.

In view of the above and looking towards the future, Lynn (1998: 231) suggested that NPM of the late 1990s has three constructive legacies for the field of public administration and for democratic theory and practice: (1) a stronger emphasis on performance motivated administration and an inclusion in the administrative canon of performance oriented institutional arrangements, structural forms, and managerial doctrines fitted to a particular context – in other words, advances in the state of the art of public management; (2) an international dialogue on and a stronger comparative dimension to the study of state design and administrative reform; and (3) the integrated use of economic, sociological, social-psychological, and other advanced conceptual models and heuristics in the study of public institutions and management, with the potential to strengthen the field's scholarship and the possibilities for theory grounded practice.

It seems that the ongoing debate about the net contribution and added value of NPM to the study and practice of public administration will continue. Whether it is a "new" approach, a partly new doctrine, or an old lady with new hat, it is obvious that NPM is responsible for some of the meaningful transformations witnessed by modern societies in the last few decades. It is also likely that the "newer" doctrines and methods will evolve along with bureaucratic, political, technological, and cultural developments. NPM has made its mark, but this is only one link in an endless chain of scientific advancement.

Nations as a marketplace: An economic decline

The discussion about NPM obviously leads to more elaboration about the role of economics in nation building. The consideration of nations and states as functioning mainly in a marketplace-oriented environment is a growing field of interest for many scholars, those who come from the administrative sciences, public administration, political science, political economy, or economics itself. Some of the most influential works on the relationship between states, bureaucracies, and the economic arena are those of Niskanen (1968; 1971; 1994) and Mises (1939, 1983; 1990) who build on public choice theory and on rational choice theory. The major question asked by them and by other scholars who emphasize the marketplace canons of nation building relates to explanations for the unique status of the public sector in what seems to be a free and liberal economic system, but in practice fails to perform very effectively. Modern bureaucracies must overcome a number of inherent contradictions in their position in modern democracies. On one hand, they are an essential part of advanced democratic systems that support the concepts of liberalization, freedom of choice and occupation, and many other democratic values, both in theory and in practice. On the other hand, they need an effective government (or governance) that is centralized enough to sometimes make unilateral decisions to advance policies that will have positive results for society. In this regard, the nation as a purely marketplace environment is a utopia. However, modern bureaucracies do follow at least a few principles of the free market system, and these principles are very valuable in explaining human behavior, group activity, and states policies in modern societies.

Theoretical approaches

Carnis (2005) suggests that in the view of both Niskanen and Mises, the raison d'être of bureaucracy is market failure or a symptom of socialism. According to Niskanen, bureaucracies exist because the market cannot supply certain goods or services. Thus, the role of bureaucracy is the regulation of needs and demands in the face of a market that is not profit oriented. Bureaucracy constitutes a means of substitution for the defective market. However, for Mises, bureaucracy is the expression of a more important evil for society: the state's continuous intrusion into private business activities and the personal life of citizens. Bureaucratic management differs from profit management with regard to the emphasis placed on rules against price system mechanisms (p. 2).

According to Niskanen, bureaucracies are based on organizational formation and a non-profit orientation. This approach implies first, that the difference between costs and revenues are not appropriated by any member of the organization and second, that the revenues of the organization do not derive solely from the sale of goods or services. Niskanen's analysis focuses on the productive dimension of bureaucracy. His purpose is to "develop a theory of "'supply'" based on a model of a purposive behavior by the manager of a single bureaucratic agency. As suggested by Carnis (2005), in Niskenan's view, bureaucracies exist because the market cannot provide certain goods or services. Market failures are the true origin of bureaucracy. The natural monopolistic situation (high fixed costs), the free riding problem (difficulty in collecting fees) and the external effects (difficulties … caused by the definition of property rights) constitute the traditional rationales for justifying governmental intervention. Niskanen's analysis goes further by asserting that, in some cases, the bureaucratic system could perform better than the market process. Loyalty *would* be superior in some ways to price mechanisms, or would be expected to be (Niskanen, 1994: 20). Niskanen also proposes a general framework for analyzing the bureaucratic relationship. This relationship is represented as a bilateral monopolistic situation between a sponsor and a bureau. It is conceived as a bargain between both agents concerning the output and the budget (Niskanen, 1994: 24). Niskanen's approach can be summed up by three points: (1) The analysis focuses on the technical problem of production and consists essentially of an inside investigation of bureaucratic organization. (2) The provision of goods and services by bureaucratic organizations finds some justification in the inability of the market process to satisfy the demand. (3) Given the specificity of these goods and services, there is a separation between the funding and the production, and the goal of these organizations is not to make a profit. Moreover, the demand is not directly expressed but interpreted by politicians, who bargain with the bureau to determine its budget and its output.

From another perspective, Mises suggests that bureaucracy can be fully understood only by comparing it with the operation of the profit motive as it functions in the capitalistic market society (Mises, 1983). Consequently, Mises' approach consists of defining bureaucracy by stressing what it is not. Bureaucracy constitutes a specific approach to managing the allocation of resources in a system that does not seek to make a profit. Unlike in the profit management system, the allocation of resources by the bureaucracy is made by obeying rules. There is no need to satisfy customers or to produce a quality product at the best cost. The system of profit and loss plays no role. Following the rules in the allocation of resources is the major concern of the bureaucratic administration, a behavior that distinguishes it from the for-profit world where entrepreneurship and the role of prices and costs are key. The rules and regulations determine the products to supply, their characteristics, their price, and the method of production. More accurately, the essential traits of bureaucratic management are the absence of a check by economic calculation. The impossibility of controlling the profitability of economic activities is the direct consequence of operating without the profit motive. In such a situation, it is not possible to put a value on production. Mises suggests that "… we must answer again that bureaucracy in itself is neither good nor bad. It is a method of management which can be applied in different spheres of human activity" (p. 48) and also notes that, "bureaucratic management is management of affairs which cannot be checked by economic calculation" (p. 52). For Mises, bureaucracy is an instrument, the price that is paid for the execution of orders and regulations. Bureaucracy constitutes an indispensable tool for the government. The state cannot perform without bureaucratic intervention; bureaucracy represents a consubstantial element of the existence of government. "There is a field, namely, the handling of the apparatus of government, in which bureaucratic methods are required by necessity" (p. 48). Consequently, the bureaucratic process is characterized by the importance of rules in the allocation of resources. The other element to take into account is the ownership dimension. Mises' analysis differentiates between private and public ownership. Hence, for Mises, bureaucracy is a mode of allocating resources, the administration of those resources resting essentially upon rules and a command–control system. Those resources are not legitimately held by the administrator. Consequently, the negation of the economic calculation reflects in fact the denial of private property rights and the freedom of people to decide for themselves. It also represents a process of substitution with a more coercive system based on rules to obey and on a command–control system of decision-making (Mises, 1983: 20). However, Mises believes that society needs a minimum of bureaucracy. In fact, Mises contends that society needs a minimum of government intervention, which should be limited to the protection of property rights, the properties themselves, and the people. Such minimal intervention is necessary to insure social cooperation among the members of society (Mises, 1983; 1998) and make peaceful interactions between people possible.

Summary: Is there a "science" of nations?

Obviously, the triple approach to the study of nation building, bureaucracy, and democracy as presented above should lead us to a more integrative view of the dilemmas ahead. Etzioni-Halevy (1983) describes this clash of structures and ideologies as a multi-source thesis of dilemmas (pp. 87–8): First, "bureaucracy generates a dilemma for democracy" because of its tendency to become "more and more independent and powerful and the rules governing the exercise of that power are not clearly defined." Thus, "bureaucracy poses a threat to the democratic political structure ... and yet, a powerful, independent bureaucracy is also necessary for the prevention of political corruption and for safeguarding of proper democratic procedures." Second, "democracy generates a dilemma for bureaucracy and the bureaucrats who run it, because democratic rules are self-contradictory and put bureaucracy in a double bind: ... bureaucracy is expected to be both independent and subservient, both responsible for its own actions and subject to ministerial responsibility, both politicized and non-politicized at one and the same time." From these two points emerges a third thesis where Etzioni-Halevy argues that these dilemmas put pressure on the political system and are almost impossible to resolve. From the public managerial perspective, Hood (1998) deals with "the art of the state" which, in my view, is very similar to the concept of nation building, where culture and rhetoric are cornerstones of the profession. In terms of management and administrative thinking, it may thus be suggested that the strategy used by most modern nations is one of *risk management*. Both democracy and bureaucracy must co-exist if modern nations seek both freedom for their people and also proper governability that promotes continuous improvement in the quality of life. The co-existence of bureaucracy and democracy carries risks, but also offers challenges. The development of a rich and enlightened study of *nation building* may serve as the basis upon which we can rebuild our communities and our nations.

Chapter 2
Dilemmas of Governability Under Democratic and Bureaucratic Constraints

Bureaucracy versus democracy in public domains: Several models

In recent decades, reforms in public administration, and especially the New Public Management (NPM) doctrine, have raised many questions as to the role of citizens and governments in our modern societies. This leading contemporary paradigm in public administration has emphasized the need to improve administrative performance and to treat citizens as clients, to create an ethos of a businesslike public sector and a market society. However, NPM has drawn fire from various fronts: from those who seek the improved governability of state agencies, from those who have prophesized a resulting decline in citizenry activism and involvement, and from those who have predicted serious damage to democratic values. The call for increased responsiveness by public agencies in some ways contradicted the basic need for strong governments and for improved governability. It was also countered by pressure for more collaboration between bureaucracies and social players. This second paradigm believes that the goal of improved performance can be accomplished only by safeguarding and advancing democratic values (Box, Marshall, Read, and Read, 2001; Vigoda, 2002a, 2002b).

In light of the above, it seems worthwhile to enlarge on the discussion about two major topics related to public administration and modern societies, namely *governability* through improved performance and *democracy* through liberal values. This chapter thus attempts to explore the conceptual territory between them. Naturally, this is a challenging task, as it tries to assimilate ideas and conceptual thinking from several disciplines such as management, public administration, politics, and sociology. In many ways such a discussion calls for a better balance between managerial/administrative theories and social/humanistic ideology, and the creation of a much more realistic understanding of public administration. Thus, despite the various points of view of and dissimilarities between each of the above disciplines, the goal of all of them is the same: to find a golden path between the needs and constraints of modern nations as market societies, and the desires and demands of the citizens of liberal states. This golden path is should lead us towards effective governability that preserves democratic values. While bureaucracy and democracy are frequently perceived as two separate concepts, they also have complementary meanings that are central and essential for the prosperous growth of our societies, states and nations.

Literature in public administration follows two complementary tracks for understanding changes and progress in the discipline: those that favor the bureaucratic framework of managed change and those that advocate a bottom-up transformation based on public choice. Similarly, there are two major theoretical models for reforming public administration: (1) administrative/bureaucracy-driven models and (2) democratic/citizen-driven or grass-roots-driven models. Both of these models imply change in the public sector, each from a different starting point. Both models are practical and possible. Neither of the models, however, is superior to the other. They are both legitimate abstractions of a very complicated reality where changes can work either way.

Administrative-driven models represent top-down governability. They view government and public administration as those who are responsible for the initiation of change and for making it work properly. On the other hand, grass-roots-driven models represent bottom-up governability. They make more demands of the people, expecting that they, instead of governments and bureaucracies, will make the first move towards change and reform. Hence, these models demonstrate how various reforms became successful when emanating from the urgent needs of individuals and groups or from the spontaneous collective support for an original, popular leader.

Administrative-driven models and top-down governability: Let the state lead

The most conventional path to governability, change, and reforms in public administration is by top-down initiatives of the state and a planned transformation from "old" to "new." A planned change by the government assumes that the state must lead national progress and development through effective tools of strategic thinking, the professionalism of public servants, and a balanced integration of political, economic, and social considerations. The idea of top-down governability is supported by the rational choice theory and by rational decision-making models. According to this approach, democracy functions to maximize the interests of all citizens and individuals of a national system. Hence, bureaucracy serves as a tool to facilitate the required change. Consequently, budgets, allocation of resources, employment of public servants, strategies for problem solving, and other core issues in state management are all subject to the rational thinking of disinterested politicians and professional public servants.

However, rational choice theory originally suggests that humans are motivated by self-interests. Based on utilitarian philosophy and game theory arguments (Boschken, 1998), it has been posited that individuals, as well as groups and institutions, generally operate according to desired goals and objectives. These may be formal or informal, but they always aim at maximizing personal benefits and minimizing costs (Ostrom, 1986). On the assumption that social players constantly seek more revenues, and at the same time attempt to reduce expenses and negative consequences, top-down initiatives may be problematic because the utopian view of collectivist vision contradicts human nature and self-centered interests. Thus, useful and long-range successful policies will emerge only in those cases where high ranking policy makers see a personal benefit (that is, political, economic, psychological) in making a process work.

As opposed to this rationality, healthy and prosperous civic societies in practice seek higher levels of cooperation among their members to increase general "public goods" and to improve the welfare and well-being of large communities. Thus, collaboration is frequently initiated from the top down and may be referred to as another mechanism for conflict management (Vigoda-Gadot, 2003a). For example, Fredericksen (1996) elaborated on the usefulness, but also the fragmentary nature, of analyzing conflict management methods in public domains as a continuum ranging from competitive to cooperative techniques. While the former represent a win-lose game, the latter are better described as win–win alternatives. Between the two extremes, several other alternatives exist such as litigation, arbitration, mediation, facilitated problem solving, and collaboration. However, these alternatives may be always subject to the basic contradiction between utilitarian human nature and the desirable altruistic nature of civic societies. For the emergence of reliable and honest leadership that plans ahead and initiates top-down ventures that accord well with citizens' needs and desires, a balanced mixture of self-interests and collective interests must be maintained. In top-down models of governability, egocentrism and communitarianism must find a way to co-exist in peace. Consequently, healthy top-down initiatives in public domains depend on rational choice models (i.e., Niskanen, 1968; 1994; Mises, 1983; 1990), on social/economic exchange theory (i.e., Blau, 1964), and on the collective vision of communal solidarism (Etzioni, 1994; 1995). Whereas false top-down initiatives are typical of non-democratic regimes, true top-down changes exist only in liberal environments and prosperous societies, those that abound in mutual understanding and acceptance of others' needs and aspirations, but that also value the idea of free markets and free exchange mechanisms among people. Wherever such acceptance and approval are sparse, there is a greater likelihood of alienation from governments, distrust, diversification, intolerance, conflict, and self-centered activity rather than concern for society at large or public solidarity. In such cases, top-down initiatives of public policy are counterproductive, and the alternative path of bottom-up initiatives flourishes.

Citizen-driven models and bottom-up governability: Let the people lead

The less conventional track for governability relies on the democratic ideal of grass-roots change and reforms. As suggested above, the grass-roots-driven models represent bottom-up governability and make more demands of the people, expecting them to be more involved, active, and innovative in determining their lives and quality of life. Citizens, instead of governments and bureaucracies, are those who need to make the first move towards change and reform because they are the ones who will be affected by those changes.

Letting the people lead involves many partners who initiate a process of change in policies, services, and administration based on the voluntary actions of citizens as individuals and as groups. As will be demonstrated in the next chapter, the meaning of citizenship and of citizenship behavior is similarly transformed to cohere with this change in mindset in modern nations. According to this approach, the administrative state no longer has the monopoly on reforms and formation of policies. The state relies quite often on the motivation and power of voluntary groups, on citizens, and on the third sector in general for performing tasks that in the past seemed to be within the purview of public officials and of politicians.

Jordan et al. (2005) suggests that at the center of the debate about models for governability is the question of "who or what steers society." As Tables 2.1 and 2.2 illustrate, public administration involves a mix of players who take on distinct roles – they fall into the "hybrid" boxes – involving both government and society, not one or the other. The strong government and strong governance boxes, in contrast, are more indicative of the "ideal" type promulgated by Max Weber.

According to Jordan et al. (2005), a distinction must be made between the meaning of government and the meaning of governance. Table 2.1 provides a typology of the complex array of sub-types on the basis of who (or what) determines the ends and means of policy. Table 2.1 focuses on the theoretical characteristics of the sub-types, rather than their actual use. However, comparison of the tables does reveal both the extensive overlap between the main sub-types and, by implication, some of the potential difficulties of clearly distinguishing government from governance. The governance debate is essentially concerned

Table 2.1   A simple typology of instrument types

	The State Specifies the Goal to be Achieved	The State Does Not Specify the Goal to be Achieved
The state specifies how the goal is to be achieved	Regulation (for example, linking emission standards to the use of a certain type of technology); fiscal incentives (for example, tax incentives for a less polluting technology)	Technology-based regulatory standards (for example, best available technology)
Non-state actors specify how the goal is to be achieved	Usually negotiated voluntary agreements; some market-based instruments; some regulations (for example, environmental quality objectives)	Environmental management systems; most market-based Instruments; some voluntary agreements; eco-labels

Source: Based on Russell and Powell (1996).

Table 2.2   A simple typology of governance types

	Government Determines Societal Goals (Ends)	Society Determines Societal Goals (Ends)
Government selects the means of policy	Strong Government: hierarchical steering from the centre	Hybrid Types
Society selects the means of policy	Hybrid Types	Strong Governance: society is "self-steering" and "self-organizing"

Source: Jordan et al. (2005; 483).

with understanding who or what steers society. Thus, under a government approach, society is steered by a central government, whereas in a governance model, "society actually does more self-steering rather than depending upon guidance from government" (Peters, 2000: 36). Both Tables 2.1 and 2.2 identify two important functions that need to be discharged when instruments are used: (1) the determination of the *means* of policy (that is, for us, the instruments of policy) and (2) the determination of the ultimate *ends* to be achieved (that is, the policy objectives). According to Jordan et al. (2005), "to suggest that a transition to governance is occurring does not necessarily imply that both of these functions are changing at the same time" (p. 485). However, "government" is located in the top left cell of Table 2.2, and the further we travel towards the bottom right cell, the more important societal self-organization and steering (that is, governance, or bottom-up governability) become.

Without a doubt, we live in an era of great challenges for democracies and for free citizens, some of which come from the duality of the meaning of government and governance. The twenty-first century will necessitate enormous changes in our conventional perceptions of governability from top-down initiatives to higher levels of citizen involvement and participation in policy making and implementation. Thus, a similar reformation of the meaning of citizenship and a redefinition of the role of citizens in democracies and in bureaucracies is expected. This process will undoubtedly have an impact on other stakeholders in the public sphere, in private sector firms, in the third sector, in the media, in academia, and all of them in the international context. All these players, and others, will need to find better ways to collaborate, innovate, and change, and it is the role of academic activity and studies to pave the way for such productive interaction.

Moreover, the growing trend of bottom-up initiatives should be encouraged by governments as it has several advantages: (1) building strong nations with stronger and more deeply involved citizens; (2) creating an active and responsible citizen, rather than a passive and dependent customer; (3) sharing the burden of caring for and improving society among the many stakeholders of society; (4) highlighting collaboration and partnership instead of conflict and dissention in democracies; and (5) encouraging grass-roots innovation from the people who will benefit from it.

Economic growth versus political distress in modern democracies: An irony

Even as modern nations grow economically, they still face increasing political and social problems. This is ironic because one would expect that increased global wealth and prosperity should reduce social problems and improve the daily lives of most people. Obviously, this is not the case if we consider the entire world because there is still an unequal distribution of global wealth. However, why is it not the case in countries that enjoy a greater share of the world's wealth? Why is discontent growing in places where governments have more to share with their people and in places where the welfare state is increasing its involvement in people's lives?

As I will try to explain in the next chapters, a major reason for such tension and discontent stems from the direct and indirect relationships between the ideological means and values for governing in a democratic environment and the operative methods of governing and managing the public sector. In my view, the discontent that we are witnessing in most modern societies is due in large part to unsuccessful strategies for bridging democracy and bureaucracy. The mishandling of the bureaucratic-democratic paradox can lead to a smoothly functioning bureaucracy that may contribute to the decline of democratic values.

If past achievements are any indication, modern democracies have many reasons to be very optimistic about the future. A quick look at economic growth

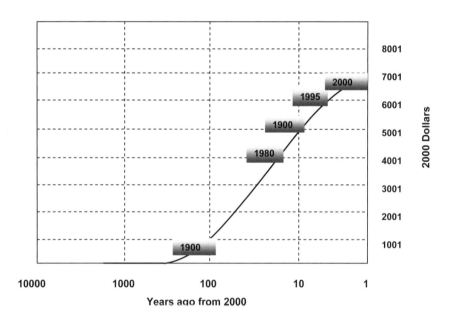

Figure 2.1   World economic growth: A historical view of gross global product per capita (GGP) portrait

Source: http://futurist.typepad.com/my_weblog/2006/02/economic_growth.html.

and development shows that in the last half of the past century most of the world has charted an almost unbroken path upward in its prosperity.

The graph in Figure 2.1 presents past and predicted world economic growth per capita. Today, the US economy is growing at a median rate of 3.5 percent per year, and the world economy at around 4.5 percent per year. This is a growth rate that we have come to take for granted and expect. But such annual growth rates were unheard of in the nineteenth century or the eighteenth century (when the world economy grew less than 1 percent per year). Things changed very little over the span of 10 or 20 years. People expected their children to have the same living standards and be surrounded by the same technology as they were.

When we look at the graph in Figure 2.1, the accelerating rate of economic growth is clear. Thousands of years of human civilization before the twentieth century produced modest wealth compared to what was produced in the much shorter interval of the twentieth century. Even within the twentieth century, there was far more growth in the latter half than in the first 50 years. Now, in 2006, 4 percent a year is assumed, and taken for granted. In fact, three billion people in the world are living in economies growing at more than 6 percent a year (China, India, Russia, Vietnam, Pakistan, Thailand, Malaysia, and others). This would have been considered amazing at any other time in history. Is this just an aberration, or has the trend line itself shifted into higher gear? Can we expect this to continue, or even accelerate, in the future? Figure 2.1 displays the global per capita GGP (Gross Global Product), starting from the year 2000 and going backwards on a logarithmic scale. It is apparent how the economic gains of the twentieth century dwarf those of all prior millennia of human civilization. Put another way, the world GGP growth of 4 percent a year seems normal today, but was less than 1 percent in the eighteenth century. If we focus on the second half of the twentieth century, the changes are even more impressive, as Figure 2.2 demonstrates.

As this growth is not just exponential, but exponential even in the second derivative (i.e., the rate of increase also increases at ever-faster rates), an expected figure for the year 2050 should look as follows (see Figure 2.3).

The breakneck speed of this development leads us to ask whether we are straining our resources ecologically, politically, financially, militarily, and socially. Having strong and growing economies is only one component of the equation for building strong nations. The discontent in modern democracies contrasts sharply with these indicators of economic growth. The sources of this discontent must lie somewhere else. Several explanations have been offered. Some would say that its roots are in the unequal distribution of economic goods among citizens. Other possible answers are the decline of the welfare state, the growing needs and demands of citizens, and overall world transformations such as political instability, cultural interactions in an ever-shrinking world, a rapid technological revolution that causes instability in the classic social hierarchy, and immense demographical changes that have a tremendous effect on the lives of every citizen on the globe.

Building Strong Nations

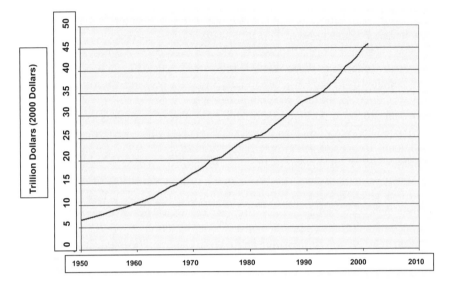

**Figure 2.2   World economic growth in the second half of the twentieth
century**

Source: http://www.sustainablescale.org/.

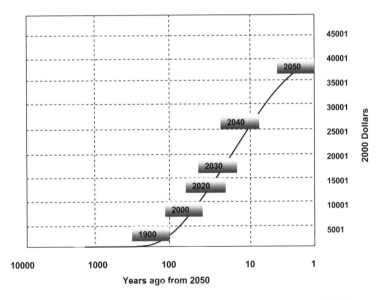

**Figure 2.3   Expected world per capita global gross product (GGP)
until 2050**

Source: http://futurist.typepad.com/my_weblog/2006/02/economic_growth.html.

Decline of the welfare state

Since the second half of the twentieth century, the welfare state in Europe, as well as in many other parts of the world, has been in decline. Many books and articles have depicted the crisis that has resulted from the movement of the state away from its former role as caregiver to its citizens.

Razin and Sadka (2005) deal with the problem of the withdrawal of the state from its commitment and responsibility to citizens. They use a political economy framework to support their rationality, which is quite accepted by most of the political science and social science community worldwide. Focusing on global processes of aging populations, migration, and globalization, they suggest that we are witnessing a deterioration of the financial system and the welfare state benefits as known today. In their view, combined forces of demographic change and globalization will make it impossible for the welfare state to maintain itself at its present level, that is, to continuously increase services to citizens and increase public expectations. As the authors argue, in much of the developed world, the proportion of the population aged 60 and over is expected to rise dramatically over the coming years – from 35 percent in 2000 to a projected 66 percent in 2050 in the European Union and from 27 percent to 47 percent in the United States – which may necessitate higher tax burdens and greater public debt to maintain national pension systems at current levels. The migration of unskilled workers produces additional strains on welfare state financing because such migrants typically receive benefits that exceed what they pay in taxes. Moreover, higher capital taxation, which could potentially be used to finance welfare benefits, is made unlikely by international tax competition brought about by globalization of the capital market. Their conclusion is simple: the political pressure from both aging and migrant populations indirectly generates political processes that favor trimming rather than expanding the welfare state. The combined pressures of aging, migration, and globalization will shift the balance of political power and generate public support from the majority of the voting population for cutting back traditional welfare state benefits.

Similarly, in a seminar organized by Observatoire Chrétien des Réalités Economiques (Paris, France, 15 October 1998), Michel Camdessus, the Managing Director of the International Monetary Fund, suggested that we are heading towards a shrinking of the welfare state in the next millennium. Camdessus argues that the twentieth century has seen countless achievements and changes. As historians look back on this period, two developments are likely to stand out as being among the most definitive of our time. The first one, which deepened as the century progressed, was the acceptance by many, indeed most, nation states of an obligation toward their citizens to provide a certain minimum level of well-being. In industrial economies, especially in Europe, this led to the emergence of the welfare state. The other development, globalization, has been rather more recent, blossoming largely in the last two decades of the twentieth century. Building on hard-won gains in trade liberalization, and aided by technological advances, a rapidly increasing volume of economic transactions now transcend national borders. Consequently, today, both the welfare state and globalization face crises of sorts. The more immediate and visible crisis relates to globalization, whose benefits to countries around the world have been undermined by widespread loss of confidence in financial markets, and consequently threatens a number of economies. The other crisis is less dramatic, less visible, but in the long-term is more profound and difficult to address. Welfare systems, based on the best possible motivation of ameliorating hardship and improving human welfare, have come to represent an enormous drain on the resources and the efficiency of many of the so-called welfare states.

In Camdessus' view, the term "welfare state" has typically been applied to countries in which public spending has risen to very high levels in order *to finance social programs*. The countries that are considered welfare states normally have governments whose expenditure is about half of their GDP. Indeed in some countries, it has risen as high as 60 percent of GDP. How did such spending levels come about? For most of the twentieth century, public spending increased because governments, especially European governments, progressively moved into activities that in the past had been left to the private sector. This trend was promoted by world wars and depressions but also by a sharp change in peoples' attitudes about the role of the modern state. The most significant changes took place in education, health, pensions, and general welfare subsidies. According to Camdessus, the extraordinary growth in public spending that accompanied the creation of the welfare state can be appreciated by the change in the share of public spending in national income that took place between the beginning and the end of the twentieth century. At the beginning of the century, the public spending of the countries now classified as welfare states was only around 10–15 percent of their national incomes. Today, it is around 50 percent or more.

As a result, social welfare has improved. The growth of public spending has reduced many risks and costs for the members of these societies: the costs of being ill, illiterate, old, poor, or unemployed. Public welfare has made great strides in terms of increased literacy and educational levels, reduced infant mortality and longer life expectancy, and reduced trauma and despair that comes with unemployment or incapacitation.

However, there were also costs associated with this process. Two types of cost may be identified. One is the direct financial or budgetary costs of providing services. The other, perhaps more controversial, and certainly more difficult to measure, is the loss of economic efficiency that is associated with some types of social services, which, for instance, reduce incentives for seeking employment. With respect to budgetary costs, the money needed to finance a welfare state must be raised mostly through taxation and, to a lesser extent, through borrowing. The tax burdens (i.e., the share of taxes in national income) have increased enormously throughout this century, reaching levels of around 45 percent of GDP in France and in Italy and even higher levels in several other European countries. In addition to increasing taxes, many countries have, over the years, also borrowed to finance their high levels of spending when tax revenues were not sufficient. France is not among the countries that have relied most heavily on this type of financing. Even so, public debt has risen over the decades to almost 60 percent of GDP. In some countries, though, spending has led to very high levels of public debt, in some cases exceeding 100 percent of GDP. This was the reason why the Maastricht Treaty imposed debt limits as a condition for being part of the European Union. A high level of debt diverts tax resources toward paying off these debts and complicates the conduct of monetary policy.

The other cost to the welfare state has to do with the reduced efficiency of the employment market. In fact, this issue has ethical, moral, and ideological ramifications for the "greater welfare state." Beyond economic outcomes, the role of the modern state in shaping citizens' lives and their quality of life has increased dramatically, creating the problem of the "passive citizen." In Europe, low levels of employment point to a reduced motivation to work. Unemployment compensation and employment protection have been twin features of the European systems for decades. Could it be that the welfare state is contributing to this situation? Unemployment benefits that replace a high proportion of previous earnings and that last for long periods must surely play a role in reducing the incentive to seek work. Employment protection legislation, high social security taxes, or excessively high minimum wages are all factors that can raise the costs of employment. Uncomfortable as it may be, the scourge of unemployment is unlikely to be removed unless these and other features of welfare systems are reviewed. Another problem that has attracted widespread attention in connection with welfare states is that, despite the best intentions of policymakers, in some countries existing programs have created a type of social segmentation. Two categories of citizens have emerged: those who are employed and are entitled to quite generous benefits if they lose their jobs, and those who are effectively excluded from the labor force and have few opportunities to re-enter the mainstream of society. The image springs to mind of a medieval city whose walls protect the citizens inside them, but leave those who are outside shut out and unprotected.

Growing needs and demands of citizens

Ironically, as the welfare state has been declining, the public has been increasing its demands for an improved quality of life and increased political freedom. The economic growth in modern democracies has a general positive effect on our lives. However, with this progress comes bottom-up pressure on the state to meet greater and more challenging goals. While this is a normal and expected process, it still creates a gap between expectations and reality that can never be bridged and gives rise to a serious reason for mistrust in government. Despite the power of bureaucracy, law, and authority (and some would also say control over resources and budgets), governments are in fact in an inferior situation compared with citizens. Whereas citizens' demands of governments may be justified and natural, the response of governments to such democratic bottom-up pressures poses many dilemmas. First, there is the normative, ethical, and ideological question of "should we meet the demands"? Then comes the practical, economic question of "can we meet the demands"? Finally, there is the technical question of "who will meet the demands"? Unsurprisingly, and in accordance with the main approaches of the disciplines defined earlier in this book as nation building, the answers come from three different sources. The normative question of "should we" must look to the socio-political framework of ideology and ethics for an answer. The practical question of "can we" relates to economic resources and the availability of budgets. Finally, the technical question of "who will" must be answered within the organizational, managerial, and administrative framework.

Governability and world transformations

The discontent in modern nations, however, also arises from the immense worldwide transformations in culture, politics, technology, and demographics. In recent years, this issue has been discussed extensively in the literature on governance and administration (i.e., Giddens, 1990; Osborne and Gaebler, 1992). I have mentioned the problem of globalization in the previous sections but this is just a mirror of the deeper cultural and political changes in many of today's developed states.

Socio-cultural transformations and governability   Many of the current problems of governability in the developed, but also in the less developed world, are strongly affected by social and cultural changes in the structure of nations and in the life-style of our societies. Socio-demographic transformations such as the changing nature of populations in demographic terms (for example, the need to handle the pressures of mass immigration from less developed countries, to deal with elderly populations, change of careers and the nature of jobs, greater demand for education and knowledge), the effect of the media revolution, the time and energy citizens tend to spend on activities that are not directly related to the production of goods and services (for example, leisure time, volunteering, and work for the community) have all changed the world in which we live. However, there are also influential cultural dynamics that may affect governability such as the almost unrestricted flow of norms and values among nations and societies and the liberal jargon of the modernized democratic society that permits behaviors and new types of life-styles that were unacceptable in the past. Moreover, the socio-cultural revolution facing many states is affected by changes in other societies and cultures and by the rapid and almost unrestricted flow of knowledge and information from one part of the world to the other.

These are all challenges to modern governability as they set new goals for policies and create new problems with which governments of the past had not dealt in any way. First, when the structure and type of populations is in flux, governments need to respond by adjusting their policies and goals to the new audience. The change in the structure of society, in the demographic characteristics of age, health, aspirations, and urbanization call for a variety of responses on the part of governments and greater flexibility of their mechanisms. These are all goals that are difficult to realize, as in any other organization that loses its old clients and needs to adjust to a new market. The only difference here is that governability is expected to answer our needs and demands as citizens in all aspects of our lives, not merely one "market" or another. In addition, given the massive change in cultures, governability is facing growing levels of uncertainty, and pressures to do things differently and according to new norms and values. Governments operate within the framework of a set of values. When those values change, the attitude of officials and the policies they promote must change as well, which is a not simple task, to say the least. Globalization adds yet another issue by forcing governments to operate in an environment that is constantly in flux, much like changing the tires on a car that never stops moving. When one policy in a specific field is proved successful (or unsuccessful) in one nation, other nations are often tempted to try it, sometimes with disastrous consequences. While we can learn a great deal from policies implemented in other states or cultures, we must recognize that every culture functions in a unique context. Ideas usually cannot be imported wholesale to another culture without some adjustments.

Political transformations and governability   Clearly, governability is also affected by political changes across the globe and in the internal arena of each state and nation. In fact, politics and governability are quite synonymous in their meaning, as the political sphere is the place where governments work and their policies are implemented. Furthermore, the legitimacy of governments is based on political and judicial arrangements that are acceptable in a given state. Therefore, when the political arena is in turmoil, governability is ultimately affected.

While the example of the immense changes in Eastern Europe as it transitioned towards democracy (or in other states in Asia or Africa that have experienced political transformations in recent years) springs to mind, our discussion focuses more on the political transformations *within* the democratic sphere. For example, in a parliamentary democracy, the capacity to govern is frequently determined by the balance among the parties. When electoral balance clearly gives one party (or a small number of parties) the mandate to rule and shape public policy, governability is much stronger than when more parties are involved in the process of governing. This point is simple and self-evident. However, reality is much more complicated and does not allow interpretations of governability merely based on electoral parameters. In other words, the balance of a coalition is only one aspect of the capacity to govern. The power of governments is also determined by other factors in political life such as the type of political leadership and the personality of the political cadre of leaders, the presidents, the prime minister or the chancellor. In other words, political stability is not just a substitute for the power of coalitions. Political disorder and problems of governability can also arise when citizens make greater demands of the government and changing events pit the public against the government, either on a temporary or continuous basis. When the political order is challenged by contentious decisions of the political leadership, by its moral standing as a group, by the individual moral standing of its members, or by worldwide trends that force greater attention to urgent threats (for example, environmental pressures, security threats, and problems of terrorism), the capacity to govern is affected as well. It seems that, as in many conventional organizations, optimal governability may be attained in times of peace and stability for the people and the leadership. Alternatively, in more turbulent times, governability becomes more and more subject to environmental changes and to the political transformations that create new rules for both those who are expected to govern and to those who are affected by such governability.

Technological transformations and governability   Governability also is subject to the greatest revolution of recent years, the technological revolution in computers, information systems, communications, and media. Today, governments have greater access to their citizens than at any time in previous history. Similarly, citizens can interact with governmental services in a much more intensive and dynamic manner. Therefore, governments have more influence on the people, but the people have much more input into governmental decisions through a variety of means, methods, and technologies (for example, access to data sources, involvement in decision-making, the actions of pressure groups, the criticism and advocacy of policy plans and so on). Buss et al. (2006) describe the new approaches and mechanisms for modernizing democracy in times of greater change and the sophistication of bureaucracy and technology. They suggest that governability in the mass technological revolution era will necessitate not only new techniques for innovation in citizens' participation but also a shift in our collective understanding about the role of governments and citizens in building our nations. This shift will bring governments and their activities closer to the public. While this shift will make the governments' actions more open to criticism, it should also increase the number of innovative ideas for change. Information and knowledge will flow much faster and more broadly, allowing more responsive governance on one hand, but also demanding more participation by citizens and their integration into the actions of governance. Thus, in several ways the capacity to govern is enhanced by using the technological interfaces that modern society offers, but its boundaries and fields of responsibility expand, and citizens are called upon to increase their role in the process of governance.

Summary: Governability under stress and the bureaucratic–democratic paradox

Discontent in modern nations has several causes. The decline of the welfare state as a top-down transition of governments towards more restrained socio-economic policies is one side of the story. This process is accompanied by bottom-up pressures from citizens who are demanding a greater involvement of the state in shaping people's lives. The demands create a gap between the public's expectations and the ability of the government to meet these expectations given its increasingly limited resources.

Governability under stress is similar to a body under stress. The curve model of stress suggests that bodies, physical or abstract, can bear a limited amount of external pressure. To a limited extent, such pressure can be productive and constructive. However, beyond a critical point, we should expect a breakdown. Indeed, governability in many modern nations has reached, or at least is quickly approaching, that critical point. The crisis that is on the horizon is reflected in the clash between democracy and bureaucracy, a clash that is defined here as the paradox of two desirable visions battling over the same time and space. One vision seeks an effective and responsive government while the other strives for political freedom and the maximum level of choice and voice.

To summarize, Figure 2.4 presents the classical clash between the bureaucratic and the democratic ethos. While this is not a new model, it does highlight the black

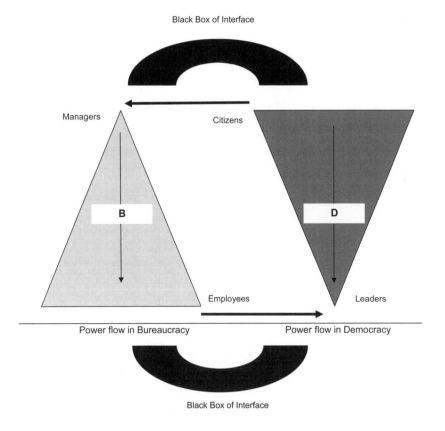

Figure 2.4   The pyramidal paradox of democracy and bureaucracy

box of interfaces between these arenas on which I plan to elaborate in the coming chapters. As suggested by Fox and Miller (1996: 15), this paradox is a reflection of the dichotomy between politics and political administration.

On the administration side are hierarchy and chain of command, enabling elected officials to both control nonelected career officials and superintend their carrying out of the people's will. Because they are not themselves elected, administrators (bureaucracy) must be neutral malleable tools so that elected officials, who embody the will of the people (democracy), can have their way and be held accountable for whatever does or does not get done.

PART II

Caught Between Democracy and Bureaucracy: An Anthology of Empirical Examinations

As demonstrated in the previous chapters, I argue for a very basic paradox between the nature of bureaucracy and democracy, this time from the perspective of governability and public management studies. This paradox may also be defined as the paradox of the nation state, as part of what may be portrayed as the process of nation building. Indeed, democracy and the bureaucracy seem to have two separate origins and differing basic assumptions about class, domination, separation of powers, and contradictory ideological understandings of how a state should be effectively run. At first glance, the gap between them seems impossible to bridge. Democracy relies on the broad, collective support of the people who hold power that can be delegated upwards to leaders. In contrast, bureaucracy is based on the power of the few and on delegation downward to employees or other individuals who make up the majority in organizations (or around them).

In this part, I explain the nature of the paradox in greater detail and the logic behind identifying this paradox both as a barrier to the effective running of democracies and also as the great promise for the future. I base this discussion on an extensive empirical study conducted recently both in Israel and also in many other developed countries in Europe, North America and beyond. In my view, Israel is one of the nations in which the results of this paradox are more extreme, extensive, and evident. The breakneck growth of the young state of Israel, a country founded on principles of multiculturalism, heterogeneity, and a strong desire to build a solid economy coupled with service oriented mechanisms typical of a welfare state have led to this outcome. I will present empirical data to try to support theoretical ideas about the meaningful relationship that exists between bureaucratic aspects of the administrative state, and its democratic nature, values, citizens' attitudes, and behaviors. This discussion should lead, in the final part of the book, to ideas about possible ways to resolve the democratic–bureaucratic paradox and to several possible remedies to the conflict.

Chapter 3

The Power of Bureaucracy:
Managerial Quality and Performance

Strong nations rely on a strong bureaucratic system. Therefore, it is not surprising that in recent decades there has been a growing interest in the development of new avenues for improving public sector performance that attests to the power, efficiency, and effectiveness of bureaucratic systems. The need to create reliable Performance Indicators (PIs) for the administrative state that are based on numerous expectations and assessments of multiple stakeholders has become an essential construct of the New Public Management (NPM) doctrine. A substantial bank of knowledge has already been accumulated in this area (e.g., Berman, 2002; Bouckaert and Peters, 2002; Halachmi, 2002; Wright-Muldrow, 2002). These dynamics have intensified and expanded, and have been applied across North America, Europe, and in other parts of the globe. They have created a much more demanding environment for evolving bureaucracies, stressing the clear need for improved measurement tools, scales, and methodologies as well as a comprehensive analysis of governmental outputs and outcomes. With the development of economic, financial, legal, and behavioral PIs, several formats for objective evaluations, especially from the point of view of citizens as clients or customers, have taken root in public administration literature and practice.

Hence, in today's rapidly changing public environment, bureaucratic systems are expected to achieve results. While the study of outputs, outcomes, and performance is a fundamental tool for the continuous development and improvement of any organization, it is an even greater challenge for public administration and public sector systems.[1] Public sector performance deserves our scholarly attention because it affects the daily life of each citizen and has an impact that transcends temporal, cultural, political, and geographic boundaries. The public sector provides services in areas in which the private sector is disinterested or is unable to operate. It functions continually and reaches places where the private sector sometimes chooses not to act. It must respond to the needs of populations who are much more diverse and scattered than those with which the private sector chooses to interact

---

1 I use the terms public sector, public administration, and public organizations interchangeably, all referring to non-profit and non-privatized organizations under the control, ownership, and financial aegis of a legitimate governance. This definition includes, for example, public education and health services, services provided by local authorities, government offices and their branches, public not-for-profit firms and government agencies, and bodies in whose financing and budgeting the country participates directly.

(Kettl, 2000). Furthermore, the public sector faces many barriers to enhanced performance. It operates in an environment that, for the most part, does not apply differential compensation criteria to employees and where decisions are made within a political system that has its own code of conduct and game rules. These barriers, as well as others, contrast sharply with the rules of the marketplace, the liberal views of a free economy, the culture of open business systems, and the competitive compensation system for both employees and customers according to which successful private organizations operate.

In the following sections we will try to track some of the performance indicators for a well performing bureaucracy. The definitions and measures that will be highlighted are core structures and principles for assessing bureaucracies in modern nations based on citizens' perceptions and attitudes. The measures presented here were used, as a whole or in a partial format, in the longitudinal project that is described in the later parts of this chapter.

Public opinions about the quality of governance and the performance of bureaucracy

Studies on the performance of modern bureaucracies and public sector organizations, especially the perceptual aspects of such performance, are based on a socio-political oriented approach to the study of public opinion. It is frequently argued that a healthy public sector is fundamental to the existence of modern and strong democracies (Thompson, 1983; Vigoda, 2002b, 2002c). While most free democracies handle public demands for improved services quite well, most non-democratic regimes lumber along with an outdated and poorly performing public sector that in the long run makes governing more difficult and unstable. The political economy approach that creates an equation between nations' political and economic status firmly supports this idea. Hence, a strong public sector is essential for the existence of a democratic culture and for the functioning of the political system (King, Feltey, and Susel, 1998; Richardson, 1997; Thompson, 1983). In order to strengthen the foundations of democracies, one must consider public opinion as a very valuable tool for information, learning, and feedback. Nonetheless, systematic empirical data is scarce in this field, as are valid and reliable measures and methodologies.

Various aspects of public opinion about government services are noted in the literature. A partial list includes topics such as (1) the scope of services offered to the citizen, (2) their quality and the public's satisfaction with them, (3) the degree to which public services comply with reasonable economic criteria regarding effectiveness and efficiency, (4) a fair distribution of public resources as citizens see it, (5) response and responsiveness to the needs and demands of the citizens, (6) sensitivity to the needs of special populations, and (7) opinions about the management style and quality of human resources in the public services' systems. Studies about such factors are growing in number, with a partial list including works by Balk (1985); Bozeman (1993); Carter (1989); Hart and Grant (1989); Local Government Training Board (1987); National Consumer Council (1986); Smith (1993); Thomas and Palfrey (1996); Vigoda, (2000a); and Winkler (1987).

These measures have been used extensively throughout the world as accurate indicators of how well bureaucracies operate. With the evolution of the New Public Management (NPM) reform (Osborne and Gaebler, 1992) such measures have become even more popular and applicable in research and in practice. The NPM reform encourages the accumulation of data regarding citizens' opinions about the quality of the services they have received from the public sector. Similarly, Kelly (2002) noted the close relationship between the need to "be reformed" and the desire to "look reformed" in the eyes of citizens. Today a consensus exists among scholars that public opinions about public sector outcomes should be studied and analyzed in light of clear-cut performance indicators (PIs). PIs may then be used to improve bureaucratic processes. Furthermore, the use of PIs reflects the increased desire of public administration to learn from private sector experiences with an eye to improving sensitivity, flexibility, and the ability to respond to changes in citizens' demands (Pollitt, 1988, 1990). The use of PIs, especially those provided by citizens in their capacity as clients, reinforces the idea that at least a minimal level of government responsiveness is essential for the existence and sustainability of democracy in modern societies (Poister and Henry, 1994; Vigoda, 2000a).

Managerial quality and performance: A global citizens perspective

Over the years, several initiatives for the study of managerial quality and public performance have been launched. Among the empirically oriented efforts one should note a few meaningful ventures: The *American Customer Satisfaction Index* (http://www.theacsi.org), The *Georgia State Poll*, the *Public Confidence in Government and Government Service Delivery* (Sims, 2001), the *Client Satisfaction Survey in Canada* (Schmidt and Strickland, 1998), the *Satisfaction with Public Services* project in the UK (Donovan et al., 2001), the *European Customer Satisfaction Index* (http://www.efqm.org/pressrel/custsat.htm), and others. These projects have used multiple methodologies and approaches to evaluate citizens' needs, satisfaction, and trust in government and in the public sector. However, they all fall short of suggesting a comprehensive strategy that is based on multiple scales and measures of performance on the micro and macro levels. Another shortcoming of these reports is their tendency to treat the public as one integral unit. In reality "the public" is made up of various groups and sectors with individual preferences and needs that should be carefully considered. Although the general voice of the public is politically and socially meaningful, much can be learned, both politically and administratively, from a closer examination of the particular preferences of smaller socio-economic and demographic groups.

Managerial quality

The managerial quality of public service worldwide is a complex concept. Studies in business management found managerial quality to be a multifaceted concept. Its complexity derives from two major approaches: (1) the economic market-derived approach, and (2) the behavioral and human resource management approach. According to the more conventional, market-derived view, managerial quality is defined by financial measures. The quality of a managerial cadre is best expressed by financial indicators such as pay, salaries, and profits. For example, Kahn (1993) defined organizational quality as predicted pay based on the salary of managers. He found positive relationships between managerial quality and baseball players' performance and concluded that managerial quality is a prime asset for every organization due to its impact on performance. In addition, Koch and Cabula (1994) examined managerial quality in American firms from 33 industries. They found that highly profitable firms, less risky firms, and firms that grow faster as well as better reward their stockholders and are perceived by corporate CEOs as better managed. However, these variables explained only about 30 percent of the variance in management quality and excellence. Thus, Koch and Cabula (1994) suggested that financial and market-derived measures are not sufficient to explain the wider meaning of managerial quality that, according to their view, remains a complex variable.

An alternative human resource approach treats managerial quality quite differently. According to this view, managerial quality denotes the success of managers as leaders of people and the proficiency of their activities as decision-makers. This definition comprises various human skills, selected organizational strategies, managerial culture, norms, and entrepreneurial ventures. It represents accessible human assets and inputs that every effective organization should have. A review of the relevant literature reveals several core elements of managerial quality. These are (1) human quality and professionalism, (2) acceptance of transparency and accountability as leading administrative values, (3) commitment of organizational members to morality and ethics as desirable codes of behavior, as well as (4) innovation and creativity of public personnel. The actual meaning of these constructs and the way they relate to each other needs better explanation and will be elaborated upon below.

Human quality refers to the merit and *professionalism* of public personnel as seen by objective assessors. It also refers to *leadership* skills of the higher ranks and of those public officials who are responsible for articulating and implementing the sector's vision and goals. Excellent managers in all sectors are expected to provide employees with adequate and supportive work environments. It is the managers' responsibility to provide a vision, but at the same time, to suggest tools for translating this vision into actions. As mentioned in various other studies, an efficient, skillful, professional, and committed public service supports governments in their functioning (e.g., Hart and Grant, 1989; Holzer, 1989; Holzer and Rabin, 1987; Staats, 1988; Vigoda, 2000a). In addition, *accountability and transparency* provide an indication as to internal mechanisms of managerial self-criticism and willingness to improve existing processes and procedures. Transparency is usually crucial in financial and budgetary policy, but it is also recommended as a good strategy for building commitment among clients and citizens.

Along with the need for professionalism, leadership, transparency, and accountability, managerial quality is also based on a broader set of values, norms, and unwritten rules that create a fair and just administrative culture. Hence, high standards of *morality and ethics* as well as serious efforts to minimize *internal politics* may be seen as the hidden underbelly of bureaucracies. While every bureaucracy is characterized by a formal set of regulations and laws, their implementation is weighted by the way in which they are interpreted by managers (DeLeon, 1996; Gawthrop, 1976; Lui and Cooper, 1997; Nigro, 1991; Richardson and Nigro, 1991; Suzuki, 1995; Wilenski, 1980). All the above studies have agreed that managerial quality also encompasses ethical standards, integrity, fair and equal treatment of citizens as clients, and appropriate criteria for rewards to public servants.

Finally, a significant component of managerial quality is *innovation and creativity*, which serves as an essential engine for renewal, development, and continuous advancement towards the collective organizational vision. Traditionally, public sector organizations are viewed as uncreative and stagnant entities. Still, managerial innovation and creativity are essential for those administrators and systems who seek to perform better and compete successfully with other organizations from the private sector or from the third sector (Golembiewski and Vigoda, 2000; Schall, 1997).

In the next sections, I will try to elaborate on the meaning of these factors and on their integration and use in advanced studies of the field. In addition to explanations about the essence of each factor, I pay special attention to the *operative measurement* that can be used in empirical studies. The reader may well be aware that this attempt to relate the conceptual and the empirical spheres is much in line with the current trend in public administration of measuring everything that seems measurable and worthy of evaluation for purposes of comparative analysis and continuous learning.

Human qualities: Professionalism and leadership

Many studies have elaborated on the importance of creating an efficient, skillful, professional, and committed public service to assist the government in its functioning (e.g., Hart and Grant, 1989; Holzer, 1989; Holzer and Rabin, 1987; Staats, 1988). However, the quality of public servants is frequently criticized by scholars and practitioners. For example, Holzer and Rabin (1987) claimed that sustained attacks on the public service encourage many top students to pursue careers in the private sector, lower morale and increase the attrition of public servants. As a result, elected officials try to minimize pay rises for career officials and thereby discourage recruitment and retention of the most able public servants.

The quality of leadership and management significantly influences the success or failure of every organization. Lane (1987) argues that leadership in the public sector has become more important especially since the 1980s. Its growing importance is related to the fiscal crisis of the state that has emerged since about 1975, as well as to the attempt to insert more private sector principles into the public sector. Modern organizations put a great deal of effort into improving managers' skills, particularly their aptitude for business and their ability to deal effectively with people. Since this layer of employees is responsible for the continuous long-range operation and healthy functioning of the organization, it is of major importance that we evaluate its image in the eyes of citizens. Despite the fact that citizens do not always have sufficient knowledge about the abilities and professionalism of public managers, they still serve as objective and honest evaluators of services they are entitled to receive. In many cases, citizens' criticism is not directed towards the immediate service provider but toward the public system and its leaders as a whole. The democratic process in general, and particularly the free media, help create better accountability and improve public awareness. This is particularly true at the local government level where the operation of public agencies is more relevant to citizens' day-to-day life. Hence, we should ask several questions. Do citizens trust public servants and have faith in their leadership? Do they believe in their professionalism and capability to implement public policy as required? The assessment of employees as qualified and effective in fulfilling their duties is another aspect of the interface with the public. While managers have the most influence over the operation of public administration, it is the front-line employees who interact with the public and need to provide immediate answers to their requests. Being in the front lines, employees must demonstrate a service orientation, professionalism, knowledge, patience, and understanding of the citizens' changing needs. This study maintains that while the public may not be able to assess how well the manager performs his or her job, they can certainly evaluate how well the employees function. An operative measurement of human qualities is thus built of professionalism and leadership in the public sector:

Measuring perceived professionalism and leadership in the public sector The measurement devised to make this assessment is based on two sub-scales: (1) the quality of the administrative leadership, and (2) the quality of the employees. The first sub-scale reflects citizens' views as to the quality and professionalism of the leading administrative group, managers, and senior bureaucrats. Three items were used in this sub-scale: (1) "Public leadership and senior management in the Israeli public service are well qualified and have high professional standards," (2) "The Israeli public service is managed appropriately and is in good order," and (3) "The leaders of the Israeli public service have a clear vision and long range view as to where we are going." The second sub-scale reflects citizens' views as to the quality and professionalism of front-line employees in the public service. This sub-scale was also measured by three items: (1) "Employees of the Israeli public service are professionals and highly qualified," (2) "Employees of the Israeli public service show understanding, care, and willingness to serve the citizens," and (3) "The Israeli public service employs only high quality individuals." Respondents were asked to provide their attitudes on a 5-point scale ranging from 1 (strongly disagree) to 5 (strongly agree).

Accountability and transparency

As mentioned earlier, accountability and transparency have important issues that appear frequently in the discussion about public sector management. They testify to the quality of public sector management by pointing to self-critical awareness and the willingness to improve existing processes and procedures. Transparency is crucial in economic, financial, and budgetary policy, and is further recommended as a good strategy for building trust, commitment, and faith among clients and citizens. Bureaucracy that is willing to work under transparent conditions signals that it has nothing to hide, that it is based on quality foundations strong enough to squelch criticism by the public, and that it constantly seeks self-improvement (Finkelstein, 2000). Accountability relies on transparency, and the two terms go hand in hand when seeking to explore new avenues for organizational improvement and development. Accountability refers to the duty of governments and public officials to report their actions to citizens, and the right of the citizens to take steps against those actions, if they find them unsatisfactory. As suggested by Halachmi (2002), accountability requires us to discern who is accountable, for what, to whom, in what respect, and how to assess it. Undoubtedly, both transparency and accountability are crucial elements of quality management in modern democracies.

Measuring perceived accountability and transparency in the public sector Accountability and transparency represents the acceptance of criticism, a sincere desire to improve poorly functioning programs or performance in state services, and a willingness to be exposed to outside evaluators in order to improve future results (Finkelstein, 2000; Halachmi, 2002). It was measured by five items: (1) "Israeli public administration takes public criticism and suggestions for improvement seriously," (2) "Today, more than ever before, the public system is willing to be exposed to the public and to the media," (3) "Public administration treats defects found by the state comptroller seriously," (4) "Public administration sees criticism as an important tool for future service improvement," and (5) "Israeli public administration encourages public employees to accept criticism and use it to improve services for citizens." Respondents were asked to provide their attitudes on a 5-point scale ranging from 1 (strongly disagree) to 5 (strongly agree).

Innovation and creativity

Innovation and creativity represents the degree to which public policy is flexible, takes initiative, and is willing to adopt new ideas. These constructs of managerial quality serve as an essential engine for renewal, development, and continuous advancement towards the collective organizational vision. The conventional perception among the public is that governments and their executive bodies and institutions are uncreative, conservative, and unaware of innovations and required changes or reforms. Still, studies demonstrate how managerial innovation and creativity are essential for those administrators and systems who seek to perform better and compete successfully with other organizations from the private sector or from the third sector (Golembiewski and Vigoda, 2000; Schall, 1997).

Surprisingly, despite the seeming lack of incentive to innovate, innovation is very much expected in the public sector. It offers serious added value not only for the public agencies, but also for the citizens and the society they serve (Borins, 2000; 2001; Kimberly, 1981; Vigoda-Gadot et al., 2005b). "Surprisingly," because public organizations have traditionally been perceived as inefficient, bureaucratic, and hierarchical, yet, they function in complex environments that reflect a great deal of uncertainty, much of which their well-defined tasks are not designed to handle.

Contradictorily, however, today's' public organizations are forced to act in a forward-thinking manner. They jointly exhibit a mixture of characteristics that represent bureaucratic forces (for example, hierarchy, specialization, and impersonality) and innovative practices (such as flexibility, adaptability, creativity, and risk taking). In many respects, innovation is no longer the provenance of the private sector only; on the contrary, innovation is recognized in governmental and non-governmental organizations alike, such as voluntary and non-profit organizations (VNPOs) (Vigoda-Gadot et al., 2005b).

Innovation exists in any modern governmental organization, be it social security, health and welfare, urban planning or defense, to name a few. For example, public health programs provide vaccinations to all newborns, and advanced care to the needy. They use first class technology to assist the disabled, to reduce the effects of aging or to develop cures for diseases (such as cancer, AIDS, and SARS). Globalization further stimulates public sector innovation through economic liberalization, advanced technology, and post managerial ideologies (for example, NPM). These stimulate fast access to information and immediate solutions.

Measuring perceived innovation in the public sector   Public sector innovation reflects entrepreneurial actions, flexibility, the willingness to adopt new ideas, and the initiation of original enterprises by public servants in order to improve services to the people. It was measured by a 3-item scale: (1) "Israeli public administration formulates promising new ideas which improve citizens' quality of life," (2) "Compared with other countries, Israel occupies a leading position in developing useful projects for the public," and (3) "Advanced technology is used to improve the quality of service in this country." Respondents were asked to report the degree to which they agreed with the items on a scale from 1 (strongly disagree) to 5 (strongly agree).

Ethics and morality

Public policy is mutually related to administrative culture, ethics, norms, and behaviors of public servants. For example, along with governmental operations, questions of ethical standards, integrity, fair and equal treatment of clients, or appropriate criteria for rewards to public servants become more relevant. Today, public services in Europe are more expansive than ever before (Gladstone, 1995). As a result, public servants manage growing budgets. They control the transfer of more capital to and from the state treasury. Access to such large quantities of money exposes many of them to ethical dilemmas as to how to properly manage, distribute, and redistribute economical wealth. Other ethical difficulties arise as a result of the instability between business and social requirements in the public environment. For example, when the cost of certain medicines is too high for citizens to purchase, should the state take responsibility and help them? When state prisons are overcrowded with convicted prisoners, should the state release some of them to create more places for others? Responding to such moral issues is difficult. However, public policy that neglects considerations of ethics, equal treatment of the public, or basic justice and fairness creates a self-destructive process that may damage its functioning in the long run (Wilenski, 1980).

The last two decades have witnessed a growing interest in issues of administrative ethics and fairness (DeLeon, 1996; Gawthrop, 1976; Lui and Cooper, 1997; Richardson and Nigro, 1991; Suzuki, 1995; Wilenski, 1980). Generally, citizens are sensitive to and aware of such unhealthy processes, although most have little or no opportunity to use their collective opinion in order to influence decision makers. While the media, the auditing system, the state comptroller, and even the legal authorities in Western societies are those that should play an important part in criticizing public policy and administrative culture, citizens themselves are rarely asked about their feelings and attitudes on such topics. Do they feel that public administration operates effectively and ethically? Are they being treated fairly by public servants? Nonetheless, the absence of a direct public voice does not imply that citizens have given up their potential power. Most people seem to have an opinion about the internal processes in public agencies (such as, do they work to high standards of morality and ethics? Do they treat all citizens fairly?). Citizens as clients increasingly develop independent opinions about the type of culture public administration encourages and how this culture accords with general morality. This study argues that the policy and culture of public administration affect citizens' feelings and beliefs about the responsiveness of public agencies.

Measuring perceived ethics and morality in the public sector   Ethics and morality in public sector organizations describes general attitudes towards fair treatment, honesty, integrity and the general fairness of civil servants. It consists of three items: (1) "In Israeli public administration, most civil servants are impartial and honest," (2) "Citizens of this country receive equal and fair treatment from public officials," and (3) "In Israeli public administration, deviations from good moral norms are rare." Respondents were asked to report the degree to which they agreed with these items. The scale ranged from 1 (strongly disagree) to 5 (strongly agree) with higher scores representing a more positive view of the public service as moral and ethical.

Internal politics and perceptions of organizational politics

Closely related to ethics and morality in the public sector, but still independent stand from them is internal politics in public organizations. In recent decades, organizational politics, especially the way it is perceived by employees and managers, has became a field of great interest in business administration, management, and applied psychology. The term "organizational politics" has its roots in both political science theory that promoted research into individuals' political behavior (i.e., Almond and Verba, 1965; Verba et al., 1995) and in conventional management studies that recognized the importance of the informal power game in the workplace (i.e., Mintzberg, 1983; Pfeffer, 1992). Studies emphasized that it is essential to know more about the covert side of individuals' interest–promotion dynamics in various arenas, which is frequently the essence of any political behavior (Peterson, 1990). As far as management theory is concerned, it became evident that gauging the political climate of a work unit is a complex task, but it is crucial for a better understanding of organizations, their effectiveness, efficiency, and general performance (Gandz and Murray, 1980).

Studies have usually defined organizational politics as behavior strategically designed to maximize self-interests (Ferris, Russ, and Fandt, 1989) and, by implication, in conflict with the collective organizational goals, or the interests of other individuals. Block (1988: 5) mentioned politics (in organizations) as basically a negative process and argued that, "If I told you you were a very political person, you would take it either as an insult or at best as a mixed blessing." Gandz and Murray (1980) and Medison et al. (1980) observed that when individuals were asked to describe workplace politics, they typically listed self-serving and manipulative activities that are not perceived positively. A series of studies by Kipnis and his colleagues as well as others (Erez and Rim, 1982; Kipnis et al., 1980; Kipnis and Schmidt, 1982, 1983, 1988) promoted the behavioral understanding of organizational politics by typologyzing and analyzing the concept of influence tactics. These studies argued that organizational politics was perceived as self-serving behavior by employees to achieve self-interests, advantages, and benefits at the expense of others, sometimes contrary to the interests of the entire organization or work unit. This behavior was frequently associated with manipulation, defamation, subversiveness, and illegitimate ways of using power to attain one's objectives. Therefore, organizational politics was labeled as unethical and even immoral or corrupt behavior.

Faced with the difficulty of measuring organizational politics empirically, Ferris et al. (1989) suggested the concept of the *perception* of organizational politics as a useful gauge of this phenomenon. Kacmar and Ferris (1991: 193–4) and Ferris and Kacmar (1992: 93) promoted a cognitive approach and argued that the stronger the perception of politics by organizational members, the less likely they were to believe the organization to be just, equitable, or fair. More recent studies (Ferris et al., 1996; Harris and Kacmar, 2004; Vigoda-Gadot, 2003c; Vigoda-Gadot and Drory, 2006) have used the theory of procedural justice to argue that organizational politics is related to the efficiency of human resource systems and to decision-making processes. Lack of minimal justice and fairness in these systems was found to be a leading cause of higher perceptions of organizational politics and therefore of impaired organizational outcomes. All these studies draw on the classic works by Kurt Lewin (1936) who argued that people respond to their perceptions of reality, not to reality itself. Likewise, politics in organizations should be understood in terms of what people think of it rather than what it actually represents.

Measuring perceived internal politics in public administration   Ferris et al. (1989) defined organizational politics from the perspective of the employee. According to their view, this variable represents the degree to which respondents view their work environment as political, and therefore unjust and unfair. Based on this view and on other studies that followed (i.e., Kacmar and Carlson, 1994; Kacmar and Ferris, 1991; Vigoda-Gadot, 2003c; Vigoda-Gadot and Drory, 2006), I took a different approach that focused on citizens' perspectives of this phenomenon that reflected the level of political considerations in administrative work and decision-making. A 3-item scale, using the following statements, was used to test this variable. (1) "The actions of the public administration serve the purposes of only a few individuals, not the public system or the public interest;" (2) "Favoritism rather than professionalism determines the decisions made in public administration;" and (3) "Generally speaking, the public administration operates appropriately and is not affected by political pressures" (reversed score). Respondents were asked to assess the public sector in general and report the degree to which they agreed with the items on a scale from 1 (strongly disagree) to 5 (strongly agree). A higher score meant a higher perception of organizational politics.

Additional potential indicators: Communication channels and stress

Moreover, one must also consider the citizens' reactions when contacting public administration agencies. Is this an activity they dread or do they find it relatively painless? While there has been a growing interest in recent years in the stress and strain of public employees in the fields of education, health care and welfare (e.g., Crank, 1991; Friesen and Sarros, 1989; Israel et al., 1989), almost no attention has been given to citizens'/clients' stress in their relationship with public institutions. When public servants are skilled and professional, we expect citizens to feel more comfortable and endure less stress and strain when confronting public officials. However, when those officials are unskilled, incompetent, and indifferent, they may treat citizens insensitively and thus encourage reactions of dissatisfaction, helplessness, or even anger towards the public system as a whole. Such expectations are indeed in keeping with contemporary psychological theory. Studies have long argued and empirically validated a negative relationship between a supportive environment and reduced levels of stress and strain in organizations (e.g., El-Bassel, Guterman, Bargal, and Su-Kuo, 1998; Jayaratne and Chess, 1984; Punch and Tuetteman, 1996;). When the individual is surrounded by an emphatic and supportive environment, levels of stress, strain, and anxiety dramatically decrease. Therefore, gauging the level of stress endured by citizens when contacting public agencies should contribute to a better understanding of the human side of public administration. Hence, the factors of communication channels and the psychological status of citizens as clients is of prime importance if one seeks a better understanding of the nexus between bureaucratic machinery and the democratic sphere.

Nonetheless, measuring communication channels and stress is a rather complex task. Given that the public administration literature has not yet paid enough attention to such scales, I could not find an established scale for measuring communication channels in the public sector and the stress levels they induce. Therefore, I looked to a sister discipline, that of management and applied psychology. Creating such measurement tool is one of my major goals. However, to date it has not yet been fully developed, so I decided not to include it in the empirical section of this book. I therefore leave it as an open project for future studies, and definitely a very promising and challenging one.

Performance in the public sector

Building Performance Indicators (PI)

While it is not obvious that the accumulated wisdom of the private sector is transferable to the public sector (Pollitt, 1988; Smith, 1993), still the inevitable interactions between the two spheres are productive for both. However, this book is more interested in how the public sector can benefit from the experience of private organizations in managing large bureaucracies. This question has received much attention in the New Public Management literature, which has been rapidly developing in Western societies since the 1980s (Stewart and Ranson, 1994). A considerable effort has been devoted to identifying and defining new criteria that may help determine the extent to which public agencies succeed in meeting the growing needs of the public. As a result, New Public Management has shown great interest in specific Performance Indicators (PIs) used in private organizations. It has recommended that they be applied in the public sector (e.g., Carter, 1989; Smith, 1993), arguing that these indicators could function as milestones along the road to better efficiency and effectiveness of public administration.

Over the past few decades, performance indicators have become a central concern of administrative systems seeking renewal, reform, and change. It is a common view today that a better understanding of public sector performance should rely on enriching and improving our "toolbox" of PIs. Thus, public sector performance and PIs are evaluated according to various economic parameters with tools borrowed from the policy evaluation field. In addition, however, performance evaluation also utilizes the attitudinal–behavioral approach that uses non-economic parameters as measurements. This approach argues that the traditional economic approach cannot supply all the required information needed for a comprehensive performance evaluation. Such a comprehensive evaluation must also take into consideration the attitudes of the citizens, who are often defined as the customers or consumers of public service, as well as the attitudes of the public administrators themselves. Our article follows this theoretical line of thinking.

The attitudinal–behavioral approach is applied to many aspects of public sector management and performance. Some of these areas include the scope and quality of services offered to citizens and public satisfaction with them, effectiveness and efficiency, and the equitable distribution of public resources. This approach also considers the public's willingness to contribute to the advancement of prioritized social and public values that public administration finds difficult to deal with or does not wish to handle, and opinions about the management style and quality of human resources in the public service systems (for more detailed examples see: Balk, 1985; Carter, 1989; Hart and Grant, 1989; Local Government Training Board, 1987; National Consumer Council, 1986; Smith, 1993; Thomas and Palfrey, 1996; Winkler, 1987). In line with recent reforms in public administration, especially those stemming from the New Public Management paradigm, many performance indicators have been developed to evaluate administrative performance (e.g., Berman, 1997; Nyhan, 1995). Nonetheless, two of the most commonly used perceptual measures are (1) attitudes towards the general responsiveness of governments and public administration, and (2) detailed evaluations of citizens' satisfaction with governmental services.

For example, Smith (1993) mentions two different indicators for measuring public sector performance, those internal and external to the organization. Measures of internal performance, such as managerial processes, routines and formal procedures, are of limited interest to ordinary citizens yet are also those that attract more attention in management literature. Their main objective is to enable the central government to maintain closer control of devolved management teams (Carter, 1989). However, Smith argues that these studies are less concerned with external indicators (outcome-related), which are intended to enhance the *accountability* of public organizations to external interested parties (for example, service users, the electorate, taxpayers, the central government). The role of such outcome indicators is to furnish external users with information about the consequences of public sector activity so that citizens can make better judgments about the organization's performance.

In accordance with this approach, Anthony and Young (1984: 649) claimed that more active interest in the effective and efficient functioning of public organizations by its governing boards is essential for the improvement of management in nonprofit organizations. Citizens' awareness will increase the political pressure placed on elected and appointed representatives on governing boards, thereby enhancing both managerial efficiency and the effective allocation of resources in the public sector. Smith (1993) compares this process of public accountability to stakeholders/ citizens to the role adopted by financial reporting in the private/corporate sector. As in the private sector, increasing external-related outcomes, such as the responsiveness of public authorities to citizens demands, will have a profound impact on internal control mechanisms, as managers and public servants become more sensitive to their duties and strongly committed to serving the people.

Management theory, as well as political science theory, defines this process of "controlling" or "monitoring" as the collection and analysis of relevant data about organizations' achievements and the implementation of actions to improve future performance (Thomas and Palfrey, 1996). Control and monitoring is frequently identical to accountability when public needs and interests are involved. As was argued by Stewart and Ranson (1994), organizations in the public domain exercise substantial power for which they are accountable. Public accountability must involve a political process that responds to the many voices of citizens/clients. A response of *voice* is defined by Hirschman (1980) as a purely political action compared with *exit,* which represents more of an economic action. Since citizens generally do not have the option of exit in a public market, the option of voice becomes more relevant and significant. Moreover, Western democracies seem to be facing pressures for greater rather than less accountability to their citizens. Traditionally, large public bureaucracies use a variety of formal control systems (such as general and internal auditing, accounting, and special departments that deal with citizens' requests and complaints) that are aimed at providing the organization with better information on which to base internal performance indicators. However, hardly any effort has been made to actively obtain external performance indicators such as citizens' opinion of actual public operations and services. Moreover, even when such steps are taken, the main motive is political rather than professional or administrative.

As the NPM doctrine evolved, measuring success in the public sector became a key issue. The search for better performance in public administration systems draws on a continuous exploration of measurable output and outcome indicators. The NPM doctrine, as implemented in the public sector, implies that *if you can't measure a public output/outcome, it probably isn't worth consideration.* In line with recent reforms in public administration, especially those stemming from the NPM paradigm, many performance indicators have been developed to evaluate administrative performance (e.g., Berman, 2000; Nyhan, 1995). Nonetheless, two of the most commonly used perceptual measures are (1) attitudes towards the general responsiveness of governments and public administration, and (2) detailed evaluations of citizens' satisfaction with governmental services.

Responsiveness to citizens as clients may be regarded as the Holy Grail of modern public administration. A responsive bureaucracy delivers services and goods to its destinations with optimal speed and accuracy (Chi, 1999; Vigoda,

2000a, 2002a). Thomas and Palfrey (1996) argued that responsiveness attests to the speed and accuracy with which a service provider replies to a request for action or for information. Speed can refer to the waiting time between citizens' request for action and the reply of the public agency. Accuracy means the extent to which the provider's response is appropriate to the needs or wishes of the service user (Rourke, 1992; Stewart and Ranson, 1994). The political environment of public organizations restricts its professional flexibility and capability to appropriately responding to citizens' demands. As was noted by Palfrey et al. (1992: 133), "enhanced awareness of consumers' views offers elected members the opportunity to increase their chances of re-election and prospective members of being elected." It seems that the political sphere is responsible for the somewhat negative image of responsiveness in the eyes of many administrators and scholars. Since the strongest motive of politicians in every democracy is to be (re)elected, outcomes of public activity are normally examined and presented for public criticism only prior to the coming elections. It is only when elections are looming that politicians concern themselves with citizens' satisfaction. Frequently, these assessments do not rely on objective or scientific data bases and serve only the politicians' narrow interests. Moreover, Winkler (1987) has criticized the superficiality of current consumerism in the public sector for being just a little more than a public relations exercise aimed at recruiting voters. When consumerism and consumers become a tool in the political game, the reliability of public surveys made for political purposes is damaged and their implications should be treated with considerable suspicion.

Given the above factors, it is not surprising that evaluating responsiveness in public agencies is a complex task. Private organizations must always be aware of clients' satisfaction in order to make adjustments that help the organizations respond better. On the other hand, public organizations are less concerned with citizens' demands because usually the latter do not have a real "exit" alternative for obtaining services they want in areas such as security, transportation, ecology, health, education, and so on. Even when such alternatives exist, they are usually partial, limited in quantity, relatively more expensive, and beyond the financial capability of ordinary citizens.

Beyond the idea of measuring the general responsiveness of public agencies, there is also a need to more closely evaluate satisfaction with services received. In other words, evaluating administrative performance means a comprehensive, distinctive, reliable, and continuous assessment of citizens' satisfaction with government operations in various fields. In recent decades satisfaction measures have became prevalent in state and federal agencies. They were largely prompted by the client canon of NPM and by the vision of "putting citizens first" (Caiden and Caiden, 2002). Hence, public administration encourages the use of satisfaction measures as part of performance evaluations both inside public agencies and around them (e.g., Poister and Henry, 1994; Swindell and Kelly, 2000). It should also be noted that this strategy has been adopted despite some limitations it has and some criticism it needs to address (Stipak, 1979, 1980).

Nevertheless, as New Public Management evolves, public administration must become more pro-active and take the initiative in measuring its own performance. For example, Pollitt (1990) suggested a taxonomy for measuring performance in the public sector by: (a) measuring performance as an activity aimed at renewing or reinforcing political and public legitimacy, and (consequently) attracting political allocations of resources; (b) measuring performance as an aid to management in making decisions about how to adjust organizational structure and processes, and allocating internal resources to support these changes; and (c) measuring performance in order to provide customers and clients with information about the quality, effectiveness, accessibility, or efficiency of the services being provided. While the first two types of performance measurements remain the dominant concern of the literature, the third has received little attention. New Public Management argues that citizens/consumers represent a new actor – and a most important one – in the performance evaluation game.

Citizens' satisfaction

Citizens' satisfaction is a frequent measure of performance in the public sector. Over the years, satisfaction with public services, especially that of the citizenry, has become a useful tool for assessing the outcomes of governmental agencies of various types, on the local, national, and federal level (Van Ryzin, 2005; Van Ryzin and Freeman, 1997; Van Ryzin, Muzzio, and Immerwahr, 2004a, 2004b). This interest has intensified especially with the evolvement of the NPM doctrine, which advocated the view of citizens as customers or clients. Along with other performance indicators, and perhaps due to the weaknesses of some hard data that do not tell the whole story about meeting citizens' needs and demands, satisfaction indexes have become became very popular in the study of public sector performance, despite the limitations they have (Stipak, 1977, 1980).

A variety of data and measures of citizens' satisfaction are mentioned in the literature. Several leading initiatives are the Canadian Common Measurement Tool (Institute for Citizen Centered Service 2005 – http://www.iccs-isac.org/ eng/cmt-about.htm), The United States National Citizens Survey (International City/County Management Association 2005 – http://www.comcate.com/home/ newsandevents/events/icma2007.html). Other initiatives also resulted in reliable and acceptable scales and methods that have enjoyed widespread public and scientific recognition (for example, specific measures in the ACSI – American Customer Satisfaction Index – http://www.theacsi.org, The European Values Survey – http://www.europeanvalues.nl/index2.htm, The World Value Survey – http://www.worldvaluessurvey.org, and The Euro-Barometer – http://ec.europa.eu/ public_opinion), but they all share the common denominator of closely evaluating the satisfaction with services received in greater detail.

Measuring citizens' satisfaction with the public sector   Van Ryzin (2004c) reviews the various methods for measuring citizens' satisfaction with public services. He mentions single item measures, the ACSI scale, the EVL–EVLN (Exit/Voice/Loyalty and Exit/Voice/Loyalty/Neglect) scale (based on Hirschman, 1970), and short and long Likert scales. Today The EVL/EVLN is considered an independent scale for *reactions* to satisfaction/dissatisfaction, and the single item scales are unacceptable due to redundancy and over simplicity. Currently, the most common and reliable scales are multi-item measures (mostly Likert based) that cover a variety of public services and can gather data systematically from various perspectives.

Thus, in order to measure citizens' satisfaction with various public sector agencies, we assembled detailed information about a long list of governmental services on the national and communal level. Respondents were given a list of public institutions and organizations that deliver different services. They were asked to report how satisfied they were with the treatment they received either when they personally arrived at the public offices or contacted them by phone. The services that were studied were: (1) hospitals and public clinics, (2) public schools, (3) courts, (4) Ministry of the Interior, (5) labor ministry and employment services, (6) police, (7) transportation ministry, (8) public transport/buses, (9) public transport/rails, (10) public transport/ El-Al Israel Airlines, (11) public transport/airport authority, (12) public postal system, (13) local municipality, (14) electricity company, (15) Ministry of Religious Affairs, (16) welfare system and national security, (17) telecommunication services, and (18) tax system. Answers ranged from 1 (very unsatisfied) to 5 (very satisfied).

Responsiveness

Approaches to the understanding of public administration's responsiveness are controversial. Some studies describe responsiveness as, at best, a necessary evil that appears to compromise professional effectiveness and, at worst, an indication of political expediency if not outright corruption (Rourke, 1992). According to this line of research, responsiveness damages professionalism because it forces public servants to satisfy citizens even when such actions contradict the collective public interest. To satisfy the public, short-term considerations and popular decisions are overemphasized, while other long-term issues receive little or no attention at all. However, other studies suggest that democracy would seem to demand administrators who are responsive to the popular will, at least through legislatures and politicians if not directly to the people (Stewart and Ranson, 1994; Stivers, 1994). While responsiveness is occasionally considered a problematic concept in public administration literature, it is undoubtedly critical to politicians, bureaucrats, and citizens alike. A responsive politician or bureaucrat must be reactive, sympathetic, sensitive, and capable of feeling the public's needs and opinions. Since the needs and demands of a heterogeneous society are dynamic, it is vital to develop systematic approaches for its understanding. In many ways this is the key for securing a fair social contract between citizens and rulers.

A clear consensus exists among many scholars and practitioners that the opinions of service receivers need to be taken seriously by policy makers (DHSS, 1979; National Consumer Council, 1986; Palfrey et al., 1992; Winkler, 1987). This information can help to: (1) understand and establish public needs; (2) develop, communicate, and distribute public services and; (3) assess the degree of satisfaction with services (Palfrey et al., 1992: 128). Thomas and Palfrey (1996) argue that citizens are the clients and main beneficiaries of public sector operations and therefore should be involved in every process of performance evaluation. In their study, responsiveness of the public sector to citizens' demands is mentioned as an important part of performance *control* because it refers to the speed and accuracy with which a service provider replies to a request for action or for information. According to this definition, speed can refer to the waiting time between citizens' request for action and the reply of the public agency. Accuracy means the extent to which the provider's response is appropriate to the needs or wishes of the service user. Nonetheless, while speed is relatively a simple factor to measure, accuracy is a more complicated one.

Unlike the private sector, public service accuracy must take into consideration social welfare, equity, equal opportunities, and the fair distribution of "public goods" to all citizens. Rhodes (1987) and Palfrey et al. (1992) suggested these criteria in addition to the efficiency, effectiveness, and service that characterize market-driven processes. To test for the accuracy of governmental endeavors, one must examine how citizens feel when using public services. A well accepted method is to use responsiveness as complementary to satisfaction measures such as those presented earlier.

Measuring responsiveness to citizens' needs   Responsiveness refers directly to the accuracy and speed of public sector reaction to citizens' demands. Relying on the theoretical conception of Thomas and Palfrey (1996), this variable was measured by four items aimed at evaluating the speed and accuracy of public services provided to the citizens by the authorities. The items were: (1) "Israeli public administration responds to public requests quickly," (2) "Israeli public administration is efficient and provides quality solutions for public needs," (3) "Israeli public administration is sensitive to public opinions and makes a sincere effort to support those citizens who need help," and (4) "Citizens' appeals to public agencies are treated properly, concisely, and within a reasonable period of time." Respondents were asked to report the degree to which they agreed with the items. The response scale ranged from 1 (strongly disagree) to 5 (strongly agree).

Additional potential indicators: Image and reputation

The image of the public sector and its reputation are subject to growing interest and criticism. This interest has expanded and paralleled similar developments in the more generic managerial and organizational context. Organizational image has become a prime concern of managers, executives, and administrators in all sectors, professions, and regions across the globe during the twentieth century. In a rapidly growing market society, people are flooded with information and data about goods and services. The improved standard of living in the developed world increases the number of choices people need to make in their daily life, from choosing a soap or a shirt to buying a house or a car, accepting a job offer, or deciding on a neighborhood in which to live. As suggested by the cognitive psychological approach (Lewin, 1936) and modern decision-making theories (Janis, 1968; Simon, 1976), people tend to make decisions and business choices based on a complex set of perceptions or attitudes that frequently reflect a general "image" of the product or service rather than the actual quality of that product or service. Most of us buy a car based on the recommendation or experience of friends, the evaluations and statements sent to us in the media, or based on marketing campaigns that are targeted at improving our image of the product. The assumption is that if this image is positive, I will be more inclined to purchase the product instead of choosing alternative options that are also available on the market.

Thus, it is only natural to find that the origins of the study of organizational image are in the literature of public affairs and marketing (e.g., Selama and Selama, 1988). Over the years, studies have suggested numerous definitions and related, but distinctive, terminologies for this phenomenon (Browne and Golembiewski, 1974; Dowling, 1994; Dutton and Dukerich, 1991; Fombrun and Shanley, 1990; Fomburn, 1996; Gioia, Schultz, and Corley, 2000; Riordan, Gatewood, and Bill, 1997; Thompson, 1967; Treadwell and Harrison, 1994). For example, Riordan et al. (1997) suggested that organizational image reflects individuals' perceptions of the actions, activities, and the accomplishments of the organization, and this image ranks the organization in comparison with other organizations. Their study followed Miles (1987) and Fombrun and Shanley (1990) who used the term *reputation*, and Dutton and Dukerich (1991) and Dutton, Dukerich, and Harquail (1994), who referred to *corporate image* as synonyms for organizational image. These studies and others advanced the notion that organizational image reflects: (1) the stability of the organization and its reputation in the marketplace and society, (2) the quality of the organization's outputs and outcomes as seen by clients, (3) the organization's position as a manufacturer or service provider in comparison with other competing organizations, and (4) the general willingness of various stakeholders to become engaged in the actions of the organization as customers, clients, or employees.

Moreover, nearly four decades ago Thompson's (1967) argued that an organization does not present one image, but multiple images, because "each assessor is inclined to employ a different kind of yardstick" (p. 88). An organization may have one image as an employer, another as a service provider, and yet another as a social institution. Following this line of thought, the image of organizations should be treated as a multi-focal concept derived from various perceptions such as those of employees, customers, contractors, and suppliers. When considering the image of public sector groups, citizens also become significant stakeholders. Nonetheless, most studies have still used an internal rating strategy to determine organizational image, turning to employees and asking them about (1) how they view the organization and its activities, and (2) how they think others view the organization from the outside. For example, Browne and Golembiewski (1974) explained organizational image as a comparative structural frame that each employee develops to rate his or her department or organization in comparison with other departments or organizations. This intra-organizational perspective of organizational image is built upon a set of constructs such as the common experiences of the employees, the common knowledge that they share, expectations from the job, and the quality of mutual interactions. Note, however, that the operative aspect of measuring perceived public sector image relies heavily on generic managerial and organizational tools. As this study was not focused on image and reputation in the public sector, I will not develop this construct any further in the current book. However, I do believe that it is an additional aspect of public sector performance that should be developed in future studies.

Summary: Core terminology in the bureaucratic discourse and its measurement

This chapter presented a perceptual terminology and conceptualization for dealing with bureaucracy and its operative meaning in the public administration of the modern nation state. I firmly believe that taking a perceptual view is not the only way to analyze these arenas. Indeed, the economic approach as well as the technical and judicial point of views may add a great deal that will help us better explain the meaning of the bureaucratic and the democratic systems. However, the perceptual approach puts citizens at the front and center of the entire issue. This book, like most of the works it relies on, maintains that reality is very much in the eyes of the beholder. Similarly, better understanding of the bureaucratic phenomena can be gained by analyzed its meaning for the involved stakeholders. As with many other political ideas and processes, people feel they know what bureaucracy means in daily life. For many, it reflects order, fine structures, public regulations, and systematic control over resources and services. From a less favorable point of view, bureaucracy synonymous with red tape, high fences, slow moving administrative actions, and lackluster responsiveness, all of which impinge on public satisfaction. Yet, an empirical scientific approach must consider all these perceptions objectively and measure them in a valid and reliable manner so that worthwhile knowledge can be accumulated.

Chapter 4

The Charm of Democracy: Building on Democratic Values and Good Citizenship[1]

Democracy and citizenship behavior: Obedience, loyalty, and participation

Fox and Miller (1996) present the "loop model of democracy" that puts citizens and citizenship at the center (p. 15): (1) The people/citizens are aware of what they want or need; (2) Competing candidates (or parties) for electoral office – political entrepreneurs – offer alternative packages of wants or needs that can be satisfied by a particular method; (3) People/citizens choose a representative by voting for whatever alternative package seems the best match with their preferences; (4) Coalitions of winning entrepreneurs pass laws reflecting the people's/citizens' choice; (5) A vigilant populace pays enough attention to the process and the results to judge the elected representatives as either successful or wanting; (6) If satisfied with the results, people/citizens will reward incumbents with their votes; if unsatisfied, they will vote for alternative entrepreneurs offering alternative packages.

This process is the conventional compromise of modern nations for ruling and being ruled in return. People (the citizens) and the leaders (the politicians and the senior bureaucrats) must obey the rules of the democratic game. They are expected to be loyal to the system and to its terms. Furthermore, they are called upon to actively take part in making the process work and the system operate wisely and fairly. This is the essence of "citizenship behavior" in modern democracies.

At first glance, citizenship behavior and effective governance that is based on principles of neo-managerialism, such as New Public Management (NPM), may seem an odd couple. Citizenship in modern society draws its substance from ideas such as political participation, community involvement and communitarianism, social justice, humanitarianism, voluntarism, and shared responsibilities of individuals (Box, 1998; Fredrickson, 1997). By contrast, effective managerialism and the NPM approach, which has become so important in contemporary public administration, centers on different forces and mechanisms: competition and businesslike operations, the effectiveness and efficiency of public organizations, and quality of services (Bozeman, 1993; Lynn, 1998; Perry and Kraemer, 1983;

1 Some sections of this chapter are based on E. Vigoda and R.T. Golembiewski, "Citizenship Behavior and the Spirit of New Managerialsim: A Theoretical Framework and Challenge for Governance," *American Review of Public Administration* (2001).

Pollitt, 1988). This chapter attempts to explain, however, why and how these two important streams in management thinking can and should be related.

Citizenship behavior is a powerful construct of human activity that deserves more attention in the study of public administration and management. Beyond the basic constructs of obedience and loyalty, constructive citizenship behavior in modern societies encompasses active participation, involvement, and voluntary actions of the people in managing their lives. Nonetheless, this idea has so far received scant consideration in NPM thinking. Until the 1980s, only a few attempts had been made to develop a comprehensive analysis of citizenship behavior that could be related to general management science, and especially to images of public administration theory and action. Studies concerned with exploring the citizenship–management connection took a relatively narrow perspective. One line of research focused on citizens' involvement, participation, and empowerment in the national and local environments (e.g., Barber, 1984; Pateman, 1970). More recent studies fostered the notion that voluntarism and spontaneous actions of individuals are useful tools for governments in their efforts to overcome budgetary difficulties, advance stability, and promote effectiveness in public arenas (Box, 1998, 1999; Brudney, 1990; Fredrickson,1997; Rimmerman, 1997). Other studies, mainly in management and organizational psychology, emphasized the valuable self-motivated contributions of employees that can lead to better efficacy and success inside the workplace. Prosocial, altruistic behaviors (e.g., Brief and Motowidlo, 1986) and organizational citizenship behavior (OCB; e.g., Morrison, 1996; Organ, 1988; Smith, Organ, and Near, 1983) have been identified as necessary for the creation of a healthy organizational atmosphere, particularly for promoting service quality and enhancing the general outcomes of public organizations (Podsakoff and MacKenzie, 1997). In addition, a budding interdisciplinary approach elaborated on the possibility that higher levels of citizens' involvement on the state or community level are related to more involvement in the job and to enhanced organizational democracy that improves organizational outcomes (Peterson, 1990; Putnam, 1993; Sobel, 1993). Organizational democracy and a participatory climate were found to be good predictors of employees' performance in private and public systems, and thus received increased attention in recent years (Cohen and Vigoda, 1999, 2000; Cotton et al., 1988). All the above studies pointed to the added value of citizenship behavior, in its many forms and settings, to management in general and to public organizations in particular. Regretfully, these efforts have not matured into a broader perspective on the overall relationships between characteristics of citizenship behavior and new trends in modern managerialism. Knowledge about different aspects of the citizenship–management connection have not been combined in an effective way that could lead to a better understanding of both fields. Hence, the advantages of such mutual enrichment have been overlooked and left as "unfinished business."

Reviewing theoretical and empirical studies on NPM, citizenship behavior, and the potential interrelationships between them, the present study elaborates on several questions. What is so important about the relationship between multi-dimensional citizenship and new managerialism, especially in the public sector?

What are the variants of citizenship behavior in and around organizations that can be used to enhance public management goals? On what theoretical grounding can we assume that citizenship behavior and NPM are in fact related? Who should be involved in fostering citizens' involvement and participation that may promote what I define as "a spirit of new managerialism," and what duties and responsibilities should each participant have? Answers to these questions may contribute to the development of more responsive public administration and healthier democratic societies. Our theoretical discussion also leads to a model for understanding the field. It suggests that planned strategic co-operation and a genuine partnership among players in the political, administrative, and social arenas is crucial and possible. In our view, it is a prime managerial challenge for the future.

Citizenship, governability, and New Public Management: A critique

In the modern world, strong nations are expected to demonstrate effectiveness, efficiency, and a sense of governability. This goal can be fostered by a variety of methods and models, one of which is the tendency to incorporate ideas of the NPM doctrine. However, NPM may be criticized for not doing enough to usher in the idea of citizenship behavior through the main entrance of modern managerial halls. Unlike traditional public management approaches, the NPM movement focuses on citizens as sophisticated clients in complex environments. Relying heavily on private sector management, citizens of modern democracies are perceived more and more as clients with multiple alternatives for consuming high-level services. Public authorities must treat the public well, not only because of their presumed administrative responsibility for quality in action but also because of their obligation to democratic rules, to accountability demands, transparency criteria, and sometimes even because of their fear of losing clients in a increasingly competitive businesslike arena. Hence, NPM opposes the more classical approach to governance and public administration that used to see citizens as simply constituents or voters. However, NPM creates a different obstacle to productive citizenship behavior that must be recognized and overcome. I argue that NPM encourages passivity among the citizenry because citizens acquire the power of *exit* (which indeed was virtually unavailable in the past), but at the same time NPM discourages the use of the original power of *voice* by citizens who may have much to contribute to their communities.

To improve our arguments about and criticism of the current status of NPM, I want to focus on two major groups of players that are involved in governmental and administrative processes in democracies. Each of these groups has a special function and a unique set of duties. One group comprises rulers and public administrators who are responsible for the proper management of large organizations and bureaucratic agencies. The second is the public, the "citizens," particularly those authentic citizen-leaders who agree to be managed by "others" and must develop and sustain the appropriate control, involvement, and participation in the administrative process. Hobbes argued that these groups are tightly bound in a kind of mutual agreement.

According to Hobbes, the people and their government have a *hidden social contract*, which calls for the people's obedience and loyalty to the government in return for government's commitment to provide for some of their basic "natural" rights. In its elementary configuration, this contract advocates bi-directional transactions of human resources promoting the mutual interests of citizens, states, and society.

While recent developments in the study of NPM focused on the responsibilities of the first group (rulers and administrators), they paid much less attention to the second (citizens). NPM favors a massive socialization of business management practices in the public sector to provide rulers with better tools for policy implementation (e.g., Lynn, 1998; Pollitt, 1988). The only problem is that these orientations and practices have, thus far, simply not been integrated with another key construct of healthy democratic systems. That construct is the active role of the public, its participation and involvement in running its own life more effectively, and the responsibility of administrators to encourage such public contributions. This underestimation of active and constructive citizenship behavior is a weakness in contemporary NPM theory.

For example, Box (1998: 73–4) suggests that NPM takes a very clear and unfavorable approach to active citizenship involvement in the administrative process. According to Box, there are three types of citizens classified along a continuum of desire to affect the public policy process: (1) "freeriders," those consumers of public services who receive public goods for free and let others do the work of citizenship; (2) "activists," who, in contrast, are deeply involved in public life and in citizenship activities aimed at the betterment of the community; and (3) "watchdogs," in the middle of the continuum, who are involved only in key issues of relevance to themselves personally. Practically and theoretically, NPM mainly encourages the "freeriders" and perhaps some of the "watchdogs." It does not, however, elaborate on the significance of "activists." So far, NPM has not emphasized the need for a better reciprocal linkage between rulers and citizens. At most, it has concentrated only on one direction of the flow of influence, from rulers to citizens. In many respects, this position does not adequately consider the positive effect of citizens' action on (new) public systems.

Why and how has such a tendency occurred? When we examine the evolutionary development of modern public administration, several answers to this question emerge. During the 1960s and 1970s, a growing number of observers perceived public administration as an antiquated and dying discipline that no longer could provide the public with satisfactory answers to its needs and demands. The contract between rulers and citizens, once a fundamental principle of democratic societies, seemed to have lost its glory. Governments and rulers in Europe and in America became unpopular in the eyes of many citizens as well as those of the elites (Rainey, 1990: 157). Public administration seemed to have no adequate answers for problems in education, transportation, employment, crime, natural resources, and other salient social issues. These inadequacies tarnished the image of public administration. Theoreticians and practitioners were left with epidemic social dilemmas waiting for new solutions.

In the search for alternative answers, business management theory was proposed as a source for new and invigorating ideas (Bozeman, 1993). It was suggested that *public management* (or *New* Public Management), rather than public administration, could offer a new understanding of how to run governments more efficiently, how to improve their relationships with citizens as clients, and thereby overcome some of society's pandemic ills. Today, despite the popularity in America and Europe of the theme of running the government like a business, this approach has encountered some unexpected difficulties. NPM has taken the lead in the study and practice of public systems, highlighting its main theme about the flow of responsibilities: the commitment and obligation of public institutions to citizens as passive clients. Conversely, however, the idealized relationship between citizens and governments has been described more in terms of a *uni-directional treaty* rather than the *bi-directional relationship* consistent with representative democracy. Administrators are encouraged to assume greater responsibility toward citizens, while citizens' participation and involvement in the administrative process is perceived by politicians and public servants as problematic. As King, Feltey, and Susel (1998: 319) argued, "although many public administrators view close relationships with citizens as both necessary and desirable, most of them do not actively seek public involvement. If they do seek it, they do not use public input in making administrative decisions ... (and) believe that greater citizen participation increases inefficiency, ... delays, and red tape."

Hence, NPM tends to overlook the importance of self-derived, spontaneous, and voluntary actions that are both vital and economically efficient for prosperous societies (Etzioni, 1994, 1995) as well as successful organizations (Katz and Kahn, 1966). Ironically, this behavior has enjoyed considerable attention in the business management literature, which served as a role model for NPM but has never been properly utilized in its original form. For example, since the early 1980s many studies of organizational behavior elaborated on the importance of pro-social and extra-role activities, later known as "Organizational Citizenship Behavior" (OCB). Organ (1988) defined this behavior as the "good soldier syndrome," and other scholars sought to relate it to a broader concept of citizenship on the national and community levels. A progressive definition of citizenship behavior refers to voluntary actions inside and outside the workplace that can be beneficial for private or public organizations (e.g., Graham, 1991; Organ, 1988; Van Dyne, Graham, and Dienesch, 1994). Still, many issues have been overlooked in the NPM literature, including engaging the public in administrative processes, encouraging citizens to take an active part in managing local governance, OCB and the spontaneous involvement of public employees inside the workplace, and the general promotion of citizenship and altruistic behavior at all social levels.

Consequently, NPM traditionally does not elaborate on the advantages of citizenship behavior within or around the public system. Most of the writing in the field focuses on simple businesslike orientations; these are necessary and important, but they fail to effectively cultivate the many dimensions of human enterprise. The conventional perspective of NPM calls for a massive implementation of business standards in the public sector by strategies of privatization, outsourcing, PIs (Performance Indicators), and an orientation to quality service. It does call for improved communication channels with citizens, but only as passive clients (Pollitt, 1988). It also views rulers and administrators as the major agents of managerial change. In this view, public administration adopts a "patronage" position towards citizens who are left with only minor responsibilities, such as becoming "good customers" or "sensible clients." NPM does not, however, encourage more voluntary active effort and participation by citizens in the administrative process.

In a groundbreaking work, Fredrickson (1997) in *The Spirit of Public Administration* suggests that a revitalized spirit of *new* public administration is necessary. In line with this idea, I further argue that a balanced reciprocal relationship between citizens and rulers may lead to the creation of *"a spirit of new managerialism."* This spirit is relevant to the twenty-first century and may flourish only in soil rich in mutual contributions by different parties. There is a need to develop the theory of the advantages of multi-dimensional citizenship behavior and to elaborate on its contribution to modern societies via NPM. Our argument is that citizenship behavior is vital for any public system and administrative bureaucracy that is seeking effectiveness, efficiency, fairness, social justice, and overall healthy growth and development. Citizenship behavior, whatever form it takes, has significant value for the general society.

A more comprehensive inclusion of citizenship behavior in the study of new managerialism is also in line with the contemporary business management approach because of the relatively low costs of voluntary action (Brudney, 1990; Brudney and Duncombe, 1992). From an economics viewpoint, the NPM approach does not take advantage of its most powerful, valuable, and inexpensive resources: good will, civic virtue, spontaneous initiatives, and innovation by individuals. Even in its own business-oriented terminology, contemporary NPM theory is limited and incomplete. It needs a much more sound understanding of how to relate citizenship behavior with the management of public systems. In the following sections, I try to portray this multi-dimensionality of citizenship behavior and to prepare the ground for a model of integration between citizenship and NPM. Such a discussion is vital to a better understanding of how to incorporate numerous voluntary enterprises in modern public management.

Dimensionality of citizenship behavior

Previous research has pointed to three core elements of general citizenship behavior: obedience of the people to social rules, loyalty to social institutions, and participation in social life (Marshall, 1950). While obedience and loyalty naturally belong to a worldwide definition of citizenship, the essence of citizenship behavior is *participation*. Participation means the active involvement of citizens in three main settings: governance (a *national* arena), local lives (a *communal* arena), and the workplace (an *organizational* arena).

The national and communal arenas　Montesquieu in *The Spirit of the Laws* argued that a state based upon popular participation, as distinct from other forms of government (for example, those based on obedience or loyalty), depends for its stability on the civic virtue of its good citizens. Rousseau emphasized the importance of citizens' freedom, political participation, and a "general will," which calls for making contributions to the governing and administrative process without gaining any personal advantages, only the common interest. Active citizens assist in safeguarding and supporting sound governance (for example, by holding or electing others to executive positions) and in adjudicating violations (for instance, by serving on juries). They also participate (directly or through representatives) in changing laws in response to new needs and in evolving an understanding of the common interest. Consequently, citizenship behavior includes devoting time and effort to the responsibilities of governance and administration, keeping well informed, sharing information and ideas with others, engaging in discussions about controversial issues, voting in whatever manner is provided under the law, and encouraging others to do likewise (Graham, 1991; Putnam, 1993; Van Dyne et al., 1994).

Community involvement and participation in local administrative processes constitute another unique aspect of participatory citizenship. Communal citizenship represents more informal participation than activity at the national level (Sobel, 1993). Some people may be disinclined or indifferent to participation in citizenship behavior at the national level. They may prefer a closer, perhaps more personal domain such as the community. While much research has been conducted to identify the mechanisms of individual voluntary action at the national level (e.g., Almond and Verba, 1963; Milbrath, 1965; Verba and Nie, 1972), recent studies have emphasized the importance of citizenship participation and voluntary action at the communal level (Barber, 1984; Etzioni, 1994, 1995; Hurd, 1989; King and Stivers, 1998; Putnam, 1993). For example, Barber (1984: 303) argued that "... political participation in common action is more easily achieved at the neighborhood level, where there are a variety of opportunities for engagement ..." and Hurd (1989) noted that "the need to foster responsible citizenship is obvious. Freedom can only flourish within a community where shared values, common loyalties and mutual obligations provide a framework of order and self-discipline, otherwise, liberty can quickly degenerate into narrow self-interest and license." King and Stivers (1998: 195–6) argued that "active citizenship is different from voting, paying taxes, or using government services ... in active citizenship citizens rule and are ruled in turn." Putnam (1993) concluded that communities with higher levels of voluntarism and civic engagement become better places to live, characterized by more trust in government, better government performance, and positive relations between citizens and the state.

The organizational arena　Beyond the national and communal spheres, active citizenship participation also has an organizational aspect. Studies in organizational behavior have long argued that more participation in the workplace, increased job involvement, and opportunities to use an effective voice may lead to improved job satisfaction, reduced turnover and absenteeism, and better organizational performance (Keller, 1997; Lum et al., 1998). Other studies found that public organizations that promote the values of employees' empowerment and participation in decision-making are more likely to enhance communication throughout units, increase the commitment of stakeholders, and improve productivity as well as the quality of services (Berman, 1995; Young, Worchel, and Woehr, 1998). Hence, an analysis of citizenship behavior in modern societies entails a broader conceptual discussion, applicable not only to nations, states, and communities but also to organizations, bureaucracies, and public agencies. In a rapidly changing environment, organizations and the workplace have an important task. Organizations' productivity leads to a significant improvement in quality of life. Citizens' demands and needs grow faster and reach farther than ever before. The expansion of welfare services provided by the state to its citizens, directly or by proxy, must cohere with such demands and satisfy more people more frequently and more extensively. In practice, organizational change in these agencies only partly matches the rapid transformation of the environment, and needs better support from quasi-public and non-public organizations (the "third sector"). Therefore, the idea that self-derived citizenship activity should be related to management and organizational sciences, as well as to public administration operations, has attracted growing attention in recent decades (Katz and Kahn, 1966; Organ, 1988).

Two basic patterns of relationship between citizenship behavior and the organizational arena should be mentioned in this regard. First, the enhanced involvement of citizens in the administrative process (for example, becoming members or supporters of public or third sector agencies) generates commitment to a healthy public service, proper understanding of what is right and what is wrong in managing public organizations, and education leading towards constructive participatory democracy. Second, improved intra-organizational citizenship behavior by public employees improves performance by public and third sector agencies. The benefits of self-inspired contributions by employees reach far beyond the merits of formal authority and bureaucratic mechanisms. Recently, Rimmerman (1997: 19) suggested that increased citizens' participation in workplace decision-making processes is important if people are to recognize their roles and responsibilities as citizens within the larger community. This idea is consistent with an earlier work of Pateman (1970), who argued that through participation in decision-making (on the state, community, and organization levels) the individual learns to be a public as well as a private citizen.

We thus suggest that participation in multiple settings such as the national or communal arena, as well as participation inside organizations, should be borne in mind when NPM strategies are developed. The involvement in and contribution of citizens to the state, community, workplace, and society in general are valuable. Citizens' involvement has the advantage of being the least costly input in the administrative process. Participation also enhances individuals' commitment to their environment and approval of public administration's legitimacy. Also, an increase in political participation bodes well for political stability and the accountability of the public sector (King and Stivers, 1998). Stability and accountability create services to the people that are responsive and effective.

Citizenship behavior: Levels of analysis

Citizens' participation is manifested in two major ways: personal initiatives and organized action. McKevitt (1998: 42) suggests that participation and active citizenship are frequently portrayed as individual qualities, but at the same time they have strong overtones of collective responsibility. Box (1998: 71–4) also emphasizes the centrality and current trends in individualism and collectivism, especially in communities. Like McKevitt, Box identifies the struggle for "a point of balance" between individualism and collectivism that influences the nature of citizenship in America. The tension between the individualistic and the collectivist ideas of citizenship is real, and disagreement exists over its boundaries. Following this approach, I identify two levels of active citizenship behavior that are discussed in the psychological, sociological, managerial, and administrative literature: (1) *individual:* altruism and voluntarism of persons in national, communal, and organizational settings; (2) *collective:* organized or semi-organized citizenship behavior as represented by interest groups, volunteer associations, volunteer programs, not-for-profit organizations, and the third sector. Together, these levels comprise the citizenship behavior hierarchy of modern societies.

The individual level Individual citizenship behavior refers to the very basic construct of personal actions and reactions taken by individual citizens. These are spontaneous actions of unorganized persons who engage in altruistic actions aimed at enhancing the prosperity and development of their environment. Citizens may show compassion for other citizens, contribute time, money, and other resources to help those less capable or less fortunate, and provide assistance for others whenever the situation requires it without seeking any personal advantage or compensation (e.g., Conover, Crewe, and Searing, 1993; Monroe, 1994; Piliavin and Charng, 1990). Moreover, inside public organizations citizens–employees may exert additional effort to help fellow employees fulfill their duties and serve the public without seeking any personal rewards. General management literature has defined these enterprises as Organizational Citizenship Behavior (OCB), which reflects an informal contribution that participants can choose to make or withhold without regard to sanctions or formal incentives. As noted in previous studies (e.g., Organ, 1988; Organ and Konovsky, 1989; Podsakof and MacKenzie, 1997), many of these contributions, aggregated over time and persons, considerably enhance organizational efficiency and effectiveness. Further studies concluded that given the multiple pressures under which they work, public organizations should seek a better understanding of the relationship among citizenship behavior inside and outside the workplace, management, and organizational outcomes (Cohen and

Vigoda, 1999, 2000; Graham, 1991). Encouragement of citizenship behavior in and around public agencies may contribute to these organizations' productivity, competence, and success, and hence to society in general.

The collective level   This level of citizenship behavior comprises semi-organized and fully organized actions initiated by groups of individuals. Usually, citizenship behavior at this level emerges when a group shares mutual interests and all members are willing to be actively involved in collective voluntary endeavors. The group's ambition is high, and there is recognition that it would be almost impossible to achieve most of the joint goals as individuals. Among these groups one finds neighborhood associations, ad hoc groups that seek limited ecological goals, volunteer programs inside organizations, and even altruistic support groups offering help to those in need from others who have experienced similar needs (for example, quitting smoking, avoiding drugs or alcohol, supporting families in distress, and so forth). Previous research has demonstrated that the emergence, growth, and decline of voluntary groups can be explained by human capital variables, the emergence of leadership, socioeconomic status, and competition with other groups (Janoski and Wilson, 1995; McPherson and Rotolo, 1996). Membership in voluntary groups also increases forms of political expression and participation (Michael, 1981). Furthermore, membership in volunteer programs in the public sector has economic value for public organizations as well as symbolic rewards for citizens' participation (Brudney, 1990; Brudney and Duncombe, 1992).

Apart from the semi-organized citizenship actions, the collective level of analysis also includes highly organized and fully institutional collective endeavors. The most obvious representative of this sub-category is the organized not-for-profit sector, which has grown rapidly in recent decades. Collective institutional citizenship derives from ambitious interests of large groups that have undergone a relatively complicated process of institutionalization and formalization. Management and public administration sciences have devoted considerable attention to this field (Brinton, 1994; Coble, 1999; O'Connell, 1989; Smith and Lipsky, 1993). In many ways, these organizations (also known as non-profit or voluntary organizations) represent increased public involvement aimed at providing services in areas in which the state is unable or unwilling to play a significant role. This "third sector" is distinct from the traditional public and private sectors (Gidron and Kramer, 1992). In recent years, voluntary organizations and the third sector constituted about 10 percent of the economic size of all governmental activities in the US (O'Connell, 1989) and their relative size continues to grow. Such figures may indicate that citizens of modern societies have more needs and demands and that they are disappointed with governments' operation and inability to provide satisfactory welfare services. Hence, it seems that today, more than ever before, citizens are willing to engage in collective voluntary actions (both semi-organized and fully organized) to fulfill their needs (King, Feltey, and Susel, 1998).

A multi-dimensional model of citizenship behavior and public administration

The complex construct of modern citizenship behavior and its limited employment in NPM theory calls for a revised conceptual framework that can unite this "odd couple." This framework should advocate the co-existence of as well as mutual solidarity between the public as represented by citizens on the one hand, and the administration as reflected in NPM on the other. Figure 4.1 presents a suggested model of multi-dimensional citizenship behavior and its effect on public service systems as stemming from the NPM approach. Based on the location of citizenry action (communal and national versus organizational) and on the levels of analysis (individual versus collective action), I distinguish four types of citizenship behavior: Micro-citizenship (MC1), Midi-citizenship (MC2), Macro-citizenship (MC3), and Meta-citizenship (MC4). Each type is then related to the relevant construct of managerial operation and outcomes. Together they are intended to provide a synthesis of the fields.

	Organizational	Communal & National
Individual	Micro-citizenship → Employees' Performance	Macro-citizenship → Personal Welfare
Collective	Midi-citizenship → Organizational Performance	Meta-citizenship → Social Welfare

Figure 4.1   Good citizenship behavior: Dimensionality and level of analysis

Micro-citizenship Micro-citizenship (MC1) is the very basic image of citizenship actions as taken by individuals in the limited sphere of the workplace. Employees may actively participate in workplace activities and express a greater willingness to support others even when not asked or ordered to do so. These employees may be defined as good organizational citizens (Organ, 1988). They differ from other individuals who show lower levels of citizenship behavior or withhold such positive behaviors entirely. Some of these employees may even engage in organizational misbehaviors, such as stealing organizational property or sabotaging the work itself (Vardi and Wiener, 1996). The micro-citizenship of individuals inside the workplace has been shown to have a direct and significant impact on employees' performance (Vigoda-Gadot and Cohen, 2004). Findings suggest that organizations benefit from using measures of OCB as an integral part of their routine performance evaluation strategy because of the valuable information they provide on employees' informal contributions (Morrison, 1996).

Hence, a challenge for management theory in general, and particularly for (new) public management, is the development of valid and reliable research tools that can distinguish different types of public employees or "organizational citizens" in public agencies. Such indicators are expected to increase the explanatory power and predictability of organizational behavior models. In the public sector, it is extremely important that good organizational citizens be those who interact with the public to create a responsive environment and, as highlighted in NPM theory, serve citizens as clients. Enriching the public sector with employees who are better organizational citizens may also have an educative spillover effect on the public, improve the image of public administration, and make contact with citizens more fruitful and efficient both economically and socially.

Midi-citizenship Midi-citizenship (MC2) also refers to actions taken inside organizations, but they arise from the collective voice of groups of individuals rather than from independent individual actions. Whereas micro-citizenship has the greatest effect on other individuals, the midi-citizenship pattern is fashioned by groups for the sake of other groups or units, or for the sake of the organization as a whole. Midi-citizenship focuses on the attainment of broader objectives and goals in the workplace, not only personal targets and interests. The involvement and general voice of groups in the manufacturing process is valuable. Studies have demonstrated that more involvement of organized individuals in decision-making processes contributes to better operation in private as well as in public organizations (Erez, Earley, and Hulin, 1985). Methods such as quality circles, team-building strategies, and MBO (Management by Objectives) emphasize the general encouragement of work groups' becoming more active as well as entrepreneurial in the various stages of production (Drucker, 1966; Hirschman, 1970). Midi-citizenship is accordingly built upon micro-citizenship but is far more ambitious in its effort to increase and improve the general performance of public organizations. Furthermore, groups are more powerful than separate individuals and set more challenging goals, which are later translated into massive improvement of goods and services. The collective action also enhances the feeling of communitarianism and the sense of cooperation that can spillover into the extra-organizational environment (Peterson, 1990; Sobel, 1993). In this way, organizations in general, and especially public agencies, serve as habitats for the growth of citizenship awareness and the development of sensitivity toward others, be it other work units or various social groups.

Macro-citizenship I defined macro-citizenship (MC3) as altruistic endeavors of individuals in the national and communal settings, those that express self-initiated contributions for the sake of others in the wider society. Moving beyond the narrow organizational arena, individuals use similar tendencies of altruism and willingness to help fellow citizens in the national and communal spheres. As elucidated earlier, the active citizenship of individuals outside the workplace is characterized by independent enterprises focused on assisting others who may need help. Such spontaneous actions by unorganized people aim at enhancing the prosperity and development of the environment in general, thereby increasing the welfare of their fellow citizens. This is why macro-citizenship is related, in our model, to personal welfare in the national and communal arenas. Citizens may help other citizens by showing tenderness, kindness, and generosity. They can contribute a variety of diverse resources, such as time or money, to help the less able or the less fortunate. They may also provide assistance for the elderly, for children in need, for minorities, or for other disadvantaged groups. In so doing, they seek no personal rewards or compensation in return (Monroe, 1994; Piliavin and Charng, 1990). Studies have also suggested that some practices and skills gained in intra-organizational experiences may be useful for these initiatives. Citizens in the intimate setting of the workplace may learn how to use their personal resources more effectively, and then transfer them into the wider society (Peterson, 1990). Macro-citizenship is also characterized by people engaging only in one-on-one or one-on-group activities, avoiding (intentionally or not) any relationship with organized groups of volunteer associations.

Meta-citizenship   Meta-citizenship (MC4) is the term I decided to use for collective citizenry action in the wider society. With the exception of ideas like universal citizenship (Oliver and Heater, 1994), this is perhaps the highest level of participatory and constructive citizenship behavior identifiable. Meta-citizenship represents collective actions at the communal and national levels that stem from deep altruistic dispositions, conscientiousness, and general acceptance of the constructive value of citizenship duties and responsibilities.

As noted by Fredrickson (1997), collective actions by interest groups, by political parties, or by citizens' lobbies are the most acceptable and widely studied aspects of citizenship behavior in contemporary political science literature. However, during the nineteenth century, citizens (especially in America) functioned in a more direct way, through town meetings, raising a militia for defense, and engaging in Midwestern barn raising (p. 12). In earlier centuries, citizens' associations were the most powerful image of American society, becoming less popular from late 1800s to the mid-1900s with the emergence of the reform movement in public administration. The founding fathers of modern public administration, such as W. Wilson and D. Waldo, urged that the discipline become a formal field of knowledge and an independent science among all other social sciences. The reform movement introduced specialization, professionalism, merit-based appointment and promotion, and the application of management sciences into government. Citizens continued to play a role, but a less direct one. They continued to organize, albeit less and less, to solve problems or provide services and increasingly formed interest groups to influence government. As Fredrickson indicates, in the 1950s "pluralism" emerged as the best term to describe the connection between citizens and governments. Thus the indirect relationship between the public and the administrators became even more widespread. The tradition of citizenship as involving an energized and self-directed public had essentially been lost.

Citizenship behavior was reconstructed only in the 1970s when citizens resumed their functions in associations and NPOs (Non-profit Organizations), later known as the emerging "third sector." Hence, patterns of meta-citizenship were transformed over the years, but they continued to represent the overt, pure, and broad connection between organized citizens and governments. More specifically, meta-citizenship has had a major impact on public sector services by creating an awareness of social welfare. Today, more and more organized citizens are taking action when the state is unable or unwilling to do what it ought to do for the public. Meta-citizenship is advanced as supplementary to governmental policy, and in some cases as an accelerator of processes already in progress.

Citizenship behavior, governability, and public management: A synthesis

We suggest that incorporating the idea of citizenship into new governability and NPM thinking can be achieved more successfully through a multi-dimensional model, such as the one presented here. The model provides a classification that may better map voluntary enterprises in modern society and offer better explanations for them from a theoretical standpoint. Another contribution of our model may be the examination of the relationship among different dimensions of citizenship behavior in and around public organizations. Here we may look at literature in political theory and management science that argues that citizenship behaviors at the state, community, and organizational levels are related (Graham, 1991; Peterson, 1990; Sobel, 1993). An alternative theory may suggest that such a relationship is not possible, and further studies should subject the three perspectives to a comprehensive empirical evaluation. The results of this effort may discern the nature of the constructive "citizenship syndrome" and illuminate the bases for voluntary actions in society.

So far, I have demonstrated that citizenship behavior has many faces. However, it has only one source, namely the people and their willingness to engage in constructive activities. Building a spirit of new managerialism means bringing the citizens closer to their original role as equal members in the administrative process. In so doing, they may transform bureaucracies and stagnant public services into more flexible, responsive, and vital entities upon whose broad shoulders modern societies can safely rest. The final sections of this chapter elaborate on the nature of this spirit and the challenges it poses for the future.

The spirit of new managerialism: Added value through new citizenship behavior

The four types of citizenship behavior suggested here may be viewed as one alternative typology of human activism and voluntary actions that are revitalizing administration in modern society. As Joyce (1994) and Box (1998) argued, people in America and other developed democracies are ready for "a new citizenship" that will liberate and empower them. This new citizenship calls for a revitalized relationship with governance, or "citizen centered governance" (CCG). Citizens should be encouraged to become part of governance, taking on more responsibilities for running their lives rather than treating the administrative process as something separate, and themselves as customers to be "served" or antagonists to be opposed (Ostrom, 1993). According to Schachter (1997), "a new citizenship" must be related to the process of reinventing government, which is a way of creating change through managerial techniques (Box, 1998). Referring to the Clinton administration's National Performance Review, Schachter describes a situation in which "current reform proposals do not include a wake-up call to the public to assume its obligations since customers have no obligations to the enterprise from which they buy products and services ... Citizens can sit back comfortably in their rocking chairs and watch government improve to meet their expectations" (p. 90). Schachter criticizes this view because it encourages passive citizenship, equivalent to Box's "freeriders," instead of yielding productive involvement and participation. He then suggests a model of "citizen owners" and "active citizenship" that may be the basis for a "new citizenship." In all, these perspectives and models lead to robust citizen reliance on public management's commitment to increasing agency effectiveness and responsiveness. Active citizenship behavior on the individual or collective level that emerges in national, communal, and organizational arenas represents people engaged in deliberations to influence public sector decision-making. It shapes the political agenda, ponders the goals that governments should pursue, and evaluates how well particular public-sector programs work (Box, 1998: 73).

Nowadays NPM literature tries to identify and define new criteria that may help determine the extent to which public agencies succeed in keeping pace with the growing needs of the citizens (Pollitt, 1988; Smith, 1993). Nevertheless, it has not fully considered the potential advantage of multi-dimensional models or "new citizenship" involvement (Box, 1999). The prime advantage of such citizenship involvement is its long-term effect and continuity. More involvement, participation, and voluntarism by citizens (as individuals or collectively as groups and organized institutions) in different settings (state, community, or organization) is a valuable resource that new managerialism should not ignore.

Smith (1993) provides reasoning and support for this notion, arguing that citizens' participation, involvement, and awareness of the performance of public services should be a core element of NPM. It can increase the political pressure put on elected and appointed public servants, thereby enhancing both managerial efficiency and the effective allocation of resources in the public sector. This process of public accountability to stakeholders/citizens is comparable to the role adopted by financial reporting in the private/corporate sector. As in the private sector, externally related outcomes (such as citizens' satisfaction, perceptions of public administration's responsiveness, perceptions of public personnel's morality and fairness) have a more profound impact on internal control mechanisms. Managers and public servants become more sensitive to their duties and more deeply committed to serving their public customers. Greater citizenship involvement, altruistic and voluntary activity, participation, and engagement in national or local managerial processes may breed internal organizational involvement, commitment, and innovation by public servants. Furthermore, public employees may become more willing to engage in extra-role behavior, pro-social behavior, and organizational citizenship behavior (Brief and Motowidlo, 1986; Organ, 1988; Podsakoff and MacKenzie, 1997) to support the common goals of citizens, governments, and the public service. In return, it is expected that citizens will develop deeper loyalty and commitment and increase their participation. They will exert additional effort and contribute to the general good of their environment.

A challenge for governance: Citizenship-infused governability

A multi-dimensional analysis of citizenship behavior and its relationship with NPM creates a major challenge for governance – to create a citizenship-infused governability that goes hand in hand with a desire to improve efficiency and market orientations while maintaining and encouraging principles of open democracy. What guidelines should governments follow to respond properly to these challenges? Several suggestions can be defined: (1) enhancing the partnership with and empowerment of citizens by various means that are not manipulated by the state. In general, these actions must stimulate environmental conditions that are necessary to generate spontaneous behavior by citizens as individuals or groups or as part of organized institutions (such as through education, participatory experience in community aid, and financial support to organized groups); (2) programs of involvement must be governed by citizens and administered by practitioners who understand them; (3) public service practitioners must operate as advisers and helpers to citizens rather than as controllers of public organizations (Box, 1998; Rimmerman, 1997); (4) public administration must be responsible for evaluating these initiatives and learning about their outcomes. All programs in which citizens are involved should be under continuous evaluation by unbiased professionals from academia or the private sector, and (5) on the intra-organizational level, public administration is responsible for creating a spirit of help and service beyond formal procedures (but not in contradiction to them). Improved organizational citizenship behavior among public employees can become an effective tool in the relationship between citizens and public servants (Morrison, 1996).

Several programs and techniques can be applied to achieve these goals. First, volunteer programs in the fields of health, welfare services, education, and security should receive national and federal support. Adequate training programs of volunteers as well as volunteer leadership and management should be developed and implemented by professionals. Second, educational efforts that emphasize the importance of voluntarism should start in the very first years of school and create an awareness in the very young of the value of citizenship involvement. A good example is the local democratic club that was established in Culver City, California and contributes to greater citizenship involvement in community life (http://www.culvercityonline.com/). Without such an extensive educational effort, long-term initiatives will remain limited and incomplete. Governments should also be responsible for the coordination of cooperation among different voluntary groups and institutions. Coordination may increase the efficiency of volunteer groups and organizations to get more value for effort. However, government's role should not be coercive but must remain consultative. Using their delegated authority, governments can establish public volunteers' committees to coordinate the voluntary activity at the local and national levels. This goal can be accomplished with the benefit of the experience gained in several countries, such as Denmark and Israel, which increased citizenship involvement through "citizens conferences" and "citizens committees" that deal with actual public concerns and try to influence decisions on issues that are not fully addressed by governments (for example, see http://www.zippori.org.il/English/index.html). Governments will maintain their advisory position, providing the citizens with the conditions and experience to make their ideas a reality.

Citizens and citizens' leaders, for their part, play several roles in the process of generating the new spirit of managerialism. The most elementary role is taking an active part in running their own lives and encouraging others to do likewise. As proposed above, this can be accomplished on the individual or collective level. Participating in neighborhood associations or voluntary groups, active involvement in parents' committees at schools, donating money, time, or effort for the development of community services, and encouraging others to take part in such activities are all valuable and important missions. In addition, all citizens should contribute constructive criticism of the public system to provide feedback for politicians and public servants, thereby increasing their responsiveness and sense of responsibility. Finally, citizens and citizens' leaders should serve as socialization agents of voluntary actions. The educational mission of citizens is to avoid passivity and to motivate future generations to become involved, thereby promoting an understanding of shared responsibilities in social life.

Good citizenship and strong nations

Fredrickson (1997) suggests that the spirit of public administration must develop a theory of the public that goes beyond interest-group pluralism, beyond public choice theory or representative democracy, and beyond a customer service orientation, to a refined and expanded idea of citizenship. In accordance with this idea, this chapter has presented a new perspective on modern citizenship that may be a starting point for the spirit of *new* public administration.

According to Marshall (1990), the center of the art and science of administration is the citizen being served. However, should the flow of services be a one-way one or a bi-directional one that involves taking responsibility for oneself and the active involvement of citizens? Marshall argues that there is a definite need for enhanced citizenship in the administrative process. The good citizen is interested in, active in, and responsible for his/her place in society. Box (1998) attempts to "bring public administration back to democracy by drawing on new roles for practitioners and citizens in the governance of their own communities" (p. xi). He challenges the idea, drawn from the private sector, that local residents are only *consumers* of public services, people who should be treated like customers, as the NPM literature argues. Instead, Box suggests that individuals are returning to their earlier role as *(good) citizens,* people who are the owners of the community and take responsibility for its governance (p. 3).

In line with these ideas, I developed a multi-dimensional perspective of citizenship behavior that does not necessarily contradict but indeed meshes well with the trends of new managerialism and NPM. This perspective elaborated on (1) settings of citizenship (national/communal and organizational), (2) levels of analysis (individual and collective), and (3) integration of these dimensions with NPM ideas to create a "spirit of new managerialism." This spirit may be defined as a mutual power of MC1, MC2, MC3, and MC4. It asks that governments take strategic steps to promote citizenship values at all levels, and that citizens actively participate in spontaneous initiatives and in the process of building the society. The structure and culture of public administration must become more flexible and responsive to citizens' needs (Vigoda, 2000a). To achieve this goal it, should become pro-active and entrepreneurial in the initiation of partnerships between public servants and citizens. The focus of NPM should adjust itself to include the transformation of "good will" into "effective operations." In contrast with "old" managerialism, the new spirit of public management must call for multivariate citizenry action. Public administration, through its professional cadre, should initiate this process and take the lessons learned to heart. Investment in spontaneous behavior is less expensive and more cost effective than other reform efforts, so it should receive a higher priority on the NPM agenda than calls for improved performance of public agencies.

Furthermore, cultivating this mini-citizenship pattern may lead to improvement in all other patterns (midi-, micro-, and meta-citizenship). Organizational behavior theory and general management literature can provide additional guidelines as to the nature of this phenomenon and its recommended application in the public sector (Podsakoff and MacKenzie, 1997). Citizenship behavior should be an integral part of NPM as well as of any other new reform in the public sector. Similarly, much can be learned from research on communitarianism, organizational citizenship behavior, volunteer groups and programs, the third sector, and various other aspects of individuals' altruistic behavior. As suggested by Kramer (1999) and King and Stivers (1998), building relationships among citizens, administrators, and politicians is a long-term and continuous project. For truly democratic government, administrators and citizens must engage each other directly on a regular basis in full blown, unrestricted public dialogue, with neither side holding back anything important. Democratic public administration involves active citizenship and active administration that uses its discretionary authority to foster collaborative work with citizens. In sum, this section maintains that, unlike other managerial practices, NPM has unique properties that make citizenship behavior a natural factor to incorporate within it. Thus, the challenge for strong nations, modern governance, and new managerialism is a more comprehensive application of this valuable knowledge in public administration strategies.

Trust in government and in public administration

With respect to the above description of citizens' participation, trust in government and in administrative agencies represents a different aspect of the democratic machinery. Coulson (1998) describes it as an essential ingredient for building the "contract" between citizens and governance in the public sector management era. Thus, trust is a less active but still essential dimension that legitimizes democratic actions and institutions. Open societies rely on citizens' trust. The failure of that trust to reach a critical level signals the desire for political change. In fact, in recent years we have witnessed a massive proliferation of the concept of trust both in public administration and in the social sciences. There are also numerous definitions of the term "trust" (Bouckaert et al., 2002; Luhmann, 1988). Among these definitions, the one that views trust as the "faith people have in their government" (Citrin and Muste, 1999) has been adopted by public administration studies and applied to the administrative agencies that are an indispensable and central part of government. Notwithstanding, like participation and involvement, trust may also have a negative aspect. Studies note that overly trusting attitudes towards the government lead to a decline in the healthy criticism of the government and its policies. While a certain level of trust is essential for the legitimization of democratic institutions, overly trusting attitudes may reflect the stagnation of the citizenry, a situation that endangers the basic elements of a democratic system (Citrin and Muste, 1999; Coulson, 1998; Luhmann, 1988).

Levels of trust are generally measured by surveys and interviews using several indicators. As the literature proves, trust may be studied and measured at the macro and/or at the micro level. At the macro level, it is considered acceptable to look at trust in the government as a whole, which is a relative and vague concept. At the micro level, one may look at trust in the governmental and administrative agencies that represent modern bureaucracy, which is much easier to conceptualize and measure (Bouckaert and Van de Walle, 2003). This study focuses on the micro-level meaning of trust. However, the core assumption is that the micro and macro levels are mutually related and thus, as the trust of citizens in administrative agencies increases, their confidence in democracy and in other governmental institutions increases commensurately.

The common explanation of trust at the micro level is the micro-performance hypothesis about trust in government (Bouckaert et al., 2002; Bouckaert and Van de Walle, 2003). This hypothesis simply states that as citizens grow more satisfied with public sector performance, their level of trust in the government increases. Recent studies in the Israeli setting found empirical evidence that supports this claim (Vigoda, 2002a; Vigoda-Gadot and Yuval, 2003a, 2003b). While this hypothesis may be less theoretically valid when the general term "trust in government" is used, it is much more theoretically valid when referring to trust in a specific administrative agency based on its performance. Therefore, this study will refer to specific administrative agencies when evaluating the level of citizen trust.

Measuring trust in government and in public administration

Trust in government and in public administration refers to the level of faith or confidence citizens have in state authorities and in administrative branches of various kinds (Citrin and Muste, 1999). To measure trust in government and in public administration, I used an 18-item scale that focused on state bodies and administrative agencies such as: (1) Ministry of Health; (2) public hospitals; (3) public clinics; (4) public kindergartens and schools; (5) higher education (colleges and universities); (6) judiciary system; (7) Israel Defense Forces; (8) secret security services; (9) police and prisons; (10) public broadcasting system; (11) Ministry of Transportation; (12) Ministry of National Infrastructures; (13) authorities for the management of water system and national lands; (14) Ministry of the Environment; (15) State comptroller's office; (16) religious services system; (17) State treasury and tax system; (18) the central bank (Bank of Israel). Respondents were provided with a list of various state agencies and public organizations. They were asked to indicate how much trust they had in each of them on a 5-point scale from 1 (very little trust) to 5 (a great deal of trust). For the seven-year research period, the reliability of this scale ranged between .85 and .89, with an overall value of .88.

Participation in decision-making

The appropriate role of the public in public administration has recently received significant attention from both practitioners and academics (Ebdon, 2002; King et al., 1998; Thomas, 1995; Weeks, 2000). This interest is basically the result of public disenchantment and apathy at the end of the twentieth century, which expressed itself as a reduced level of trust in the governments of many Western democracies (Putnam, 1993; Simonsen and Robbins, 2000). Whereas some scholars suggest that higher levels of citizenship involvement (for example, participation in administrative decision-making, political participation, or community involvement) may lead to increased conflict over policy making and implementation (i.e., Thomas, 1995), there are also other, more positive, perceptions about the function of such involvement. Today, most studies assume that citizens' participation at the administrative level can improve public sector performance. The same logic is suggested for increasing levels of political participation and community involvement that urge policy makers to create innovative strategies for the people. Thus, recent studies have concentrated on finding the most efficient methods of participation – usually at the local/communal level and/or in the budgeting process (Berner, 2003; Church et al., 2002; Franklin and Ebdon, 2004; Irvin and Stansbury, 2004; Orosz, 2002; Simonsen and Robbins, 2000). For example, public hearings are one of the most frequently used formats for participation, yet such public participation proves inefficient in several ways (Berner, 2003). Arnstein (1969) and Church et al. (2002) suggest viewing community input as a spectrum or "ladder" of participation. The lower rungs of the participation ladder comprise processes in which power holders seek to educate the public about particular issues. Higher up on the ladder are processes through which power holders consult those individuals or groups who could potentially be affected by a proposed or current policy. Still higher up on the ladder, power holders and interested parties agree to share or delegate responsibilities for decision-making. At the top rungs of the ladder, lay individuals dominate decision-making. This level of participation requires a transfer of decision-making power from traditional decision makers to lay individuals.

Irvin and Stansbury (2004) weigh the advantages and disadvantages of citizens' involvement at the organizational/administrative level and conclude that the ideal conditions for its emergence are based on strong community ties, small groups organized locally, a willingness to volunteer, and the urgency of the issues at stake. A more radical approach characterizes the work of King et al. (1998) who, based on interviews and focus group discussions, develop the concept of authentic participation, that is, deep and continuous involvement in administrative processes with the potential for all involved to have an effect on the situation. The key elements of this concept are defined as focus, commitment, trust, and open and honest discussion. It requires that administrators focus on both process and outcome, meaning that participation is an integral part of administration, rather than an add-on to existing practices. The public is part of the deliberation process from issue framing to decision-making. Authentic participation places the citizen next to the issue and the administrative structures and processes furthest away, while the administrator is the bridge between the two. Despite criticism of intensive citizen involvement in administrative decision-making that has been voiced by other researchers, this study considers such involvement an essential stage for building healthy and balanced administrative systems. Furthermore, the study characterizes this involvement as a crucial step for building a stronger democracy. It seeks to demonstrate how such involvement may have an effect on positive attitudes towards government and towards public administration as well as encourage higher levels of democratic participatory behaviors (such as political participation and community involvement). The next section will therefore expand on the meaning of democratic participatory behavior and trust in modern nations.

Measuring perceived participation in decision-making

This variable was based on previous measures of involvement and participation in decision-making as applied in the discipline of organizational behavior and management (i.e., Aiken and Hage, 1966). It was defined as the degree of input and participation in administrative processes aimed at determining policies, strategies, plans, or actions of public agencies and was measured by two items: (1) "The public administration is interested in involving the public in important decision-making processes," and (2) "The public administration treats citizens as a central partner in decision-making processes aimed at improved public performance and efficiency." Respondents were asked to report the degree to which they agreed with the items on a scale from 1 (strongly disagree) to 5 (strongly agree).

Political participation

Brady (1999: 737) argues that participation is "surely one of the central concepts in the study of mass politics" and that all definitions include four basic concepts: activities or actions, citizens, politics, and influence. The classic definition by Verba and Nie (1972: 2) suggests that political participation refers to "those activities by private citizens that are more or less directly aimed at influencing the selection of governmental personnel and/or the decisions they take." However, more recent definitions have extended this scope somewhat. For example, Nagel (1987: 1) described participation as "actions through which ordinary members of a political system influence or attempt to influence outcomes," and Kaase and Marsh (1979: 42) suggest that participation includes "all voluntary activities by individual citizens intended to influence either directly or indirectly political choices at various levels of the political system." These latter definitions extend the meaning of participation beyond the conventional electoral system to the executive level of government and administration. Thus, a definition of participatory behavior in a democratic system that is both suitable and balanced for our purposes may be termed "democratic participatory behavior" (DPB) and be characterized by the level of active and passive involvement of citizens in various social activities directed at making the political or communal systems function more effectively.

Measuring political participation

This variable refers to "those activities by private citizens that are more or less directly aimed at influencing the selection of governmental personnel and/or the actions they make" (Verba and Nie, 1972: 2) or actions through which ordinary members of a political system influence or attempt to influence outcomes (Nagel, 1987). An 8-item scale was used, based on similar measures developed elsewhere (Almond and Verba, 1965; Brady et al., 1999; Milbrath and Goel, 1977; Verba et al., 1995). Respondents were asked to report the frequency of their involvement in these political activities on a 3-point scale: 1 (never been active), 2 (had been active in the past but not today), 3 (active today). The items that were used are as follows: (1) being a member of a political party; (2) keeping informed about politics; (3) voting regularly in general elections; (4) sending support/protest letters to politicians or to different newspapers; (5) being an active member of a public organization (public committee, political party and so forth); (6) taking part in demonstrations or political meetings; (7) engaging in political discussions; (8) being a candidate for public office; (9) signing petitions on political issues. The total score for each respondent was calculated by summing the responses for each item.

Community involvement

Barber (1984) argued that "... political participation in common action is more easily achieved at the neighborhood level, where there is a variety of opportunities for engagement ..." (p. 303). Recent political science and sociological literature has strongly developed the concept of communitarian involvement as a separate and important dimension of political participation (Barber, 1984; Etzioni, 1994, 1995). Community activity is considered more informal participation than national activity (Sobel, 1993). While certain individual characteristics promote both national and local participation, other personal as well as local community characteristics primarily stimulate participation in local politics (Pettersen and Rose, 1996). Some people may decline to participate in political activities because of dislike or indifference. They may prefer a closer, perhaps more personal domain, the community, with activities such as membership in a tenants' committee or in a parents' school committee. People who are active in their community will presumably demonstrate higher levels of good citizenship behavior and may also benefit from skills they acquire, networking opportunities and personal enrichment (Sieber, 1974).

Measuring community involvement

According to Brady (1999) and Barber (1984), this measure is operationalized as being involved in communal activities. Respondents were asked to report the frequency of their involvement in these community related political activities on a 3-point scale: 1 (never been active), 2 (had been active in the past but not today), 3 (active today). A 6-item scale was used as follows: (1) being a member of a voluntary organization in the community; (2) being a member of a tenants' committee; (3) being a member of a parents' school committee; (4) taking part in community cultural activities; (5) writing letters to the mayor or to other local officials about different issues; (6) writing letters to the local newspaper regarding community affairs.

Political efficacy

Niemi, Craig and Mattei (1991) argued that among the various concepts dealing with individuals' attitudes towards politics, political efficacy is the most important and therefore has received much attention in the literature. Political efficacy refers to the individual's perception of her/his ability to influence political officials and the political system (Barner and Rosenwein, 1985). Milbrath and Goel (1977) argued that political efficacy is part of the sense of mastery a child acquires during socialization. Political efficacy includes two related dimensions: internal efficacy and external efficacy (McPherson, Welch and Clark, 1977). Internal efficacy refers to one's belief in one's ability and competence to understand political processes and to take part in them. External efficacy refers to one's belief that the political system and political officials are responsive to one's attempts to influence it and that citizens' demands do affect governance. Conceptually, political efficacy should be related to political participation. An individual with high levels of internal and external efficacy will be strongly motivated to participate in the political system. Therefore, there is strong empirical support for a positive relationship between political efficacy and political participation (Burn and Konrad, 1987; Guyton, 1988; Nassi and Abramowitz, 1980; Paulsen, 1991).

Measuring political efficacy

This variable was defined and measured in accordance with Guyton (1988), who defined it as one's perceptions of one's capability to understand and influence the decision-making process in the political system. I decided to focus on external efficacy and to drop the internal efficacy items. Hence, the following five items used were: (1) "The public has a great deal of control over what public servants do in office," (2) "The average person can make a difference by talking to public officials," (3) "The average citizen has considerable influence over state affairs and governmental policy," (4) "State leaders are usually sensitive to public opinion," (5) "The average person has a major say in how the local government is run." However, it should be noted that there is a need for future studies to investigate the role of internal political efficacy with items suggested by Niemi, Craig and Mattei (1991) such as: (1) "I consider myself to be well qualified to participate in politics," (2) "I feel that I could do as good a job in public office as most other people," (3) "People like me don't have any say about what the government does," and (4) "I don't think public officials care much what people like me think." Each of the items was measured on a 5-point scale (1=strongly disagree, to 5=strongly agree).

Additional potential indicators: Representation and discrimination

Beyond trust in government and the active participatory behaviors in which citizens may choose to be involved (or withhold), there are other democratic values that express opinions and behavior intentions that are worthy of examination. Finkel, Stigelman, and Humphries (1999) suggest a list of additional democratic values such as political tolerance, support for democracy, and repression potential. In addition, other two major indicators are perception of representation and discrimination. Although these were not central to the empirical examination, they are undoubtedly relevant for future studies in the field and are even more relevant for a better understanding of the bureaucratic–democratic paradox in modern nations. In many respects, representation and discrimination are also closely related. Wherever a lack of representation occurs, one should expect higher levels of perceptions of discrimination. Those parties or groups, in the national or communal arena, who are left unrepresented or even underrepresented will probably feel discriminated against, differentiated from, and separated from those who are better represented. Given that in modern political and administrative bodies, representation in democracy is a vehicle for making one's voice heard and maximizing interests of various types, it becomes essential that citizens *be* represented and *feel* represented properly. How representation and discrimination may affect bureaucratic indicators of managerial quality, satisfaction, responsiveness, or performance of public agencies is also worthy of study. The common wisdom suggests that actual (or perceived) under-representation and a sense of discrimination (by minorities or other groups in society) leads to lower levels of satisfaction, perceived responsiveness, or perceived managerial quality. However, one should keep in mind that the opposite effect is also possible, whereby those who perceive bureaucracy as functioning poorly will also tend to *feel* under-represented (or ill-represented) and discriminated against at least in practice. To date, literature is equivocal about the exact flow of causality in this regard, so my assumption about the bi-directional nature of this interaction is worthy of examination.

Summary: Core terminology in the democratic discourse and its measurement

This chapter tried to suggest a perceptual terminology and conceptualization for dealing with democracy in the modern state. I began by elaborating on the meaning of citizenship and citizenship behavior and on the democratic values that result, which reflect what democracy means for ordinary people. Beyond obedience, I emphasize the normative aspects of loyalty, trust, and active participation of citizens. Trust has received much attention in political science and public administration literature because it is one of the core elements of governments' legitimacy. Participation is a more complicated phenomenon because it is an active behavior rather than an attitude or opinion towards government. Furthermore, it involves an investment of time, energy, and dedication by citizens. Together with additional aspects of democratic values, such as representation, discrimination, political efficacy, and trust in citizenship involvement they constitute a broad backdrop against which to depict the democratic profile of modern societies and strong nations.

Chapter 5

Empirical Evidence: A Longitudinal National Study of Bureaucracy and Democracy in Israel

Strangely enough, empirical evidence for the nexus between democracy and bureaucracy in modern nations is scarce. For this reason, seven years ago I initiated a national, longitudinal project that tracks developments in this arena. The project started as a research seminar for graduate students in the division of Public Administration and Policy at the University of Haifa. The students took an active part in formulating the research agenda, the assessments of the state of Israeli bureaucracy, and the potential effects on the stability and values of democracy. In the years that followed, the idea was extended, and the data set we collected gradually grew to include a representative national sample of Israeli citizens from across the nation. Since then, it has led to several studies, some of which are described here.

Hence, in this chapter, I focus on four empirical attempts to tackle the relationship between bureaucracy and democracy in the context of the Israeli public arena. All four studies demonstrate how a theoretical relationship between bureaucracy and democracy can be developed and tested empirically. I first develop a rationale for the examination of the type of relationship between two essential constructs of bureaucracy and democracy – citizens' satisfaction with public services, and citizens' trust in government and in public administration systems. In the second section I turn to a more comprehensive model that includes variables such as managerial quality and other democratic outputs. The third study uses the allegory of a tango dance to express the gradual progress in this relationship. This theoretical development is followed by an empirical examination of two samples (citizens and public sector employees) based on a similar model. In this study we also make use of an advanced statistical method – SEM (Structural Equation Modeling) – to assess three alternative models and compare them. Finally, in the fourth study we extend the discussion to include factors such as ethics, morality, justice, and organizational politics in the public sector and hypothesize about their potential effect on performance and democratic values. I believe that this four-fold empirical examination makes a significant contribution to the literature by identifying several missing links in the relationship between bureaucracy and democracy and exploring some inner dynamics typical of the "black box of interface" noted in Figure 2.6.

Bureaucracy and democracy in Israel: A longitudinal study

In 2001, a long-range effort was initiated, aimed at studying the nature of bureaucracy and democracy in Israel, as perceived by ordinary citizens. This longitudinal study had several goals: (1) to systematically collect data about the citizens' attitudes towards public services, (2) to collect the data using the skills and experiences of academic scholars from an independent non-governmental agency, (3) to gather this data over a number of years so that a comparative analysis could be conducted, (3) to allow the use of this data in other studies on bureaucracy and democracy in Israel and in international analysis, and (4) to incorporate these attitudes when making and implementing policy and to encourage government agencies to consider involving citizens in the creation of public policy.

The method used in this research has several elements. First, the research tool is based on a questionnaire and data gathered in Israel over seven successive years, from 2001 until 2007. In 2000, we produced the first draft of a questionnaire that was tested on a limited number of residents in the city of Haifa. Based on the results of this pilot study, we rebuilt the questionnaire in a newer and more effective format. The new format was distributed nationwide for the first time in 2001. A complete version of this questionnaire is available in the appendix. The questionnaire was designed to examine bureaucratic aspects of citizens' perceptions of government and public administration, as well as various democratic values and participatory behavior. In total, 3,360 individuals participated in the study – 345 in 2001, 502 in 2002; 490 in 2003; 446 in 2004; 498 in 2005; 505 in 2006; and 574 in 2007. The response rate for these years ranged between 80 percent and 85 percent due to a very effective direct sampling method that we used systematically over the years. In accordance with this method, citizens were approached by one of the research assistants and were asked if they were willing to take part in the study. The response rate was calculated as the ratio between those participants who ultimately took part in the study and those who agreed to listen to our basic explanation of the study and reviewed the questions. Data were collected between May and July of each year by a random sampling method. Various cities and other population areas were sampled based on geographic location and the size and structure of the population. Representative samplings were included from larger and smaller cities, rural settlements, the northern, southern, and central areas of the country, as well as from individuals from a variety of socio-economic levels. Interviewers met the participants in various locations such as public venues, governmental institutions, and private homes. Citizens were asked to provide their perceptions of and attitudes toward public administration, public services, and public officials on the national and local levels. More specifically, participants were asked to provide information about their attitudes regarding the bureaucratic aspects of managerial quality, responsiveness of public sector agencies, satisfaction with services, and trust in various administrative and governmental institutions. Participants also provided information about their democratic values and participatory behaviors. However, this data was available for only some of the years (for example, data on citizens' perceptions of involvement and participation in administrative decision-making were available only for 2005 and data about political participation and community involvement were available only for the years 2003 to 2005).

Table 5.1 presents the psychometric characteristics of the measures and variables that were mentioned in the previous chapter. To simplify the presentation of the data, I used the most updated files we have for 2007. Following this summary of the sample's descriptive statistics, I will describe a series of empirical analyses that were conducted over the years to explore the linkages between bureaucracy and democracy as citizens perceive them. Each of the following sections thus suggests a vehicle for a better understanding of the gray area in which bureaucratic mechanisms and democratic ideology live together in modern nations.

Table 5.1   Psychometric characteristics of the variables over time

Variable	2001–2007 (N=3360)		
	Mean	S.D.	α
The power of bureaucracy			
Managerial Quality (MQ)			
1. Human qualities: Professionalism and Leadership (HQ)	2.51	0.86	0.80
2. Accountability and Transparency (TA)	2.55	0.84	0.86
3. Innovation and Creativity (IC)	2.74	0.89	0.75
4. Ethics and Morality (EM)	2.71	0.93	0.70
5. Internal/Organizational Politics (IP/OP)	3.59	0.99	0.62
Public Sector Performance (PSP)			
1. Citizens' Satisfaction (ST)	3.11	0.54	0.83
2. Responsiveness (RS)	2.22	0.75	0.86
The charm of democracy			
Democratic Values (DV)			
1. Trust in Government and in Public Administration (TRST)	2.81	0.52	0.87
2. Participation in Decision-Making (PDM)*	2.22	0.98	0.80
3. Political Efficacy (PE)*	2.19	0.79	0.77
Democratic Participatory Behaviors (DPB)			
1. Political Participation (PP)#|*	1.82	0.41	0.72
2. Community Involvement (CI)#*	1.66	0.47	0.68

Notes: #Scale ranged from 1–3; *Data is available for only some of the years.

Empirical evidence (1): Satisfaction and trust – Can we point to causality?[1]

Whereas citizens' satisfaction with services is largely an outcome of public policy, trust is a psycho-political concept with much broader implications. To trust a person, a group, or an institution is to assume their reliability, to believe that they will act "as they should" (Barber, 1983; Citrin and Muste, 1999). Psychologically, trust is an informal contract between at least two parties that brings some certainty into relationships. If you trust someone, you expect him/her to fulfill certain unwritten agreements, and thus, you feel free to plan and act under the assumption that the agreement will be honored. Hence, trust has some major political implications that are relevant for national-level and community-level relationships such as those between citizens and central or local government or citizens and public administration (Nye, Zelikow, and Philip, 1997).

As suggested by Citrin and Muste (1999), political trust refers to the faith people have in their government and to the level of support that citizens give to leaders, policy makers, and the entire political and executive system. Trust also reflects the citizens' belief that the government operates fairly and is deserving of respect and obedience. Thus, trust is related to the effectiveness of government policies. The level of political trust can affect the stability of the institutions that make or enforce these policies. Such stability is necessary for the creation of growth and progress in governments and in their operative branches (such as public administration) that are obligated to serve the public on the basis of the "hidden agreement" between rulers and the people.

Nonetheless, the linkage between political trust and administrative performance is open to debate. Some studies suggest that building trust in government is possible only when quality managerial foundations promote an administrative system that operates at a higher level of efficiency and effectiveness. According to this view, political trust cannot be created and maintained when governments fail to deliver satisfactory services and goods to the public (Erber and Lau, 1990; Vigoda, 2002a). However, another approach treats trust in the government as a key to the emergence of high performing agencies of public administration. This view suggests that building trust with citizens offers state leaders enough legitimacy to make decisions that are impossible without massive public agreement. Similarly, Citrin and Muste (1999) suggest that "governments enjoying greater public support are able to function more smoothly and effectively than those with less public trust" (p. 465). Similarly, Ruscio (1997) stated that effective organizations require learning and knowledge, and learning requires trust. Moreover, widespread public trust also infuses the political system with a basic source of power that enables more extensive administrative operations aimed

---

1 Some sections of this chapter are based on E. Vigoda-Gadot and F. Yuval "Managerial quality, administrative performance, and trust in governance: Can we point to causality?," *Australian Journal of Public Administration* (2003) and on "Managerial quality, administrative performance, and trust in governance revisited: A follow-up study of causality," *International Journal of Public Sector Management* (2003).

at the interests of the public. Thus, if we want high performing organizations, we need to find ways to promote trust. Hence, the paradoxical question remains: Is trust a result of quality management and efficient administrative systems or is it a mediating factor between various constructs of managerial quality and administrative performance? I try to suggest a few insights into this question based on several empirical studies that I have conducted in recent years. I describe this as a paradox of performance and trust, and suggest two alternative models and an extra midrange one to try to explain it.

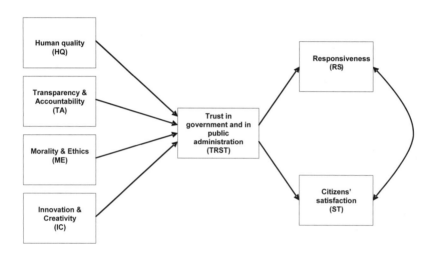

Model 1 – Trust leads to performance.

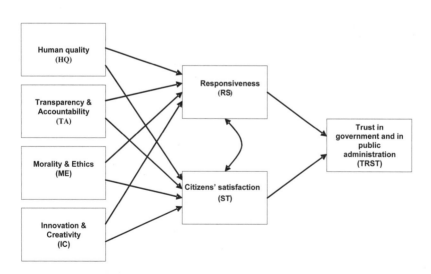

Model 2 – Performance leads to trust.

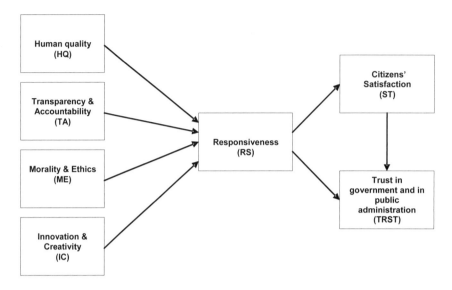

Model 3 –Midrange effects.

Figure 5.1   The relationship between trust and public sector performance

Figure 5.1 presents the three alternative models for the relationship among managerial quality, administrative performance, and trust in government and in public administration. This is both a simplified and richer version of the five models suggested by Van de Walle and Bouckaert (2003). Assuming that managerial quality is an independent variable responsible for variance in both administrative performance and/or trust in government, I first suggest two alternative models: (1) trust in government leads to higher levels of perceived administrative performance, namely to responsiveness and citizens' satisfaction, and (2) perceived administrative performance (responsiveness and citizens' satisfaction) leads to higher levels of trust in government. In addition, a third model is depicted which hypothesizes that: (3) trust in government is affected independently by responsiveness and satisfaction, yet responsiveness also has a clear effect on citizens' satisfaction. Let us explain the three models in more detail:

Model 1: Trust leads to performance

According to model 1, trust in government and in public administration mediates the relationship between a set of variables representing managerial quality and the two components of administrative performance, namely responsiveness and citizens' satisfaction. This model follows the line adopted by Citrin and Muste (1999) and Ruscio (1997). It represents the thesis that trust is a precondition for the emergence of better performance. According to this idea, citizens' perceptions of governmental responsiveness as well as their degree of satisfaction regarding services received are both affected by the level of political faith and trust among the people. Responsiveness and satisfaction are built only when a reasonable level of political trust is maintained, and individuals have good reason to assume that state leaders and public officers are doing their best to promote services for the people.

Model 2: Performance leads to trust

Model 2 represents the alternative relationship where various components of managerial quality affect administrative performance, leading to higher levels of citizens' trust in government and in public administration. This model is more in line with the view of Erber and Lau (1990) as well as Nye et al. (1997) who treat political trust among citizens as another consequence of the operation of the state and its administrative branches. In fact, this is the more prevalent view in political science and has been adopted by Verba, Schlozman, and Brady (1995). To create trust in government and in the public service, state leaders and public officers need to improve outputs and outcomes to a level that builds a positive image of the government and satisfies its people. Only then can a real level of trust can be achieved, a level necessary to support the democratic foundations of the state.

Model 3: Midrange effects

In addition to models 1 and 2, model 3 offers a more complex pattern of relationships. As with model 1 and 2, this model also assumes that responsiveness and satisfaction are aspects of administrative performance that need to be treated separately. Moreover, as indicated in model 2, trust is again suggested as a dependent variable resulting from administrative performance. However, unlike model 2, this model distinguishes between the two sub-scales of administrative performance to create an additional midrange effect where responsiveness leads directly to satisfaction. This contrasts sharply with model 2, which hypothesizes only a general correlation between these factors. Thus, a clear causal path is delineated where citizens' satisfaction results from governmental responsiveness. It is this satisfaction with responsiveness alone that may lead to changes in the peoples' level of trust.

Empirical findings

The findings of the study are described below. Table 5.2 presents descriptive statistics as well as inter-correlations among the variables for each of the samples. Means, standard deviations, and Cronbach alpha levels were within reasonable limits and were quite similar in both studies, indicating the validity of the measures. The correlations between the variables were relatively high, but did not exceed a level of .70 that in other cases indicates a problem of multicollinearity.

Table 5.2   Descriptive statistics and inter-correlations for the study variables (reliabilities in parentheses)

Variable	Mean		S.D.		1		2		3		4		5		6		7	
	Test1	Test2	Test1	Test2	Test1	Test2	Test1	Test2	Test1	Test2	Test1	Test2	Test1	Test2	Test1	Test2	Test1	Test2
1. Human Quality (HQ)	2.71	2.45	.73	.72	(.87)	(.87)												
2. Transparency and Accountability (TA)	2.72	2.43	.78	.77	.60*	.67*	(.84)	(.85)										
3. Morality and Ethics (ME)	2.64	2.39	.85	.80	.57*	.60*	.47*	.58*	(.77)	(.78)								
4. Innovation and Creativity (IC)	2.70	2.53	.83	.79	.58*	.63*	.61*	.62*	.53*	.55*	(.77)	(.76)						
5. Responsiveness (RS)	2.40	2.14	.81	.73	.68*	.70*	.67*	.69*	.58*	.60*	.68*	.68*	(.88)	(.86)				
6. Citizens' Satisfaction (ST)	3.11	3.00	.51	.49	.47*	.41*	.33*	.37*	.40*	.37*	.38*	.34*	.48*	.38*	(.85)	(.87)		
7. Trust in Government and in Public Administration (TRST)	3.02	2.86	.55	.58	.47*	.43*	.43*	.41*	.40*	.44*	.38*	.358	.48*	.41*	.63*	.61*	(.81)	(.81)

N1=345 (Test1), N2=502 (Test2)   *P<.001.

Table 5.3   Goodness of fit summary for the research models

Model/ Description	Df		X^2		P		X^2/df		RFI		NFI		NNFI		CFI		GFI	
	Test1	Test2	Test1	Test2	Test1	Test2	Test1	Test2	Test1	Test2	Test1	Test2	Test1	Test2	Test1	Test2	Test1	Test2
1. Trust leads to performance	8	8	216.34	276.30	0000	.0000	27.04	34.53	0.45	0.44	0.79	0.79	0.46	0.44	0.79	0.79	0.85	0.86
2. Performance leads to trust	4	4	6.47	9.17	0.17	.057	1.62	2.29	0.97	0.97	0.99	0.99	0.99	0.98	1.00	1.00	0.99	0.99
3. Midrange effects	7	7	23.15	29.21	.0016	.0001	3.31	4.17	0.94	0.95	0.98	0.98	0.96	0.96	0.99	0.99	0.98	0.98

N1=345 (Test1), N2=502 (Test2)   P=Significance.

Table 5.4   Path coefficients and explained variance (R2) for the models

Model/Description	Model 1: Trust leads to performance		Model 2: Performance leads to trust		Model 3: Midrange effects	
	Test1 n1=345	Test2 n2=502	Test1 N1=345	Test2 n2=502	Test1 n1=345	Test2 n2=502
HQ→RS	-	-	.30*	.22*	.33*	.25*
HQ→ST	-	-	.25*	.21*	-	-
HQ→TRST	.21*	.21*	-	-	-	-
TA→RS	-	-	.28*	.25*	.23*	.23*
TA→ST	-	-	-.04	.04		-
TA→TRST	.14	.09	-	-		-
ME→RS	-	-	.12	.12*	.13*	.13*
ME→ST	-	-	.13*	.15*		-
ME→TRST	.14*	.25*	-	-		-
IC→RS	-	-	.34*	.34*	.35*	.32*
IC→ST	-	-	.07	-.02		-
IC→TRST	.04	-.02	-	-		-
TRST→RS	.96*	.68*	-	-		-
TRST→ST	.73*	.64*	-	-		-
RS→TRST	-	-	.17*	.17*	.15*	.16*
ST→TRST	-	-	.68*	.76*	.68*	.74*
RS→ST	-	-		-	.37*	.36*
$R^{2\#}$						
RS	.43	.30	.80	.80	**.81**	**.82**
ST	.60	.56	**.62**	**.59**	.35	.27
TRST	.44	.39	.34	.28	**.60**	**.56**

* P≤.05   # Highest values of explained variance in rows are in bold.

Table 5.3 presents the major fit indicators that testify to the quality of the models. As clearly shown, model 2 (performance leads to trust) best fits the data. Its chi-square value was not significant, and the chi-square to df ratio was less than 2. RFI, NFI, NNFI, CFI, and GFI were relatively high and ranged between .97 and 1.00. All of these values indicate that the model fits the data better than models 1 and 3. Both models 1 and 3 had a significantly poorer fit with the data and had to be rejected. Their chi-square test produced significant values, indicating that the models did not cohere with the data; the chi-square to df ratio (X^2/df) was close to 5 and 8 (respectively), which exceeds the recommended value of 2. RFI, NFI, NNFI, CFI and GFI were all lower than in model 2.

Table 5.4 presents path coefficients and explained variance for the models. As can be seen, all path coefficients were in the expected positive direction. Human quality was positively related to responsiveness in models 2 and 3 (.30 and .33 respectively) and to satisfaction and trust (.25 and .21 respectively in model 2 and in model 1). Transparency and accountability were positively related to responsiveness in models 2 and 3 (.28 and .23 respectively). Morality and ethics were positively related to responsiveness, satisfaction, and trust in models 3, 2, and 1 (.13, .13, and .14 respectively). Innovation and creativity were positively related to responsiveness in models 2 and 3 (.34 and .35 respectively). Furthermore, trust was positively related to responsiveness and satisfaction in model 1 (.96 and .73 respectively), as well as in model 2 (.17 and .68 respectively) and in model 3 (.15 and .68 respectively). Finally, responsiveness and satisfaction were also positively related in model 3 (.37).

However, an analysis of the explained variance raises some questions as to the superiority of model 2. As is evident, it was model 3 that exhibited the highest explained variance for the variable "trust in government and in public administration" ($R^2=.60$) and for the variable "responsiveness" ($R^2=81$). These values were higher than the levels achieved by model 2 ($R^2=.80$ and $R^2=.34$ respectively). Model 2 showed a higher level of explained variance only for the variable "satisfaction" ($R^2=.62$), and model 1 displayed a higher level of explained variance than model 2 for the variable "trust." Consequently, while model 2 best fit the data, it is still not a perfect model in terms of explained variance. Indeed, model 3 has an advantage in this regard.

Despite some weaknesses in model 2, especially its limited level of explained variance in the variable "trust," I concluded that this was the best model among all those examined here. This model, which demonstrates the effect of managerial quality on administrative performance and only subsequently on trust in government and in public administration, was better than the other two models. It proved a very good fit with the data, demonstrating a strong magnitude of path coefficients in the expected directions, a reasonable level of explained variance, and a sound theoretical adaptability to the conceptual framework. Nonetheless, model 3, which depicts a set of relationships similar to those of model 2, also had its advantages. It indicates that the hypothesis that administrative performance leads to trust is more credible than the alternative theory that trust influences performance. Moreover, it re-emphasizes that the decision to demonstrate a clear causal link where responsiveness leads to satisfaction (rather than a general bi-directional linkage between these factors) has merit.

Can we point to causality?

In an attempt to resolve the paradox of interrelationships between bureaucracy and democracy in modern nations, this section has revisited one question of causality among managerial quality, administrative performance, and citizens' trust in governments and in public administration. It asked whether administrative performance leads to a higher degree of trust in the government and in public administration or vice versa. Using a recent sample of Israeli citizens, I have tried to re-evaluate three theoretical models. All models specifically implied one type of causality and were tested against each other across two years of data collection and two different samples. In general, this section gives considerable support to most of the previous findings (Vigoda-Gadot and Yuval, 2003a) where performance leads to trust more than trust leads to performance. Hence, it also supports the conclusions of various studies in the field that found similar relationships. One of these recent studies (Ulbig, 2002) suggested that "satisfaction with the procedures and people of government ... helps to boost feelings of trust in government" (p. 801) because citizens who are satisfied with governmental policies also have a meaningful voice alternative, viewing the process as efficient and neutral, and perceiving the authorities as fair, honest, and trustworthy.

As a result, these findings have potential merit in several ways. First, they again highlight the role of managerial quality as a precondition for the enhancement of administrative performance and trust in government. Second, they confirm that performance leads to trust rather than trust leading to more positive evaluations of performance. Nonetheless, the findings of this study provide no clear-cut conclusions. The accurate relationship between these variables still remains unclear, even if some definitive answers seem to emerge.

Moreover, as stated in a previous study (Vigoda-Gadot and Yuval, 2003a), studying causality paths between quality, performance, and trust in government is a complex task. There are at least two explanations for such complexity. First is the inherent tension between democracy and bureaucracy. As suggested by Thompson (1983) "democracy does not suffer bureaucracy gladly: Many of the values I associate with democracy such as criticism, trust, participation, and individuality stand sharply opposed to hierarchy, specialization, and impersonality I ascribe to modern bureaucracy" (p. 235). Second is the long standing dilemma in the social sciences about good explanations and the search for causality. Are there clear-cut distinctions between social "reasons" and social "results"? More specifically, is democracy the antecedent to an improved bureaucracy or, alternatively, is an improved bureaucracy a precondition for a strong democracy?

This tension is reiterated by our study in which I tried to compare aspects of bureaucracy (for example, managerial quality and administrative performance) with aspects of democracy (such as trust in government). Following Gawthrop (1997), I also concluded that there is a great deal of confusion and hypocrisy associated with the concepts of democracy and bureaucracy. According to Dwight Waldo "when both are studied together the opportunities for confusion and delusion are multiplied, given the human capacity for irrationality and ego-serving views of the world" (p. 205).

Nevertheless, despite this complexity I argue that democracy and bureaucracy can and should be studied in relation to each other. Our follow-up study confirms that one pattern of relationships between bureaucracy and democracy is, after all, more dominant than another. According to our findings, managerial quality leads to administrative performance, while trust is a subsequent reaction by citizens to the performance of public administration. Model 2 received strong support in both surveys and also yielded a relatively high level of explained variance for citizens' satisfaction. Note, however, that the explained variance of model 3 was higher than that of model 2 for both the variables of "responsiveness" and "trust." These findings were consistent for the two samples (test1 and test2) and imply that model 2 is undoubtedly not a perfect (nor a correct) model. Some elements in model 3 seem to compete with those of model 2, but since both of them indicate that performance leads to trust, I feel confident that this is the more accurate description of cause and effect.

The findings have profound implications for new approaches to public administration. First, if administrative performance leads to a higher level of trust in the government, one can appreciate the impact and relevancy of new reforms in public administration that call for a more businesslike approach to serving the people. The New Public Management (NPM) approach, which emphasizes the role of citizens as clients or customers, is supported by this study. Based on this study's findings, the implementation of the NPM doctrine can create a substantial political impact as well as an economic and managerial one. Hence, this empirical section provides some support for advocates of the NPM paradigm who seek to improve the performance of governmental and administrative bodies with the expectation of safeguarding the principles and foundations of our democracy. An important implication of these results is that effectiveness and responsiveness in governmental agencies is a precondition to trust, a quality earnestly sought by many Western democracies, but one that has remained tantalizingly elusive.

As I have also noted in a previous study, it is important to weigh the advantages of this study against certain criticisms of the NPM approach that have recently surfaced (Box, Marshal, Reed, and Reed, 2001; Vigoda, 2002b, 2002c). Box et al. (2001) argued that "today's market model of government in the form of New Public Management goes beyond earlier "reforms," threatening to eliminate democracy as a guiding principle in public-sector management" (p. 608). Along the same lines, I criticized NPM for downplaying the willingness of citizens to engage in active political participation and seek control over administrative elites (Vigoda, 2002b). Nonetheless, the fact that NPM directs public managers and political decision-makers to utilize business measures in order to reduce financial and budgetary waste as well as to increase managerial quality and performance eventually leads to more public trust. This in itself is an important contribution to our democratic values. It is possible, however, that NPM does introduce some shortcomings into the public system, but these should not prevent us from using the NPM vision in a creative manner. The goal of NPM and other reforms in public administration is to find a balance between the economic and financial needs of the state on one hand, and the political, social, and ethical demands of citizens as individuals on the other. Thus, it seems that NPM still has much to offer to our public administration and governmental institutions.

The findings presented thus far help reveal the links between administrative and managerial variables and political variables in the democratic realm. This is an underdeveloped field of knowledge and our empirical findings may guide other studies in this field. In line with previous research (i.e., Hibbing and Theiss-Morse, 2001; Nye, Zelikow, and King, 1997), the findings of this study reconfirm the hypotheses that satisfied citizens are those who trust their governments. As I stated in the closing sections of our previous study, these citizens may become the great builders of modern democracy despite the fact that trust is not necessarily translated into political activism (Ulbig, 2002). It is more likely that citizens develop trust in government and in its executive branches when most of their essential needs and demands are fulfilled to an acceptable level. However, this trust and satisfaction does not translate into active political participation (Vigoda, 2002a; Vigoda-Gadot and Mizrahi, 2007). As demonstrated by various studies in the past, most citizens still remain on the sidelines as passive bystanders. Hence, by investigating managerial and administrative variables, this empirical section offers a better understanding of citizens' attitudes and behaviors, but much more work is needed in the future to fully explore the relationships between bureaucracy and democracy.

Empirical evidence (2): Managerial quality, performance, and democratic values[2]

To determine the relationship between managerial quality, public sector performance, and several aspects of democratic values, I tested the following model (Figure 5.2). This model has several goals that lead to specific hypothesized relationships. First, it examines the effect of citizens' involvement and participation in administrative decision-making on perceived managerial quality and on the perceived performance of the public sector. Second, it tests the effect of perceived performance on trust in administrative agencies. Third, it explores the relationship between perceived performance and political participation and community involvement as part of democratic participatory behavior. Finally, the model suggests that perceived performance mediates the relationship between perceived managerial quality and participation in decision-making on one hand and trust and democratic participatory behavior on the other.

Several hypotheses emerge from this model. First, based on the theory of the relationship between bureaucracy and democracy (Mosher, 1982; Waldo, 1977), it is suggested that citizens' involvement and participation in decision-making at the administrative level is positively related to the managerial quality of the public sector as perceived by citizens. This hypothesis is also based on the idea of authentic participation and the work of Irvin and Stansbury (2004) and King et al. (1998). It is argued that when people are deeply involved in practical administrative processes of any kind, they acquire a better understanding and more realistic perspective of specific processes, difficulties, and dilemmas that the public sector and its officials face in daily activities. As a result, these citizens will tend to have more positive perceptions about the quality of services and goods with which

---

2 Some sections of this chapter are based on E. Vigoda-Gadot and S. Mizrahi, "Public sector management and the democratic ethos: A longitudinal study of key relationships in Israel," *Journal of Public Administration Research and Theory* (2007).

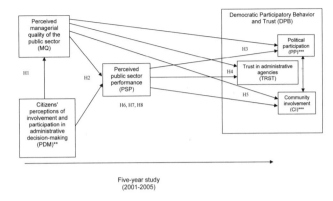

Five-year study
(2001-2005)

* All paths represent correlative relationships; no causal relationships should be inferred
** Data available for 2005 only
*** Data available for 2003-2005 only

Figure 5.2   Research model

they are provided by the public sector. Whereas distancing citizens from decision-making centers may lead to increased levels of alienation from and disaffection with public administration, bringing the customers closer to public institutions enables them to have a more realistic understanding of and appreciation for the complexity and efforts invested in making bureaucracy work properly.

Hence, I first suggest that *the perceived managerial quality of the public sector is positively related to citizens' perceptions of involvement and participation in administrative decision-making.*

Citizenry participatory theory and democratic theory further suggest that participation in decision-making processes increases the players' responsibility for the outcomes, so that players tend to accept and cooperate with the system (Dahl, 1971; Pateman, 1970; Putnam 1993). Moreover, participation in decision-making processes may strengthen the sense of group identity and correspondingly, loyalty to the group or organization (Osterman, 1999; Rose, 1999). Thus, increased citizen involvement and participation in administrative decision-making may lead to positive evaluations of performance in administrative agencies. Fornell et al. (1996) show, for example, that monopolist companies receive lower client satisfaction ratings than non-monopolists because the use of the latter companies depends on free choice. Therefore, the monopolistic, non-participatory nature of many government services alone could explain part of the public's dissatisfaction with them.

Furthermore, an engaged citizenry might become more appreciative of the tough decisions that government administrators have to make, and the improved support from the public might create a less divisive, combative populace to govern and regulate (King et al., 1998; King and Stivers, 1998; Putnam, 1993). Irvin and Stansbury (2004) explain the various advantages of citizen participation in terms of education, building trust and legitimacy, breaking gridlocks, making better policy and implementation decisions, and avoiding litigation costs. Yet, they also point to the disadvantages of citizen participation in terms of costly processes, time consuming, budget-consuming demands from strong interest groups that participate the most, and the possibility of poor decisions that are politically impossible to ignore.

From a social choice perspective, Mizrahi (2002) shows that participatory or democratic rules provide sufficient opportunities for players to change outcomes and improve their payoffs because they incorporate many players and interests. Furthermore, participatory and democratic rules are also more stable than non-participatory or less democratic rules because of the vagueness they create regarding the true connection between rules and outcomes. That is, under a complex structure of rules, a player cannot be sure what rules or norms need to be changed in order to improve outcomes, and he/she will therefore attempt to change policy within the rules and norms. The more people, interests, and alternatives involved in the decision-making processes, and the stronger the perception of participation in decision-making in one's environment, the more stable the set of rules. Moreover, as rules become more participatory and give players the opportunity to express their preferences, the more players will feel committed to the democratic/participatory process and will be more satisfied with the outcomes. In line with these arguments, I suggest that *perceived public sector performance is positively related to perceived managerial quality and to citizens' perceptions of involvement and participation in administrative decision-making.*

It may be further suggested that a high-quality managerial system, smoothly functioning public administration, and a strong democracy are factors tightly bounded together, as they all rely on productive and widespread citizenship involvement. According to some, among the advantages of the democratic system are the enhancement of individual and collective competences, the increase in self-motivation, and the expansion of equal opportunities for social mobility (which is described as the "democratic ethos"). Woller (1998) indicated that no bureaucracy or democracy can function properly without a minimal input of citizenship activity. Moreover, modern public administration, as well the NPM approach with its strong market-based orientation, is deeply rooted in a democratic heritage. It is democracy that grants legitimacy to the decisions and actions of public service, and it is democracy again that must hold the tyrannical nature of bureaucracies in check (Mosher, 1982; Waldo, 1977). Thus, our next three hypotheses try to establish a linkage between the nature of modern public administration and certain citizenry values of participation and trust. The core assumption is that quality management and a better functioning public administration will enhance trust in administrative agencies, but will be negatively related with active participation both on the national and communal levels. This latter expectation is based on the idea that higher levels of political participation, community involvement, and other forms of protest are needed when the administrative system does not perform properly. Alternatively, when public administration is meeting the expectations of the citizens, lower levels of participation and involvement are needed both on the national and communal levels. Thus I also suggest that *(1) Trust in government is positively related to perceived public sector performance and to the perceived managerial quality of the public sector; (2) Political participation is negatively related to perceived public sector performance and to the perceived managerial quality of the public sector; (3) Community involvement is negatively related to perceived public sector performance and to the perceived managerial quality of the public sector.*

According to Figure 5.2, a thorough examination of our model necessitates a test of mediation. In line with the reasoning suggested thus far, perceived public sector performance is expected to mediate the relationship between perceived managerial quality and perceived participation in decision-making on one hand and trust and democratic participatory behavior on the other. This expectation is based on the assumption that citizens in modern democracies place a growing emphasis on the outcomes of public service and measure it by results. The NPM paradigm and the overall orientation towards measuring services, developing performance indicators, and looking for tangible outputs of the public system (Halachmi, 2002; Pollitt, 1988) suggest that the improvement of effectiveness and efficiency in those systems may have a mediating effect between the objective evaluations of inputs (such as perceived managerial quality and perceived participation in decision-making) and democratic outcomes (for example, democratic participatory behavior). Hence, it may be argued that perceived public sector performance will make an independent and significant contribution to the explanation of trust and the democratic participatory behavior variables, beyond the contribution of perceived managerial quality and the control variables. In addition, I also expect a mediating effect of perceived public sector performance. I argue that *perceived public sector performance makes an independent and significant contribution to the explanation of trust in administrative agencies, political participation, and community involvement beyond the contribution of perceived managerial quality, citizens' perceptions of involvement and participation in administrative decision-making and the control variables.* I also suggest that, *in the eyes of the public, perceived public sector performance mediates the relationship between perceived managerial quality and democratic participatory behavior.* Finally, I argue that *in the eyes of the public, perceived public sector performance mediates the relationship between perceptions of involvement and participation in administrative decision-making, and democratic participatory behavior.*

Finally, several control variables were used in order to examine the generalization of the model. Gender, education, and age were used in the final analysis, based on previous knowledge about their relationship with democratic values (i.e., Almond and Verba, 1963; Verba et al., 1995). From these studies, it may be inferred that highly educated men and older individuals will demonstrate higher levels of political participation and community involvement due to their higher socio-economic status. However, no strong rationale exists for the relationships between these variables and trust in administrative agencies, especially in the Israeli setting. Therefore, as noted above, these variables were chosen mainly as control variables.

Empirical findings

Table 5.5 presents the psychometric characteristics of the research variables across the sample years. This table demonstrates that the psychometric values are reasonable across the board, with fairly normal distributions and acceptable Cronbach alpha ratios for all the variables included. The table also shows the sample size for each year and illustrates which variable was measured in which year. Table 5.6 presents descriptive statistics, zero-order correlations, and reliabilities for the research variables. As can be seen, most of the inter-correlations hold in the expected directions and none of them exceeds the maximum level of .70, which is a good indication for the absence of multicollinearity among the variables.

Table 5.7 presents the results of two multiple regression analyses where perceived managerial quality and perceived public sector performance were separately regressed on the independent and control variables. According to Table 5.7, citizens' perceptions of involvement and participation in administrative decision-making was positively related with perceived managerial quality (β=.59; p<.001) and had no relationship with perceived public sector performance. Perceived managerial quality had a positive relationship with perceived public sector performance (β=.61; p<.001). These findings support our first hypothesis but only partially support the second hypothesis (it is supported for the variable perceived managerial quality but not for citizens' perceptions of involvement and participation in administrative decision-making). In addition, according to the conditions for mediation as specified by Baron and Kenny (1986), Kenny et al. (1998), and Kenny's web page (http://davidakenny.net/cm/mediate.htm), the suspected mediating variable (PSP) was positively related with the independent variable "perceived managerial quality." Thus, it was concluded that the first condition for mediation holds for the variable "perceived managerial quality" but not for citizens' perceptions of involvement and participation in administrative decision-making. Our further analyses will therefore continue to examine a mediating effect for perceived managerial quality as an independent variable, but not for citizens' perceptions of involvement and participation in administrative decision-making because it did not fulfill the first condition of mediation.

To examine the additional two conditions for mediation, let us turn to Table 5.8. This table presents the results of four multiple hierarchical regressions in which the dependent variables are trust in administrative agencies, political participation, community involvement, and democratic participatory behavior. First, each of these variables was regressed on the control variables (step 1). Second, perceived managerial quality was added to the equations (step 2), and finally perceived performance was added (step 3) to examine the independent contribution of each of these variables to the overall explained variance of the dependent variables.

According to the first equation, trust in government was positively related with perceived managerial quality and with perceived performance (β=.13; p<.001 and β=.61; p<.001 respectively). The inclusion of perceived managerial quality in step 2 contributed 24 percent of the explained variance, and the inclusion of

Table 5.5 Psychometric characteristics of the variables in each of the yearly samples (2001–2005)

Year / Variable	2001 (N=345)			2002 (N=502)			2003 (N=490)			2004 (N=446)			2005 (N=498)			2001–2005 (N=2281)		
	Mean	S.D.	α	Mean	S.D.	α	Mean	S.D.	α	Mean	S.D.	α	Mean	S.D.	α	Mean	S.D.	α
1. Perceived managerial quality of the public sector (MQ)	2.73	.66	.83	2.46	.66	.90	2.36	.69	.90	2.48	.73	.91	2.41	.72	.91	2.47	.70	.91
2. Citizens' perceptions of involvement and participation in administrative decision-making (PDM)	-	-	-	-	-	-	-	-	-	-	-	-	2.22	.98	.80	2.22	.98	.80
3. Perceived public sector performance (PSP)	2.98	.51	.85	2.85	.48	.84	2.94	.48	.83	2.92	.51	.85	2.76	.61	.89	2.89	.52	.86
4. Trust in government and in administrative agencies (TRST)	3.01	.55	.86	2.86	.59	.87	2.96	.53	.85	2.95	.60	.89	2.84	.63	.89	2.92	.59	.88
5. Political participation (PP)	-	-	-	-	-	-	1.84	.39	.69	1.80	.41	.74	1.81	.42	.74	1.82	.41	.72
6. Community involvement (CI)	-	-	-	-	-	-	1.63	.46	.65	1.65	.45	.68	1.70	.49	.70	1.66	.47	.68

Table 5.6 Correlation matrix (pairwise deletion) for the research variables (reliabilities in parentheses)

	Mean	S.D.	N	1	2	3	4	5	6	7	8	9
1. Perceived managerial quality of the public sector (MQ)	2.47	.70	2257	(.91)								
2. Citizens' perceptions of involvement and participation in administrative decision-making (PDM)#	2.22	.98	494	.60***	(.80)							
3. Perceived public sector performance (PSP)	2.89	.52	2281	.59***	.34***	(.86)						
4. Trust in government and in administrative agencies (TRST)	2.92	.59	2279	.49***	.25***	.69***	(.88)					
5. Political participation (PP)##	1.82	.41	1429	.12***	.13***	NS	NS	(.72)				
6. Community involvement (CI)##	1.66	.47	1429	.14***	.09*	NS	NS	.57***	(.68)			
7. Democratic participatory behavior (DPB)	2.42	.58	2279	.39***	.25***	.41***	.58***	.69***	.70***	(.85)		
8. Gender (1=Female)	-	-	2204	NS	NS	.09***	.06**	-.10***	NS	NS	-	
9. Education	10.10	5.61	2209	-.11***	NS	NS	NS	.15***	.09***	.15***	.06***	-
10. Age	34.10	12.22	2204	NS	NS	NS	NS	.16***	.26***	.12**	-.09***	.18***

N=494-2279: *p<.05 **p<.01 ***p<.001 NS=Not Significant.

Data available for 2005 only ## Data available for 2003–2005 only.

Table 5.7   **Multiple regression analysis (standardized coefficients) for the effect of the independent variables on perceived managerial quality of the public sector (MQ) and on perceived public sector performance (PSP)**

Variables	Perceived Managerial Quality of the Public Sector (MQ)	Public Sector Performance (PSP)
	Results for 2005, N=498β (t)	Integrative results: 2001–2005, N=2281β (t)
1.Perceived managerial quality of the public sector (MQ)	-	.61(13.30***)
2. Citizens' perceptions of involvement and participation in administrative decision-making (PDM)	.59(16.30***)	-.02(-.36)
3.Gender (Female)	.03(.83)	.08(2.19*)
4. Education	-.07(-1.99*)	.05(1.32)
5. Age	.02(.65)	.01(.23)
R2	.37	.37
Adjusted R2	.36	.36
F	68.57***	54.57***

*p<.05   **p<.01   ***p<.001.

perceived performance in step 3 of the equation added 25 percent to the overall explained variance, which was 50 percent. These findings offer strong support for a positive relationship among trust in administrative agencies, perceived public sector performance, and perceived managerial quality. They also provide partial support for the mediating effect for the variable "trust in administrative agencies." According to the second equation, political participation was positively related with perceived managerial quality (β=.20; p<.001) and negatively related with perceived performance (β=–.10; p<.001). The inclusion of perceived managerial quality in step 2 contributed 7 percent of the explained variance, and the inclusion of perceived performance in step 3 of the equation added only 1 percent to the overall explained variance, which was 8 percent. These findings support our fourth suggestion for the variable "perceived performance" but not for "perceived managerial quality." Furthermore, they provide only marginal support for our sixth argument as far as political participation is concerned because of the small increase in the explained variance caused by perceived performance.

In the third equation, community involvement was positively related with perceived managerial quality (β=.20; p<.001) and negatively related with perceived performance (β=–.09; p<.01). The inclusion of perceived managerial quality in step 2 contributed 9 percent of the explained variance and the inclusion of perceived performance in step 3 of the equation added 1 percent to the overall explained variance, which was 10 percent. Again, these findings support our fifth argument for the variable "perceived performance" but not for "perceived managerial

Table 5.8   Multiple hierarchical regression analysis (standardized coefficients) for the relationship between the independent variables, trust in administrative agencies, and democratic participatory behavior

Variables	Trust in Government and in Administrative Agencies (TRS) β (t)			Political Participation (PP) β (t)		
	Step 1	Step 2	Step 3	Step 1	Step 2	Step 3
1. Gender (Female)	.06 (2.87**)	.06 (3.05**)	.01 (.44)	-.10 (-3.70***)	-.10 (-3.79***)	-.09 (-3.46***)
2. Education	.00 (-.03)	.05 (2.84**)	.02 (1.51)	.14 (5.10***)	.15 (5.70***)	.16 (5.90***)
3. Age	.01 (.44)	.00 (.02)	-.01 (-.33)	.13 (4.79***)	.13 (4.74***)	.13 (4.79***)
4. Perceived managerial quality of the public sector (MQ)		.50 (26.71***)	.13 (6.67***)		.14 (5.38***)	.20 (6.25***)
5. Public sector performance (PSP)			.61 (32.22***)			-.10 (-3.22***)
R^2	.01	.25	.50	.05	.07	.08
Adjusted R^2	.01	.25	.49	.05	.07	.08
ΔR^2	-	.24	.25	-	.02	.01
F	2.77*	181.21***	422.42***	24.96***	26.32***	23.28***
F for ΔR^2	-	713.76***	1038.24***	-	28.91***	10.41***

Notes: N=1389–1429 due to missing values: *p<.05   **p<.01   ***p<.001.

Table 5.8 Continued	Multiple hierarchical regression analysis (standardized coefficients) for the relationship between the independent variables, trust in administrative agencies, and democratic participatory behavior

Variables	Community Involvement (CI) β (t)			Democratic Participatory Behavior (DPB) β (t)		
	Step 1	Step 2	Step 3	Step 1	Step 2	Step 3
1. Gender (Female)	.01 (.54)	.01 (.49)	.02 (.77)	-.01 (-.32)	-.01 (-1.61)	-.04 (-1.61)
2. Education	.05 (1.82)	.06 (2.43*)	.07 (2.60**)	.10 (3.71***)	.15 (6.00***)	.13 (5.59***)
3. Age	.26 (9.75***)	.26 (9.75***)	.26 (9.81***)	.17 (6.16***)	.16 (6.49***)	.15 (6.63***)
4. Perceived managerial quality of the public sector (MQ)		.14 (5.57***)	.20 (6.16***)		.42 (17.74***)	.24 (8.44***)
5. Public sector performance (PSP)			-.09 (-2.81**)			.30 (10.55***)
R^2	.07	.09	.10	.04	.22	.28
Adjusted R^2	.07	.09	.10	.04	.22	.28
ΔR^2	-	.02	.01	-	.18	.06
F	36.17***	35.48***	30.11***	20.83***	98.14***	106.99***
F for ΔR^2	-	31.07***	7.89**	-	315.91***	111.27***

Notes: N=1389–1429 due to missing values: *$p<.05$ **$p<.01$ ***$p<.001$.

quality." Similarly, they provide only marginal support for the sixth argument as far as community involvement is concerned, because of the small increase in the explained variance caused by perceived public sector performance.

Finally, in the fourth equation, democratic participatory behavior was positively related with perceived managerial quality and with perceived performance (β=.24; p<.001 and β=.30; p<.001 respectively). Obviously, this positive relationship is due in large measure to the strong effect of trust on democratic participatory behavior. The inclusion of perceived managerial quality in step 2 contributed 22 percent of the explained variance and the inclusion of perceived performance in step 3 of the equation added 6 percent to the overall explained variance, which was 28 percent. These findings provide partial support for the third, fourth, and fifth arguments, specifically verifying the relationships between perceived managerial quality, trust, political participation, and community involvement. They do not, however, provide evidence for the relationships between perceived performance, political participation, and community involvement. In addition, the findings meet the conditions for mediation that require a relationship between the dependent and the independent variables as well as the mediators and the dependent variables. As can be seen, these relationships also worked in the expected directions.

Notwithstanding, it may also be concluded that the mediation effect was far from complete. The fourth condition for mediation mandated by Kenny et al. (1998) requires that for full mediation, the effect of the independent variable(s) on the outcome variable(s) controlling for the mediator must be zero, which was not the case here in any of the four equations. Indeed, the effect of the independent variables on the dependent variables, controlling for the mediator, declined for trust in government and for democratic participatory behavior (from .50 to .13 and from .42 to .24), but for political participation and community involvement, it increased (from .14 to .20 in both cases). These findings imply that perceived performance is a partial mediator for the relationship between perceived managerial quality and trust in government as well as between perceived managerial quality and democratic participatory behavior, but not for the relationship between perceived managerial quality and political participation or for that between perceived managerial quality and community involvement. In the latter case, a direct relationship (main effect) is more dominant than the mediating relationship (side effect). In other words, it may be concluded that our last arguments are partially supported for the variables "trust in government" and "democratic participatory behavior" and are not supported for "political participation and community involvement." I further concluded that the final argument is not supported, as perceived participation in decision-making demonstrated no direct or indirect relationship with any of the dependent variables. Thus, one may argue that perceived public sector performance significantly but partially mediated the relationship between perceived managerial quality and the dependent variables. Nonetheless, a direct effect is still dominant in the model.

Finally, some additional noteworthy relationships emerged from our analysis. At the beginning of the analysis, a broad range of demographic variables was examined that may have affected the results reported thus far. These variables included income, religion, place of birth, ethnicity, and the marital status of the participants. In the pre-hoc analysis, all of these variables proved insignificant. Only the variables of age, education, and gender had any significant effect. For example, political participation was positively related to education and age (β=.16; p<.001 and β=.13; p<.001 respectively), and men more than women tended to demonstrate higher levels of political participation (β=−.16; p<.001). In line with this, community involvement was positively related with education and age (β=.07 p<.01 and β=.26; p<.001 respectively) but not with gender. Finally, democratic participatory behavior was positively related with education and age (β=.13 p<.001 and β=.15; p<.001 respectively). These relationships were very stable across the various steps of the hierarchical procedure and are also in line with previous literature on political participation and community involvement (i.e., Verba et al., 1995), which further strengthen the validity of our measures and research design.

Bureaucracy, performance and democratic values: What have we learned?

In this section, I have dealt empirically with the emerging role of public administration as a key player in socialization processes and in building the political culture and public policy of modern nations. The major goal of the study was to examine the relationships between the managerial quality and performance of the public sector and various types of participatory democratic behavior and trust in administrative agencies. To this end, classic ideas previously suggested by Mosher (1982), Waldo (1977), and Thompson (1983) were employed. These scholars noted insightfully some paradoxes in the bureaucracy–democracy nexus. Our contribution follows the more recent theory of NPM, which has pointed to the need to expand our knowledge about the meaning of managerial reforms in public administration (Hill and Lynn, 2005; Peters, 2001; Ridder et al., 2005) and about the next steps in the field. The effect of such trends on the state of democracy and on democratic values, attitudes, and behaviors in modern nations is discussed in numerous studies (Box, 1999; Rimmerman, 1997; Yankelovich, 1991). The findings support the major relationships in our model, with the exception of one: citizens' perceptions of involvement and participation in administrative decision-making at the organizational level were found to have no relationship with the mediating and the dependent variables. Although the inter-correlations between citizens' perceptions of involvement and participation in administrative decision-making and some of the dependent variables were significant, a subsequent multivariate analysis showed that these relationships were unstable and did not hold in multiple regression analysis. Furthermore, the mediation effects were only partially supported and worked for only some of the dependent variables.

In our view, the most important findings of this study are the relationships found between perceived managerial quality and perceived public sector performance on one hand and the three elements of democratic participatory behavior on the other. Despite criticism about the need for trust and participation in democracies, most studies in political theory suggest that participatory behavior is an essential component of good citizenship and prosperous, open societies. Advanced, modern democracy consists of three citizenry principles: obedience to the law, loyalty to the state and the society, and involvement and participation in the political process (Marshall, 1965). The current study focused on the two latter principles and examined trust in government, political participation, and community involvement. Our goal was not to assess their inter-relations (they were all treated as building blocks in the construction of democratic participatory behavior), but rather how they are affected by bureaucratic actions and citizens' perceptions of the actions of public administration.

The findings show that while explained variance for trust was high (50 percent), the model's contribution for the explained variance in the other two active participatory behaviors (political participation and community involvement) was modest and did not rise above 10 percent. This is a rather low level of explained variance. Putting it another way, variables focusing on perceived managerial quality and perceived performance help to explain trust in government and also explain active participatory behaviors, although to a lesser degree. These findings are in line with the existing literature on political participation and community involvement (Almond and Verba, 1963; Verba et al., 1995). In our view, they also emphasize the need to explore other potential predictors of democratic participatory behavior, beyond those suggested here.

In the same vein, a stronger relationship has been also established between citizens' evaluations of perceived managerial quality, perceived public sector performance, and various types of trust and participatory behavior. This latter relationship is very much in keeping with the positive spillover theory (Peterson, 1990; Sobel, 1993). The findings may thus imply that actions and decisions made at the bureaucratic level by public officers leave their imprints on the social and political spheres. If citizens feel that public administration is characterized by quality managerial procedures and professional staff, as well as higher levels of ethics and morality and enhanced innovativeness, the evaluations of performance and outcomes increase accordingly. Moreover, the quality and performance of the public administration machinery is transferable and can be translated into democratic "currency," that is, greater trust in administrative agencies.

However, as the findings clearly show, it can also be translated into the more negative result of reduced levels of political participation and community involvement. When the bureaucratic system delivers high quality goods and services and meets the expectations of the people, it seems that citizen involvement and participation are less needed. Consequently, the "cozy chair" effect may emerge (Vigoda, 2002b) whereby the public becomes less interested in government because it is confident that its essential needs are being met by the bureaucracy. This effect may explain why a high level of perceived performance can result in lower levels of political participation and community involvement. In some respects, this outcome contradicts the basic democratic principles that call for public engagement in the political process. The findings thus only partially support

Thompson's (1983: 235) idea that "democracy does not suffer bureaucracy gladly" and that "many of the values I associate with democracy such as criticism, trust, participation, and individuality stand sharply opposed to hierarchy, specialization, and impersonality I ascribe to modern bureaucracy." Our view is somewhat different and describes a more complex reality. Good governance and a well-performing public administration add to democracy by increasing the public's trust, but at the same time may reduce the public's political participation and involvement in the community.

The findings presented thus far may also have implications for the new approaches to the study of public administration. First, if public sector performance has direct and mediating effects on democratic participatory behavior and on trust in administrative agencies, the new reforms in public administration that call for a more businesslike approach to serving the people are clearly relevant and valuable. For example, the NPM approach, which emphasizes the role of citizens as clients or customers, is further supported by this study. The findings suggest that greater acceptance and implementation of NPM reforms should lead to increased trust in government. Hence, this chapter provides additional support for advocates of the NPM paradigm who seek to improve the performance of public administration with the expectation of safeguarding the principles and foundations of our democracy. The chapter further implies that improving managerial quality by increasing citizens' perceptions of involvement and participation in administrative decision-making is possible and, under some conditions, may lead to more positive evaluations of public sector performance. In the long run, it may also have a direct and indirect effect on trust and democratic participatory behavior.

Interpreting the results in light of the Israeli context

The findings presented in this section should be also interpreted based on the unique characteristics of Israeli democracy and its public administration agencies. Israeli society is a multicultural society composed of immigrants from around the globe. The foundations of this democracy were laid under the rule of the British mandate during 1917–1948. In the first years of independence, during the 1950s and 1960s, Israel's political, administrative, and economic systems were highly centralized. This centralism prevented the development of strong interest groups and significantly slowed down the development of a civil society based on liberal values. During these years, Israeli society did not exert significant pressure for change, even though political participation through voting was intense. Public administration was strongly associated with the ruling Labor Party and its institutions, and citizen involvement in government was minimal. The public developed informal routes to bypass the highly centralized bureaucracy, thus partially implementing a "do-it-yourself" strategy (Shprinzak, 1986).

Socio-political processes in the 1970s and 1980s increased political fragmentation, intensified social divisions, and downgraded the rule of law as well as the functioning of public administration. These dynamics represented a crisis in the political system and the government's inability to govern efficiently and provide public services (Horowitz and Lissak, 1989). This crisis was coupled with a lack of effective channels through which citizens could influence the government. Furthermore, although the first seeds of reform and change in the management of the public sector were planted at the end of the 1970s with the political revolution that brought the conservative Likud Party to power, these seeds did not blossom into widespread systemic change and were not sufficiently nurtured by the major political parties (Galnoor, Rosenbloom and Yeroni, 1999). Consequently, large sectors of Israeli society attempted to find alternative means of solving social problems. Specifically, during the 1980s and 1990s many groups and individuals in Israeli society employed non-institutionalized initiatives to create alternatives, often illegal or semi-legal, to governmental services. Several examples from the 1980s included (1) a significant growth in the "black-market economy," particularly the illegal trade in foreign currency, (2) "gray-market medicine," particularly the semi-legal, private supply of health services using public facilities, and (3) "gray-market education," particularly the employment of privately paid teachers and the evolution of independent private schools. In the 1990s, this mode of behavior spread to other policy areas such as internal security, social welfare and communications, all of which expressed people's dissatisfaction with governmental services. Ultimately, the Israeli government responded positively to these initiatives by changing its policies in the direction demanded by these citizenry groups. The rules became more decentralized and a variety of NPM style reforms in education, medicine, welfare, and communication services were initiated. Another channel of governmental response has been strengthening the ombudsman offices where complaints against various public agencies are recorded and published (Galnoor, Rosenbloom and Yeroni, 1999). This process also emphasized the central role of the Supreme Court, which enjoyed the public's trust.

Thus, as demonstrated above, Israeli society developed complex methods to overcome significant failures of the political, administrative, and democratic systems. These unique characteristics of Israel's democracy can explain the problem of predicting participatory behaviors in this study. However, Israeli citizens still prefer democratic mechanisms to non-democratic ones. The potential of strengthening such mechanisms and values by means of good governance and effective administration are at the heart of this study. Furthermore, similar processes have been observed in other democracies such as the United States (Hacker, 2004; Pierson, 1995), meaning that the framework described in this article can be applied to other societies.

Empirical evidence (3): The bureaucracy–democracy tango[3]

Previous studies on the relationship between bureaucracy and democracy in modern societies suggest that many of the elements of one conflict with those of the other. Back in the 1970s and 1980s, this tension was discussed by Mosher (1982), Thompson (1983), and Waldo (1977). More recently, Woller (1998) encouraged finding ways for the "reconciliation of the bureaucratic and democratic ethos," as the two are basic aspects of modern life in free nations. Similarly, a recent study by Vigoda-Gadot and Mizrahi (2007) suggests a conceptual framework for the understanding of the nexus between bureaucracy and democracy. According to this line of thinking, managerial quality and participation in decision-making are essential antecedents of perceived performance in the public sector. How citizens view the performance of the public sector may, in turn, affect democratic values such as trust in government as well as participatory behavior of various types. However, their study relied on a single source of data, namely a survey of citizens' attitudes and behaviors. As far as I could find, no study since has tried to validate their findings using complementary data such as information from the intra-organizational arena and the point of view of public personnel. In the next sections, I will review the general framework of the nexus between bureaucracy and democracy and suggest an alternative validation of this framework.

The theoretical model that underpins our logic is presented in Figure 5.3. The general assumption is that a well-performing bureaucracy may significantly affect democratic attitudes and behaviors such as citizens' trust, public personnel's commitment, and the general participatory behaviors of individuals. More specifically, the model suggests direct and indirect conceptual relationships among core aspects of managerial quality, participation in decision-making, perceived performance and the democratic variables of trust, commitment, and political participation in both the intra- and extra-organizational arenas.

The model presents several theoretical bases for these relationships. First, I rely on the spillover theory identified in social science literature. Studies such as those by Wilansky (1980), and more specifically Peterson (1990) and Sobel (1993), who dealt with the spillover of political attitudes and their impact on participatory behaviors, developed the idea that perceptions, attitudes, and behaviors in one social setting can be manifested in other settings as a reflection of one's skills and experience. Thus, I suggest that the attitudes, perceptions, and views (such as participation in decision-making and perceived managerial quality) of individuals in one setting (the bureaucratic arena) may spillover and affect beliefs and views (for example, trust and political participation) in a separate, but related, setting (the democratic arena), and vice versa.

---

3 Some sections of this chapter are based on E. Vigoda-Gadot and S. Mizrahi, "The Bureaucracy–Democracy Tango: A dual-source empirical revalidation by Structural Equation Modeling in the Israeli public sector," *Policy and Politics* (2008).

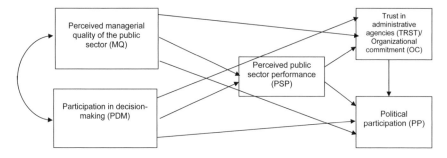

Model 1: Theoretical model

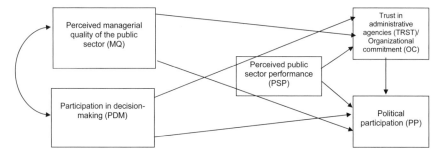

Model 2: Alternative model – Direct effects

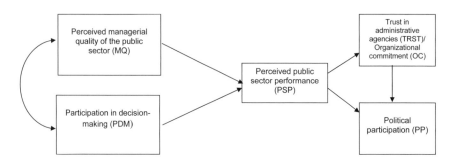

Model 3: Alternative model – Fully mediated

Figure 5.3   Three proposed models of bureaucracy-democracy interaction portrait

Second, I argue that managerial quality is largely subject to the personal skills and talent of the higher ranks in the public agency. In the quest to produce better quality public goods, senior staff members are expected to be accountable to both their subordinates and to citizens. Hence, at least cognitively, perceived managerial quality becomes central for public personnel and for the citizens when making judgments about the state of democracy. Opinions about whether the democracy is trustworthy and allows authentic citizens' involvement and participation in political processes and in shaping policies all flow from the public's view of managerial quality. This idea is in keeping with studies on the centrality of leadership and the leader's style in organizations and in the public sector (i.e., Avolio and Bass, 1991; Bass, 1985). For example, Parry (2003) specifically examined leadership styles in public sector organizations and found that a transformational leadership style has a positive effect on the innovation in and effectiveness of these organizations.

Findings from business studies about the advantages of employees' participation in decision-making and the empowerment of both public personnel and ordinary citizens in helping make organizational decisions and setting policy also bolster our argument. Participation in decision-making reflects the willingness of the leadership to delegate power to subordinates with the expectation that such actions will increase motivation among employees by emphasizing fairness and justice in the relationship between the employee and the organization (Farh, Podsakoff and Organ, 1990; Skarlicki and Latham, 1996). Participation in decision-making is also positively related to work outcomes. Schnake (1991) argued that a leader's willingness to share power may create a need in subordinates to reciprocate. One way to "pay back" a leader for his or her support is by demonstrating good citizenship through increased levels of trust and political participation. Thus, I expect that public employees' or citizens' sense of participation in decision-making will be positively related to supportive behavior by the leader and managerial quality (Niehoff and Moorman, 1993; Wayne and Green, 1993) and that both factors may affect the perceived performance of the public agency. At a later stage, these attitudes and perceptions may also be translated into trust in the public sector and active political participation.

Based on the logic above, the model first suggests that perceived managerial quality, participation in decision-making and perceived public sector performance have a direct effect on the dependent democratic variables. The indirect relationships argue for an alternative path where perceived public sector performance mediates the relationship between the independent and the dependent variables. Additional paths are suggested where citizens' trust or employees' commitment lead to active political participation. With regard to the independent variables, perceived managerial quality is related to participation in decision-making. Note also that the theoretical model makes no distinction between the direct and indirect effects and treats them equally.

Following the examination of this model, models 2 and 3 are presented and suggest partial schemes of the theoretical model. These alternative models are designed to evaluate the direct and indirect relationships separately and to further evaluate each one's fit with reality. Model 2 eliminates the indirect paths and examines a purely direct relationship alternative where all the bureaucratic properties have a direct effect on the democratic properties. Model 3 focuses on the potential mediating effect of perceived public sector performance in the relationship between the independent and the dependent variables. One should keep in mind that all three models are designed and tested for two separate samples – the citizens' sample and the public personnel sample.

Pilot study

As one of the major potential contributions of this study is the extension of a citizens-based study to the intra-organizational sphere and to public personnel, the pilot study focused on the employees of the public sector rather than on citizens. For models, data, and knowledge about citizens' perceptions of bureaucracy and democracy, I relied on previous literature such as Box et al. (2001), King and Stivers (1998), Vigoda and Yuval (2004) and others.

Thus, a pilot study was first conducted in a public energy firm. This nationwide firm, with about 12,000 employees, provides services to most of Israel's citizens; I focused on a major branch of the organization with about 503 employees, which is located in the central area of the country. Qualitative data was based on archive information and on semi-structured interviews with a cadre of managers and employees. In this stage, I interviewed ten employees and managers at all levels to make sure that our scales were clear and worthy of investigation in the next steps. All the interviews were recorded, and the transcripts were edited and analyzed to draw meaningful conclusions for the survey stage. Based on this analysis, I developed a pilot survey. In this quantitative stage, 101 employees and managers (a return rate of 87 percent) from the organization's branch office responded to a first draft of a questionnaire. The results of the qualitative stage and the pilot survey helped in formulating the final version of the questionnaire that was later distributed in three organizations: a hospital, a police unit, and a local municipality. Generally speaking, the findings of the pilot survey supported a positive relationship between managerial quality, participation in decision-making, and perceived performance by employees. These variables also had a positive, yet more modest, relationship with commitment to the organization and with active political participation.

As an extension of this stage, and prior to the survey's distribution in the other organizations, 18 managers from these organizations were interviewed. Again, all these interviews were also recorded and analyzed prior to the main survey stage. The interviews included questions about the research variables and were designed to help in formulating items for the final survey stage that were more specific. Sample questions were: (1) "Please explain, in your own words, the level of orientation towards participation in decision-making in this organization." (2) "Do you feel employees in your work environment are satisfied with their jobs? How satisfied are you with your own job? In your opinion, does the public express satisfaction with the services it receives from this organization?" (3) "Do you feel that the goals of this organization are well defined and well explained to the employees? What do you think is the meaning of managerial quality? Do these principles characterize your organization? In other words, what do you think about the managerial quality of this organization?"

(4) "In your view, what is the meaning employees' trust and citizens' trust in the organization? What do you think about the level of trust and commitment that employees have in this organization? What do you think is the level of trust that the public has in this organization?"

The study and the findings

Based on the quite extensive pilot stage described above, I composed a final version of the survey that was distributed in three organizations: (1) a central public hospital with about 2,000 employees, located in the north of the country and providing a variety of medical services to a population of 800,000; (2) a police line-unit with about 100 officers that has a close and continuous relationship with the public and is representative of the Israeli police, with a staff of about 25,000 and; (3) a local municipality in the north of the country with about 4,000 employees and a population of 300,000. Due to a relatively low number of responses in each organization, and based on our theory that argues for relationships beyond the intra-organizational level, I decided to pool the data of the organizations together, which resulted in two separate files of employees and citizens. In total, data were collected from 159 employees (a return rate of 69 percent) and from 158 citizens (a return rate of 76 percent) who appeared personally at the organizations to receive a service. Of the employees' sample, 40.1 percent were men, their average age was 39.9 (s.d.=9.1), 77.6 percent of them were married, they had, on average, 14.1 years of education (s.d.=2.1), and 94.9 percent of them were Jews. Of the citizens' sample, 57 percent were men, their average age was 39.2 (s.d=14.1), 58 percent of them were married, they had, on average, 14.3 years of education (s.d.=2.4), and 75.8 percent were not employed as public personnel elsewhere.

Table 5.9   Descriptive statistics and inter-correlations matrix (reliabilities in parentheses) for the public personnel sample

	Mean (SD)	1	2	3	4	5
1. Perceived managerial quality of the public sector (MQ)	3.34 (.84)	(.83)				
2. Employees' participation in administrative decision-making (PDM)	2.24 (.99)	.31***	(.88)			
3. Perceived public sector performance (PSP) (employees job satisfaction and responsiveness)	3.61 (.68)	.58***	.45***	(.70)		
4. Trust in the organization (TRST) (Organizational commitment – OC)	3.79 (.77)	.37***	.49***	.67***	(.81)	
5. Political participation (PP)	1.83 (.51)	.02	.15	-.07	-.05	(.86)

Notes: N=159;   *p<.05;   **p<.01;   **p<.001.

Table 5.10   Descriptive statistics and inter-correlations matrix (reliabilities in parentheses) for the citizens sample

	Mean (SD)	1	2	3	4	5
1. Perceived managerial quality of the public sector (MQ)	3.15 (.88)	(.84)				
2. Citizens' participation in administrative decision-making (PDM)	2.26 (.82)	.60***	(.83)			
3. Perceived public sector performance (PSP) (citizens' satisfaction with services and responsiveness)	2.91 (.92)	.72***	.59***	(.85)		
4. Trust in government (TRST)	2.97 (.94)	.67***	.44***	.67***	(.90)	
5. Political participation (PP)	1.93 (.42)	.21**	.27***	.16*	.25**	(.75)

Notes: N=158;   *p<.05;   **p<.01;   **p<.001.

Table 5.11   Goodness of fit indices

Model	X^2	df	X^2/df	p	NFI	RFI	TLI	CFI	RMSEA	ECVI
Public Personnel*										
Theoretical model	158.1	67	2.36	<.000	.87	.79	.87	.91	.09	1.66
Alternative model – Direct effect	200.6	69	2.91	<.000	.83	.74	.81	.88	.11	1.90
Alternative model – Fully mediated	170.3	71	2.40	<.000	.85	.78	.86	.91	.09	1.68
Citizens**										
Theoretical model	134.0	67	2.0	<.000	.90	.85	.92	.95	.08	1.52
Alternative model – Direct effect	273.1	69	3.95	<.000	.80	.70	.76	.84	.14	2.38
Alternative model – Fully mediated	136.8	71	1.92	<.000	.90	.85	.92	.95	.08	1.48

Notes: * N=159   ** N=158.

Tables 5.9 and 5.10 provide descriptive statistics and inter-correlations for the two samples. As shown, the psychometric properties of the research variables across the samples are reasonable. All variables have fairly normal distributions and acceptable Cronbach alpha ratios (.70–.90) for all the variables included. In addition, most of the inter-correlations hold in the expected directions. In both samples, perceived performance is positively related to the independent and the dependent variables. For both samples, participation in decision-making is positively related to trust and organizational commitment. An interesting bi-variate finding is that political participation is positively correlated with most of the other variables in the citizens' sample, but not in the employees' sample.

Table 5.11 provides the fit indices for the models. According to this table, the analysis of the theoretical models for both samples yielded reasonable fit indices, even if somewhat below the levels recommended in the literature (i.e., Bentler, 1990; Bentler and Bonett, 1980; Bollen, 1989; Medsker et al., 1994). As shown in Table 5.11, the fully mediated model is close to the theoretical model in both samples, whereas the direct effect model is the poorest fit of all. However, the X^2 value is significant in all the tested models, which indicates that none of them is a perfect description of the reality. In the citizens' sample, the X^2/df value is the closest to 2 (1.92 and 2.00 in the fully mediated and the theoretical model,

Table 5.12   Path coefficients and explained variance

Model Path	Public Personnel			Citizens		
	Theoretical Model	Alternative model – Direct effect	Alternative model – Fully mediated	Theoretical Model	Alternative model – Direct effect	Alternative model – Fully mediated
MQ→ PSP	.35*	-	.35*	.69*	-	.72*
MQ → TRST/OC	.02	.11*	-	.22	.35*	-
MQ →PP	.06	.05	-	.06	.02	-
PDM →PSP	.17*	-	.18*	.20*	-	.18*
PDM → TRST/OC	.05	.08	-	-.01	-.00	-
PDM → PP	.18*	.17*	-	.03	.02	-
PSP → TRST/OC	.83*	.77*	.89*	.58*	.48*	.79*
PSP → PP	-.12	-.14	-.05	-.12	-.07	-.13
TRST/OC → PP	-.02	.00	.00	.03	.03	.10
R^2						
TRST/OC	.72	.66	.73	.61	.50	.62
PP	.07	.10	.00	.04	.08	.03
PSP	.35	-	.37	.78	-	.80

Note: *<.05.

respectively). Similarly, in the public personnel sample, this ratio is also better for the fully mediated model and for the theoretical models, even if still far from the 2.00 level. For both the fully mediated and the theoretical models, in both samples, the NFI, RFI, TLI, and CFI are the closest to 1.00, and RMSEA and ECVI are the closest to 0 among all other models. Furthermore, in the fully mediated and theoretical models of the citizens' sample, RMSEA is .08, which indicates a relatively good fit of the models. Notwithstanding, the fully mediated model is superior to the theoretical one because of its parsimony and higher level of degrees of freedom. Hence, these findings indicate that for both samples, and especially for the citizens' sample, the fully mediated model is the best model. While it is far from being the "correct" model in terms of fit for either sample, it has many advantages over the other models.

In addition to the models' fit, Table 5.12 allows an in-depth comparison of the models in terms of path coefficients and explained variance (R^2). According to this table, the theoretical model of the public personnel sample is the best among all other models because it has four significant paths (MQ→PSP=.35; PDM→PSP=.17; PDM→PP=.18; PSP→TRST=.89). The mediated model in the citizens' sample and in the employees' sample is superior to all the other models across the samples. It has three significant paths with a very high magnitude in the citizens' sample (MQ→PSP=.72; PDM→PSP=.18; PSP→TRST=.79) and in the employees' sample (MQ→PSP=.35; PDM→PSP=.18; PSP→TRST=.89). The only path that exceeds these is the one between PDM and PSP in the citizens' sample (PDM→PSP=.20). Note also that these relationships work in the expected positive direction. Thus, when considering both samples, the most salient path is PSP→TRS/OC that is strongly and positively significant in all the tested models. The MQ→PSP path and the PDM→PSP path are the second best with consistent positive relationships across samples and models but with a somewhat lower magnitude. Finally, the PDM→PP path is significant only in the public personnel sample.

Furthermore, R^2 statistics show that the highest explained variance is demonstrated for the TRS/OC variable across samples and models. Its range is between 50 percent (the direct effect model of the citizens' sample) and 73 percent (the fully mediated model of the public personnel sample). The highest explained variance for PSP was 80 percent in the fully mediated model of the citizens' sample, and the lowest was 35 percent in the theoretical model of the public personnel sample. Finally, the findings for PP are much more modest. Explained variance for this variable ranged between 1 percent (fully mediated model of the public personnel sample) and 10 percent (the direct effect model of the public personnel sample). Thus, it may be concluded that, in terms of predicting public sector performance, the findings based on the citizens' sample are much more impressive than those based on the public personnel sample. For the variables of trust and organizational commitment/trust, the findings of the public personnel sample are somewhat better than those of the citizens' sample. Lastly, the findings reconfirm the obstacles in predicting political behavior but are quite encouraging in terms of predicting the relationship between the trust of citizens, the commitment and trust of public sector personnel, and public sector performance and independent variables such as managerial quality and participation in decision-making, both in the intra- and extra-organizational arenas. The implications of these findings are discussed more extensively in the final section of this chapter.

Lessons from the tango dance

The relationship between bureaucracy and democracy is similar to a tango dance where "it takes two" to make a system move forward. Bringing together the ideas of good management and a well-performing administration on one hand and a prosperous democracy with a high level of citizens' trust in government and healthy patterns of active participation on the other has become a timely and urgent challenge for our modern societies. Kelly (1998) even suggested that together with the common idea of "representative democracy" there might be a place in our modern nations for a "representative bureaucracy" where various citizenry groups gain representation in public administration bodies and have an influence on the decisions made within them. By so doing, the gap between bureaucracy and democracy can be narrowed and the potential for conflicts in values and priorities reduced. However, few studies have empirically tested the meaning and change in this gap by relating measurable elements of effective bureaucracy with those of a stable democracy.

Such a study is the goal of this chapter. It follows a theoretical framework developed in other studies (i.e., Vigoda-Gadot and Mizrahi, 2007; Vigoda-Gadot and Yuval, 2004) for relating the odd couple of bureaucracy and democracy in the context of specific public agencies. The theoretical model was empirically examined based on four in-depth field studies in Israel. It used qualitative and quantitative data collected from public personnel in the intra-organizational arena and similar data from citizens who were served by these personnel in the extra-organizational arena, to increase the similarity of the method and to maximize the comparability of the results. For analysis of the data, a structural equation modeling technique was applied and reconfirmed a solid positive relationship between elements of an effective bureaucracy and aspects of a trustworthy and active democracy. Our findings thus offer some support for previous studies in this field, including those by Mosher (1980) and Waldo (1977) who dealt elegantly with the important dilemmas stemming from the coexistence of these two social mechanisms. Moreover, the mediating model where public sector performance, both as perceived by citizens and by public personnel, mediates the bureaucratic–democratic relationship proved to be the best model for making the tango dance more explicable and understandable. In our view, this finding also accords strongly with voices calling for NPM-style reforms in public administration, particularly those reforms that highlight bureaucratic efficiency and businesslike management oriented towards performance and performance measurement (Box et al., 2001; Chi, 1999; Terry, 2005). I believe the major contribution in this context is the relationship I have demonstrated between NPM and the democratic foundations of a society or a nation.

Dancing the tango, but keeping a distance

The major finding of the study suggests that the perceived performance of the public sector serves as an important buffer between bureaucratic characteristics such as managerial quality and citizens' and public personnel's participation in decision-making, and aspects of democracy such as citizens' trust in the government, the commitment of public personnel, and active political participation. This finding is consistent not only with literature on NPM (i.e., Chi, 1999; King et al., 1998; Terry, 2005) but also with other studies that have focused on the satisfaction–trust relationship. As mentioned previously, a study by Ulbig (2002) suggested that "satisfaction with the procedures and people of government ... helps to boost feelings of trust in government" (p. 801) because citizens who are satisfied with governmental policies also have a meaningful voice alternative. Hence, the attitudes, perceptions, and views of individuals in one setting (the bureaucratic arena) may spillover and affect beliefs and views in a related but separate setting (the democratic arena), and vice versa.

A close and independent assessment of each of the samples that were used here yielded other results of interest. For example, in the intra-organizational environment, public personnel's participation in decision-making was positively and directly related to political participation. This finding is interesting, as it may imply again, based on the spillover theory, that learning, skills, and attitudes acquired in the organizational climate can be translated into more general codes of behavior on the communal and national level (Sobel, 1993). Nonetheless, this finding was not replicated in the citizens' survey, which somewhat limits its external validity. Furthermore, the relatively modest relationship that was found in this context calls for more studies in this direction. Another result of interest is the relationship between participation in decision-making and perceived performance in both samples. This finding may imply that positive perceived performance is, to a certain degree, subject to citizens' or employees' involvement in making decisions and setting policies. This finding is meaningful both in the intra- and extra-organizational contexts. It supports organizational theories on the centrality of PDM in forming a healthy job environment (i.e., Drucker, 1974; Vroom, 1964). Moreover, it is also in line with recent calls for more citizenry-infused government and for more collaboration and consultation between the state and the people, or even between these players and the private sector (i.e., Ebdon, 2002; Pierre, 1999; Thomas, 1995). While the strategy of including such players in decision-making is not always realistic, as an approach, it is one that has been little explored. Such an approach has the potential to have a strong positive effect on how the public sector is viewed and ultimately on the democratic values of trust in government and active political participation.

Dancing the tango with managerial quality and PDM

Hence, the findings reiterate the role of managerial quality and participation in decision-making in relation to democratic values and involvement. First, in both samples, perceived managerial quality emerged as a crucial antecedent to perceived performance by employees and by citizens. Therefore, the leadership of administrative bodies is potentially one of the most influential groups in society that shape people's views towards organizations, especially towards the public sector (Avolio and Bass, 1991; Bass, 1985; Parry, 2003). The fact that this finding was consistent for public sector employees and for citizens alike further increases the power of the results, as well as reconfirms the reliability and validity of the scales I used. In the longer run, these views may be translated into democratic beliefs and actions such as trust in government and political and communal participation. Theoretically, this finding is in line with the growing literature that emphasizes the role of the leadership cadre in the public sector and its immense responsibility for running state-owned organizations effectively.

Second, our findings support the importance of participation in decision-making, especially for citizens. While the literature on organizational behavior and generic management has long recognized the values of involving employees in decisions and the positive effect that this process may have on any firm's outputs and outcomes (i.e., Drucker, 1974; Porter et al., 1974; Vroom, 1964), public administration literature has only recently begun to move in the same direction. In recent years, a growing number of public administration scholars have urged governments and policy makers to find better ways to increase citizens' involvement in what previously seemed the private realm of civic servants or politicians (Box et al., 2001; King et al., 1998).

Dancing the tango: Some practical lessons

The findings of this study may also lead to some practical dance lessons for this tango. If the major theoretical implication stemming from the findings is that bureaucracy and democracy have a mutual influence on one another, then governments, policy makers, and citizens should be involved in heightening the positive aspects of both institutions. Hence, our study has three major practical recommendations: (1) Governments must make every effort to create and maintain high standards of managerial quality in the public service via investment in human resource programs and by increasing the human and social capital of the upper ranks in public agencies. This investment is crucial for improving public sector performance and the services it offers to citizens and for making citizens more willing to contribute to the common good of others in a democratic realm; (2) Governments must make every effort to encourage mechanisms of greater involvement in decision-making, both for public personnel, but especially for citizens. The literature of recent years is rich with such mechanisms, and their number is growing, especially with the evolvement of e-government (i.e., Buss,

Redburn, and Guo, 2006). The methods and mechanisms should be applied selectively to different cultures and sectors, as each has its specific needs and profile. (3) Beyond the responsibilities of governments, citizens have their role as well. Citizens' groups, citizens' organizations and the growing third sector are important partners in the bureaucracy–democracy tango. They must recognize the potential and merit of becoming more involved in government policy-making and develop their agenda in a wide range of issues relating to citizens' quality of life. These groups are expected to take an active part in formulating government policy in various fields. By affecting the bureaucratic side of the equation, they are actually also contributing to the democratic nature of their states and communities. Thus, despite the potential conflict in the bureaucracy–democracy agenda, cultivating improved public sector performance, perhaps in accordance with NPM principles, is likely to lead to a strong democracy. Demand for increased involvement by both citizens and public personnel is undoubtedly a constructive step forward in this direction, as it builds trust and encourages voice orientations of communal involvement and political participation that are essential for any healthy democracy of the twenty-first century.

Dancing the tango: future endeavors

Several limitations of this study should also be mentioned. First, it may be argued that the models tested for the citizens and the public personnel are not equivalent. For example, the variables of trust in government and the organizational commitment variables are not similar. Neither are the two satisfaction variables (that is, satisfaction with services and job satisfaction). Indeed, while it may be somewhat useful to test the exact same model with citizens and public personnel, I feel that a greater advantage of the study is its illumination of both the extra- and intra-organizational environments. I do not argue that the models should be similar in the first place. The fact that the indirect effect model received better support in both samples is in line with the expectations of the study that I would see a mediating effect of perceived performance for both samples. Second, although I applied an advanced SEM technique to test the models, the relatively moderated fit of the models and lack of significant paths among some of the variables suggest that causal implications should be made with caution, if at all. Nonetheless, the fact that the models, especially the indirect and theoretical ones, received some support across two separate but related samples, leads us to believe that the findings are reasonably robust and that the indirect relationship between bureaucracy and democracy, as formulated here, deserves further scholarly attention and empirical examination in other studies. Third, our findings are based on cross-sectional and self-report data. This technique may result in source bias (such as the social desirability effect) or common method error. The findings may also be affected by some external bias caused by events in the international, national, and even regional environment. Nevertheless, these are quite common problems when dealing with survey data. The study demonstrated sound psychometric properties in terms of the reliabilities of the research variables across the samples, which testifies to the solid structure of our measures and their construct validity. Finally, our data and model apply to only one culture, the Israeli one. Until similar measures are used in a different culture, our findings cannot be compared synchronically. Thus, further studies are needed to support our findings in other socio-political environments.

Empirical evidence (4): Internal politics, ethics and high-performing governance[4]

Another empirical illustration of the relationship between managerial quality and public sector performance is focusing on ethics and internal politics and on their relationship with public sector outcomes. Internal politics, power relations, influence tactics, and ethics are inherent to the discussion of modern public administration. Thompson and Ingraham (1996: 292) defined organizational politics as the art of competition among individuals while striving for divergent objectives. They suggested that a political analysis of organizations contrasts with rational models that portray organizations as directed towards the achievement of a single set of mutually agreed upon goals. The frequently political and unfair nature of public administration systems can be demonstrated in several ways. For example, by their very nature, public organizations are intimately tied to political and governmental systems. Thus, studies have suggested a spillover effect of political skills, attitudes, and behaviors from one arena to another (Peterson 1990; Sobel 1993). A recent study by Vigoda and Kapun (2005) examined the perceptions of politics among 336 public sector employees and 364 private sector employees. The study confirmed that public organizations are perceived as much more political in nature than private organizations. A possible explanation for this phenomenon offered by the study was based on the spillover theory.

In addition, many are familiar with the problematic question of political nominations in public administration, the complexity of requirement systems that should be professional but frequently face external political pressures, the limited internal reward system, the slow promotion processes that are often not commensurate with the actual effort of the employees, the resulting poor motivation or performance of public servants, as well as the inflexibility of such bureaucratic systems. In this context, Thompson and Ingraham (1996) investigated the reinvention labs that have been established in federal agencies and the organizational politics that accompany these attempts at innovation and organizational change. Their findings emphasize the role of organizational politics and the self-interested behavior of individuals in determining the outcomes of

---

4 Some sections in this chapter are based on E. Vigoda-Gadot, "Citizens' perceptions of organizational politics and ethics in public administration: A five-year study of their relationship to satisfaction with services, trust in governance, and voice orientations," *Journal of Public Administration Research and Theory* (2007).

organizational change. They conclude by confirming "the value of political models for understanding organizational change processes" in public administration (Thompson and Ingraham, 1996: 291). Consequently, public administration and the government are frequently criticized for their high level of internal politics that detracts from professional decision-making. It is argued that such processes and conflicts negatively affect fairness and equity in resource allocation to different populations. Federal and national agencies are occasionally accused of unfair treatment and immoral behavior by the public, accusations that stem from internal conflicts among players and from political considerations that are non-professional and irrelevant to the issues at hand.

Furthermore, organizational politics in public administration may arise from other reasons. At times, tense relations between the politically appointed rank and file and the professional ranks of the public servants develop (Nalbandian, 1980). These tense relations potentially increase the degree of citizens' suspicions of and doubts about many kinds of bureaucratic decisions and actions (Stivers, 2001). In this context, Gawthrop (1998) is concerned with the prevailing vacuity of public sector ethics and the moral disconnect between democracy and bureaucracy (Ruhil, 2000). Gawthrop further explains that a democratic "value vision" (that is, one that is based on citizens' trust, loyalty, benevolence, unselfishness, prudence, temperance, fortitude, justice, faith, hope, and even love) must be enhanced in order to promote the common good. Thus, the improvement of organizational performance and the success of public sector reforms and bureaucratic management are highly dependent on democratic values and on mutual trust between institutions and ordinary citizens. As perceptions of organizational politics and ethics represent many of these shared values towards bureaucracy, they should be studied extensively in the public sector to improve both managerialism and democratic values. In line with these ideas, it is clear why *citizens'* perceptions of politics and ethics in the public sector are crucial for a better understanding of the dynamics and outcomes of the public sector machinery.

Hence, it may be argued that ordinary citizens are acutely aware of organizational politics through various means such as the media, personal contacts with others, or through their own experience with public agencies. It is not surprising, therefore, that opinions voiced through the media and public debates identify internal politics with injustice and with unethical actions in public administration. Such actions are considered key obstacles to building a quality managerial climate that serves the people well. In support of this view, Kelly (1998) deals with the interrelations between New Public Management (NPM) reforms and the democratic polity. She suggests that "a particular public bureaucracy or administrative structure is embedded within a particular socioeconomic system" (Kelly, 1998: 201) and that, in the final analysis, politics and administration cannot be separated. In her view "there are value trade-offs and politics involved in almost all administrative decisions, and in many delivery contexts" (Kelly, 1998: 205). However, the proximity between bureaucracy and democracy, or between administration and politics, may also result in higher levels of organizational politics that may be easily observed by citizens and translate into attitudes and actions in the democratic realm.

This variable is frequently measured by items from the shorter version of the perception of organizational politics scale (POPS) that was first developed by Kacmar and Ferris (1991) and re-examined by Kacmar and Carlson (1994). The above studies, like this one, define POPS as the degree to which the respondents view a certain work environment as political, and therefore unjust and unfair.

A Model of internal politics, ethics, performance, and democratic values

A theoretical model is suggested by Vigoda-Gadot (2007) for the relationships between internal politics and ethics in public administration, performance, and several democratic values. The model is presented in Figure 5.4. Basically, it argues that citizens' perceptions of organizational politics and ethics in the public sector are important antecedents of several bureaucratic and democratic outcomes (Kelly, 1998; Thompson and Ingraham, 1996). These outcomes include both perceptual and behavioral dimensions. Trust in government and in public administration represents a perceptual dimension, whereas political efficacy and political participation are more active features of voice orientations. Among these, scholars distinguish between political participation, which is an actual behavior, and political efficacy, which reflects a belief about the effectiveness of active involvement (Niemi et al., 1991; Verba et al., 1995).

The model utilizes both direct and indirect relationships. First, a direct relationship is suggested between the independent variables and satisfaction with services. According to this line of thinking, citizens who believe that higher levels of internal politics as well as lower levels of ethics and morality exist in public administration will also demonstrate lower levels of satisfaction with the services they receive. This belief is based on studies in management and organization theory that have found a significant relationship between employees' feelings about internal politics and ethics in the workplace and their satisfaction with their jobs (Ferris and Kacmar, 1992; Kacmar et al., 1999; Witt et al., 2000). In addition, studies in public administration have suggested that public perceptions about the ethics and fairness of public officers and of public agencies are positively related to the public's level of satisfaction with services received from them (DeLeon, 1996; Vigoda, 2000a; Wilensky, 1980).

We further suggest that organizational politics and ethics, together with satisfaction with services, are good predictors of attitudes towards the democratic system. This relationship is based on the idea that ethical considerations are very significant in determining citizens' views of governments and administration (Esman, 1997; Goldoff, 1996; Webler and Tuler, 2000; Willbern, 1984). Support for this relationship is also rooted in the model used for assessing the American Customer Satisfaction Index that directly relates citizens' satisfaction with trust in government (Van Ryzin et al. 2004). Thus, when citizens perceive the bureaucracy as insensitive, feel that it promotes the interests of powerful individuals or groups based on political considerations, and believe that it engages in unfair practices, public attitudes towards democracy may become more cynical. Similarly, citizens may react negatively, either cognitively and/or behaviorally, by reducing their levels of trust and confidence in governance. More actively, these perceptions may lead to diminished belief in the value of citizenship involvement or political efficacy, negatively affecting citizens' willingness to participate in politics and discouraging them from becoming more involved in communal activities (Niemi et al., 1991; Verba et al., 1995). Consequently, the first variable to be tested in this context is trust in government. Our argument for this relationship is based on studies that have demonstrated a positive relationship between trust in government and the public's satisfaction with the services they receive from the government (Van de Walle and Bouckaert, 2003; Van Ryzin et al., 2004; Vigoda and Yuval, 2003a, 2003b; Welch 2005). Studies have also suggested that trust and satisfaction are affected by peoples' perceptions of the level of ethics, morality, and the proper handling of decision-making processes in public administration (i.e., Berman and West, 1994; Gawthrop, 1998). Thus, I suggest that perceptions of organizational politics and unethical behavior in public administration have a negative relationship with citizens' satisfaction with services and with trust in government.

Accordingly, the model posits perceptions of politics and ethics as direct antecedents of several democratic values and behaviors. The argument here is based on the works of Verba et al. (1995) and Gawthrop (1998) who argued that fairness, equity, and justice are core values in bureaucracy that have an immense effect on citizens' acceptance of the democratic ethos and thus also affect passive and active responses towards politics and towards government. Thus, higher levels of organizational politics, immorality, and unethical actions in the public sector may also lead to lower levels of political efficacy and political participation among citizens.

Finally, the model also suggests that the relationship between voice orientations and the independent variables (organizational politics and ethics) is mediated by satisfaction with services and by trust in government. Whereas conventional wisdom may suggest that citizens directly translate their views about ethics and political dynamics in the public sector into behavior intentions or actual behaviors (that is, voice orientations), the model takes a more cautious approach by also suggesting an indirect relationship. As studies in political behavior have shown (i.e., Brady et al., 1999; Milbrath and Goel, 1977; Peterson, 1990; Verba et al., 1995), political efficacy and political participation are phenomena with multiple predictors. Therefore, I argue that citizens who view public services as political in nature, unfair, and unethical, may first react by expressing lower levels of satisfaction and trust, and only then, with time and experience, translate their dissatisfaction with governance into more tangible reactions towards government and the political system. One passive reaction may be a lower level of political efficacy or trust in civic behavior. Another, more active reaction may be a reduced willingness to become involved in political processes and reduced levels of political participation. This view is strongly rooted in the cognitive approach to human behavior suggested by Lewin (1936) and is opposed to the behaviorist approach

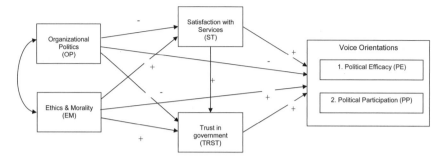

Figure 5.4   Aftermaths to organizational politics and ethics in public administration: A citizens' perspective of satisfaction, trust, and voice orientations

(i.e., Erez and Rim, 1982; Kipnis et al., 1980). In keeping with the cognitive approach, I argue that citizens' beliefs and perceptions will be translated into voice orientations and participation through a slower process of "mind change" and transformation of faith over time.

Thus, perceiving the public sector as rife with internal politics and unethical decisions will be likely to result in voice orientations of change only after dissatisfaction with services is expressed and mistrust in government is demonstrated (Van Ryzin et al., 2004). In line with this, the model suggests that citizens' satisfaction with services and trust in government mediate the relationship between organizational politics and ethics on one hand and political efficacy and political participation on the other.

Empirical findings

Figure 5.5 provides a graph that illustrates the change in the core variables over time. In addition, Table 5.13 presents a correlation matrix among the research variables for the combined sample (2001–2005). As can be seen, most of the inter-correlations hold in the expected directions and none of them exceeds the maximum level of .70, which is a good indication for the absence of multicollinearity among the variables. OP and EM correlated at the r=.31; p<.001 level. Additional factor analysis (principle components with varimax rotation) that was conducted for these two variables yielded two clear-cut factors for each of the variables, which again indicates that they are distinctive but related to each other. These zero-order correlations suggest that citizens' perceptions of organizational politics are negatively related with satisfaction with services (ST), trust in government (TRST), and political efficacy (PE) (r=–.19; p<.001, r=–.22; p<.001, and r=–.30; p<.001 respectively). The results for perceptions of ethics (EM) are even stronger. EM is positively related with ST, TRST, PE and (PP) (r=.35; p<.001, r=.39; p<.001, r=.46; p<.001, and r=.11; p<.001 respectively). In addition, ST is positively related with TRST and with PE (r=.67; *p*<.001 and r=.31; *p*<.001 respectively). TRST was further positively related with PE (r=.40; *p*<.001) and finally, PP was positively related with PE (r=.08; *p*<.01) even if quite modestly. These findings provide initial support for the direct relationship between the dependent and the independent variables. However, these relationships still need to be tested with multivariate analysis to examine their stability.

Table 5.14 presents the results of four multiple regression analyses where satisfaction with services (ST), trust in government (TRST), political efficacy (PE), and political participation (PP) were separately regressed on the independent and control variables for the combined sample. According to Table 5.14 perceived organizational politics (OP) showed a modest negative relationship with ST and TRST (β=−.09; *p*<.001 and β=−.06; *p*<.001, respectively). Again, the results for EM were even more impressive. EM had a consistent positive relationship with ST (β=.32; *p*<.001) and a somewhat weaker but still positive, noteworthy relationship with TRST (β=.17; *p*<.001). Moreover, as the model suggests, SWS was examined as another antecedent to TRST. As expected, the relationship was positive and high (β=.60; *p*<.001). All in all, these findings support the direct relationships as suggested previously. In addition, in accordance with the conditions for mediation specified by Baron and Kenny (1986), Kenny et al. (1998), and Kenny's web page, the suspected mediating variables (ST and TRST) were positively related with the independent variables, OP and EM. Thus, I further concluded that the first condition for mediation holds for the variables SWS and TRST. Our further analyses will therefore continue to examine a mediation effect for these variables.

Table 5.14 also demonstrates some of the relationships between the independent variables and voice orientations (PE and PP). As can be seen, political efficacy (PE) and political participation (PP) were separately regressed on OP, EM, and on the control variables. A direct positive relationship was found mainly between EM and voice orientations (β=.40; *p*<.001 for PE and β=.10; *p*<.001 for PP). OP was negatively related with PE (β=−.18; *p*<.001) but not with PP.

To examine the indirect relationships and the mediating effect of ST and TRST, I followed Baron and Kenny (1986) and applied a hierarchical regression analysis. This analysis is presented in Table 5.15. This table will allow us to test both of the direct relationships as suggested previously, but this time with respect to added explained variance (ΔR^2). It will also allow us to examine the additional two conditions for mediation. PE and PP were regressed on the independent variables using a three-step model. First, the dependent variable (PE and PP) was regressed on the control variables (step 1). Second, ST and TRST were added to the equations (step 2), and finally OP and EM were added (step 3) to examine the independent contribution of each of these variables to the overall explained variance of the dependent variables.

In the first step of the equations, the control variables had no significant relationship with the dependent variables. However, the second and third steps of the regressions provided very interesting findings. As can be seen from the results of the combined sample, ST was positively related with PE in the second step of the regression (β=.09; p<.001) and with PP in the third step of the regression (β=−.08; p<.05). TRST was much more strongly related with PE in the second step (β=.35; p<.001) and in the third step (β=.23; p<.001). However, its relationship with PP was significant only in the second step of the regression (β=.07; p<.05) but not in the third step, which indicates a lack of stability for this relationship. The inclusion of ST and TRST in step 2 contributed 17 percent of the explained variance in PE but made no contribution to the explained variance of PP.

Step 3 of the equations added the variables OP and EM. As can be seen, both OP and EM demonstrated a significant relationship with PE (β=−.15; p<.001 and β=.31; p<.001, respectively). In addition, EM demonstrated a positive relationship with PP (β=.11; p<.001). The inclusion of OP and EM in step 3 of the equation added 12 percent to the overall explained variance of PE, which was 30 percent. In addition, the inclusion of OP and EM in step 3 of the equation added a marginal value of 2 percent to the overall explained variance of PP, which was only 7 percent.

These findings again support a direct negative relationship between OP and perceptions of unethical behavior on one hand, and voice orientations on the other. The relationship is quite strongly supported for PE but to a much lesser extent for PP. The findings also provide partial support for the mediating effect, for the variable TRS, and to a lesser extent for the variable ST. The results also meet the conditions for mediation that require a relationship between the dependent and the independent variables as well as the mediators and the dependent variables. As can be seen, these relationships also worked in the expected directions for the variable PE, but to a much lesser extent for PP.

Moreover, to fully test the proposed mediating effect, I must return to the conditions for mediation suggested by Baron and Kenny. The fourth condition for mediation suggested by Kenny et al. (1998) requires that for full mediation, the effect of the independent variable(s) on the outcome variable(s) controlling for the mediator must be zero, which was not the case here in any of the equations. For example, the effect of the independent variables on PE controlling for the mediator(s) decreased for EM (from β=.40 to β=.31) and for OP (from β=−.18 to β=−.15). However, when I controlled for the mediator(s), the effect of the independent variables on PP showed almost no change for either EM or OP. Thus, I concluded that a mediating effect is only partially supported for the variable PE, and not supported for the variable PP. In addition, I concluded that TRST is a much better mediator than SWS, which may be considered another antecedent to trust instead of a mediator in this model.

Finally, according to Table 5.15 the control variables had a minor effect on the dependent variables throughout the stages of analysis. Men were consistently more likely than women to be involved in political participation (β=−.09; p<.001). In addition, PP was higher among more educated and older citizens (β=.14; p<.001 and β=.12; p<.001, respectively). However, whereas men showed higher levels of PE compared with women (β=−.07; p<.001), it was younger citizens and those with lower levels of education who expressed higher levels of PE (β=−.05; p<.01 and β=−.04; p<.05, respectively).

To summarize our results, I suggest two additional figures. Figure 5.5 indicates the specific significant relationships stemming from the broader theoretical model previously suggested in Figure 5.4, as well as the effect size of the relationships. Cohen (1988: 25) defined the effect size (ES or *d)* as the difference between the means, $M_1 - M_2$, divided by the standard deviation of either group. Cohen argued that the standard deviation of either group could be used when the variances of the two groups are close to each other. He further defined effect sizes as "small, *d =* .2," "medium, *d =* .5," and "large, *d =* .8." Following this approach, I calculated the effect size for the significant relationships and found most of them to be medium to high (ranging between d=.51 and d=1.85 with the exception of a few, somewhat lower relationships (ST→TRS; EM→PE; ST→PP). Our findings thus suggest that (1) OP and EM are direct predictors of ST and TRST; (2) OP is a direct predictor of PE, but not of PP; (3) ET is a direct predictor of both PE and PP; (4) ST mediates the relationship between OP and EM on one hand, and PP on the other; and (5) TRST mediates the relationship between OP and EM on one hand, and PE on the other. In addition, Figure 5.6 portrays the change in the research variables across the years of study. As can be seen, there is a great deal of correlation between bureaucratic and democratic variables that remain constant over the years. This finding should make us think again about the reasoning and the logic for building stronger nations that rely on solid democratic mechanisms accompanied by effective bureaucratic tools and methods.

Ethics, internal politics, performance and democracy: A few lessons

Nalbandian (1980) argued that the appropriate place of organizational politics in administration continues to be a topic of importance. Some two decades later, the meaning and nature of organizational politics in the public sector was discussed extensively by Vigoda-Gadot (2003c) from an interdisciplinary perspective. Vigoda-Gadot's book suggested that this arena is rife with internal politics and that its outcomes for various stakeholders can be substantially different from those in the private sector. However, the outcomes of organizational politics in terms of services to the public and the long range effect they may have on citizens of democratic nations has been overlooked in both the managerial literature and the literature of public policy and administration. The present study deals with perceptions of internal politics in public administration. However, contrary to the common method used in general management theory that focuses on the perspectives of employees and managers, our study focused on the perceptions of citizens as clients. The main rationale for this approach was based on the idea that these views are important for a better understanding of other perceptions and behaviors of citizens' towards government and towards the wider political and democratic system. Citizens' perceptions of internal politics and ethics in the administrative branches of democracies may thus prove useful in explaining trust in government as well as voice orientations such as political efficacy and political participation.

Table 5.13 Correlation matrix among the research variables for the combined sample (2001–2005)

	Mean (S.D.)	N	1	2	3	4	5	6	7	8
1.Organizational Politics (OP)	3.67 (.80)	2263	-							
2.Ethics and Morality (EM)	2.54 (.90)	2246	-.31***	-						
3.Satisfaction with services (ST)	3.04 (.55)	2279	-.19***	.35***	-					
4.Trust in government (TRST)	2.92 (.59)	2279	-.22***	.39***	.67***	-				
5.Political Efficacy (PE)	2.19 (.79)	2245	-.30***	.46***	.31***	.40***	-			
6.Political Participation (PP)#	1.82 (.41)	1429	-.03	.11***	-.02	.02	.08**	-		
7.Gender (1=women)	-	2255	-.01	-.02	.10***	.06**	-.06	-.10***	-	
8.Education	10.07 (5.61)	2209	.06**	-.01	.01	.01	-.07***	.15***	.06**	-
9.Age	34.12 (12.21)	2204	-.02	.06**	.02	.01	-.02	.16***	-.09***	.18***

Notes: N=2281; *p<.05   **p<.01   ***p<.001; # Scale ranged from 1 to 3.

Table 5.14   Multiple regression analysis for the direct effect of Organizational Politics (OP) and Ethics (ET) on Satisfaction with Services (SWS), Trust in government (TRS), Political Efficacy (PE), and Political Participation (PP) (standardized coefficients; t-test in parentheses)

	ST β (t)	TRST β (t)	PE β (t)	PP β (t)
1. Gender	.10 (5.17***)	.01 (.24)	-.06 (-2.90**)	-.10 (-3.66***)
2. Education	.02 (.75)	.01 (.25)	-.05 (-2.49**)	.14 (5.21***)
3. Age	.00 (.12)	-.02 (-1.25)	-.05 (-2.45**)	.12 (4.55***)
4. OP	-.09 (-4.22***)	-.06 (-3.66***)	-.18 (-9.00***)	-.01 (-.19)
5. EM	.32 (15.15***)	.17 (9.77***)	.40 (20.38***)	.10 (3.66***)
6. ST	-	.60 (36.28***)		
R^2	.14	.49	.25	.06
Adjusted R^2	.14	.49	.24	.06
F	68.37***	335.51***	139.78***	18.19***

Notes: N=2281: *p<.05   **p<.01   ***p<.001.

The findings of the study support some key relationships in this direction. In accordance with theories suggested in previous studies (Gawthrop, 1998; Thompson and Ingraham, 1996), I found empirically, using five years' worth of data, that both organizational politics and ethics are good predictors of citizens' satisfaction with governmental services and trust in government. The findings are also in keeping with the general managerial literature that has already firmly established the relationship between organizational politics and fairness, and employees' satisfaction and loyalty, trust, and commitment to their workplace (i.e., Bozeman et al. 1996; Cropanzano et al., 1997; Drory, 1993). An analysis across the years shows that the explained variance due to these direct relationships reached from 12 percent to 21 percent for satisfaction and 42 percent to 58 percent for trust. Obviously, the higher level of explained variance for the variable of trust was due to the contribution of satisfaction, but OP and ethics also played a significant role in this context. The study further reaffirms previous knowledge about the way in which satisfaction may lead to trust in government (Van Ryzin et al., 2004). The direct relationship between OP and ethics and voice orientations is also noteworthy. The importance of citizens' perceptions of ethics is demonstrated here with the direct relationship between EM and both PE and PP. Contrast this with the finding that citizens' perceptions of organizational politics accounted for variance only in PE but not in PP. This finding may imply that citizens' perceptions of organizational politics may have a stronger indirect relationship with voice orientations such as PE and that such relationships should be examined in future studies.

Table 5.15   Hierarchical regression analysis for the effect of Organizational Politics (OP) and Ethics Perceptions on Political Efficacy (PE) and Political Participation (PP) (standardized coefficients; t-test in parentheses)

Variable	PEβ (t)			PPβ (t)		
	Step 1	Step 2	Step 3	Step 1	Step 2	Step 3
1. Gender	-.06 (-2.66**)	-.09 (-4.42***)	-.07 (-3.97***)	-.10 (-3.70***)	-.10 (-3.61***)	-.09 (-3.41***)
2. Education	-.07 (-3.08**)	-.07 (-3.37***)	-.05 (-2.76**)	.14 (5.10***)	.14 (5.11***)	.14 (5.24***)
3. Age	-.02 (-.68)	-.02 (-1.02)	-.04 (-2.32*)	.13 (4.79***)	.13 (4.83***)	.12 (4.58***)
4. ST	-	.09 (3.28***)	.03 (1.20)	-	-.07 (-1.84)	-.08 (-2.34*)
5. TRST	-	.35 (13.00***)	.23 (9.00***)	-	.07 (2.04*)	.04 (1.03)
6. OP	-	-	-.15 (-7.80***)	-	-	-.01 (-.31)
7. EM	-	-	.31 (15.13***)	-	-	.11 (3.85***)
R²	.01	.18	.30	.05	.05	.07
Adjusted R²	.01	.17	.29	.05	.05	.06
ΔR²	-	.17	.12	-	-	.02
F	6.28***	91.13***	128.84***	24.96***	15.92***	13.84***
F for ΔR²	-	216.77***	184.75	-	2.29	8.25***

Notes: N=2281: *p<.05   **p<.01   ***p<.001.

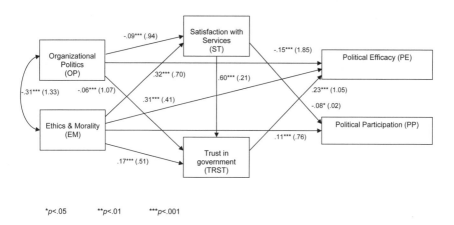

*p<.05   **p<.01   ***p<.001

Figure 5.5   A revised model: Path coefficients (β) and effect size (ES) (in parentheses)

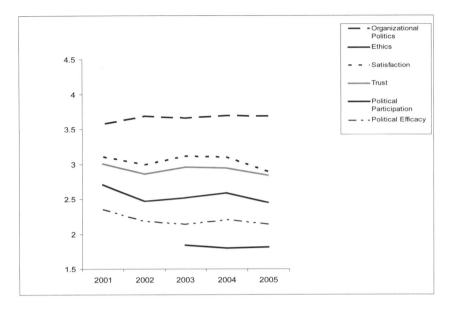

Figure 5.6   The change in the research variables during the years of the study

Furthermore, the study established a mediating role of satisfaction and trust in the relationship between the independent variables and voice orientations. While satisfaction is a partial mediator between OP and PE (beyond the direct relationship between OP and PE), it is also a mediator between EM and PP. However, according to the findings, satisfaction is not a mediator between any of the independent variables and PE. Thus, I conclude that the major power of ST is in contributing to the explanation of political participation. In contrast, the major role of trust in government is in explaining political efficacy. The revised model presented in Figure 5.5 demonstrates how ST leads only to PP, whereas TRST leads only to PE. Thus, trust in government is a good mediator between OP and EM on one hand and political efficacy on the other.

The implications of the findings are also much in line with a study by Kelly (1998) who suggests that for citizens to remain satisfied as customers, they need some broader and comprehensive information assuring that (1) either all were treated equally, or (2) that if people were treated differently, they were treated equitably and fairly according to various criteria that are accepted for valid reasons. Such a social equilibrium that is built on fairness, ethics, and a lack of predatory organizational politics is critical for social peace and a democratic society. Ruhil (2000: 834) further argues that "ethics in public administration has a long and checkered past" and that today "we need fewer calls for recognizing the lack of ethical administration and more practical roadmap to show us how we can get to our destination." According to this study, an examination over time of the public's perceptions regarding organizational politics and ethics in public administration is a first step to responding to this challenge.

Despite its contribution, this study still has certain limitations. Although survey data compiled over a five-year period was used here, the study may suffer from common method and common source bias. Thus, I recommend that future studies try to compare citizens' perceptions of organizational politics and ethics with employees' or with managers' objective perceptions. By so doing, further consideration may be given to the role of such perceptions and behaviors for organizations in general and especially for the public sector. In addition, it is important to note that no causal relationships should be inferred from our findings. The method used does not allow any time-dependent conclusions and implications should remain correlative. However, the fact that our findings were quite consistent over the years provides further justification and support for the revised model. This is clearly the advantage of our design, a format that should be encouraged in future studies of behavior in and attitudes towards the public sector. Another limitation of our study concerns the quality of the variables. For example, the acceptable but still somehow low reliability of the variable OP could create noise in the statistical analysis, and future studies will need to use a more solid measure of OP to overcome this problem. Also, data about political participation were collected only for three years rather than the full range of five years. However, this problem should be remedied in coming years as more data about political participation become available through this ongoing survey. In addition, the resulting Cronbach's alpha for the variable OP was .66, which is somehow lower than the recommended level of .70. While this value is still acceptable, I recommend that future studies try to create an even more reliable and robust scale of OP based on additional relevant items. Finally, this study relied on an Israeli sample, and therefore, its comparison with other samples, for example from other European countries or from North American settings, is limited. Nonetheless, cultural indicators may prove useful in future studies as well. For example, it is possible that organizational politics and ethics are perceived differently in various countries and thus, our findings should be treated with caution (i.e., Romm and Drory, 1988; Vigoda, 2001).

In sum, the original model and the revised model demonstrate how the relationships between organizational politics, ethics, and the tested variables may be interwoven. They illustrate the linkage between bureaucracy and democracy based on citizens' best judgments of the processes in public administration that should be ethical, fair, professional, and equitable but at the same time effective, efficient, and smoothly functioning. Our use of citizens' perspectives for measuring OP and ethics in the public sector is not very common. However, it is based on the idea that the public is aware of internal power struggles and self-seeking activities that sharply conflict with professional and ethical processes in public agencies. Our research joins other studies in public opinion research that give a great deal of consideration to the people's voice in studying the relationships and conflict between democracy and bureaucracy. According to Thompson (1983), Stivers (2001), and Gawthrop (1997), this conflict is inherent to our lives in free societies.

It reflects the essence of the contradiction between the politics of the democratic ethos and the professionalism of bureaucracy in modern nations. The five-year study reveals some core relationships in this direction that can be used in future research. The findings help us in our search to create a more functional bureaucracy in a democratic ethos and to safeguard democracy under the constraints of bureaucracy. This section also has an interdisciplinary orientation, as it tried to show how a theory from one arena (management and organizational behavior) can be used effectively in another arena (public administration and political science). This approach may promote new ideas about how to improve the management of public sector agencies. Another major contribution of this study is its exploration of an alternative viewpoint regarding the study of organizational politics and ethics. The study demonstrated that a variety of perspectives need to be considered when examining the impact of power struggles, influence tactics, and politics in the workplace. While the views of the employees are critical, the perceptions of the public should also be investigated, as they are a powerful tool in helping us understand this phenomenon and its consequences.

Summary: Implications based on an empirical longitudinal effort

In this chapter, I tried to provide some preliminary empirical support to theoretical arguments about the nexus between bureaucracy and democracy, based on a citizens-oriented longitudinal study. The first step was to establish a core relationship between citizens' satisfaction and trust in government and in administrative systems and to deal with the question of causality. The results demonstrate modest but important support for the idea that satisfaction leads to trust more than trust leads to satisfaction. Nonetheless, the alternative path is also one that deserves attention in future studies. In any case, the results of the first empirical section support the hypothesis that there is a strong relationship between the outcomes of a bureaucratic machinery and democratic outputs such as people's confidence, faith, and trust in state bodies and institutions.

In the second empirical section, I illustrated how a wider empirical model can be tested and evaluated based on the longitudinal Israeli study. This section tried to identify the links between administrative and managerial variables and political variables in the democratic realm. Gawthrop (1997) argued that there might be a great deal of confusion and hypocrisy associated with the concepts of democracy and bureaucracy. According to Dwight Waldo (1977: 16), "when both are studied together the opportunities for confusion and delusion are multiplied, given the human capacity for irrationality and ego-serving views of the world." Nevertheless, despite this complexity, one may continue to argue that democracy and bureaucracy can and should be studied in relation to each other. This is an underdeveloped field of knowledge that should be related to emerging trends in the New Public Management paradigm. Doing so will make a serious contribution to the understanding of contemporary public policy, and our empirical findings may guide other studies in this field.

The third empirical section probed a limited aspect of the enigma described by Thompson (1983) who suggested that "democracy does not suffer bureaucracy gladly: Many of the values I associate with democracy such as criticism, trust, participation, and individuality stand sharply opposed to hierarchy, specialization, and impersonality I ascribe to modern bureaucracy" (p. 235). Social mechanisms and concepts such as bureaucracy and democracy are closely related, but each has its own autonomy and independence, much like the partners in a tango. Nonetheless, in modern societies and in renewing bureaucracies they are bound together at least to the degree that a free society hopes to deliver effective quality services to the people, safeguard the elementary principles of freedom, and cultivate active citizen involvement in political and in communal processes.

The fourth study elaborated on the central role of ethics, morality, and internal politics as core elements in the bureaucracy–democracy paradox. The results of the fourth study demonstrate that the values of justice, the fair treatment of citizens and public sector employees, and an honest interpretation of bureaucratic rules by state officials is essential for better performance as well as for stronger democratic values such as political efficacy, political participation, and the involvement of citizens.

Finally, this chapter makes theoretical, methodological, and empirical contributions to the study of the tango-style relationship between bureaucracy and democracy. Based on the analogy of a tango dance presented in the third empirical study, I argue that the paradox of bureaucracy and democracy is in continuous flux, even in our times. As in the tango, players are close but not really touching, and the dance moves one step forward and two steps to the side, in a general direction of progress and restraint. I have enhanced the theoretical approach to the subject by building on the earlier model presented by Vigoda-Gadot and Mizrahi (2007), creating a more developed model with additional scales and measures that can enrich our understanding of the field. Methodologically, the dual-source approach I used for the examination of the models is unique. The two distinctive but related samples of public personnel and citizens who receive services in four Israeli governmental agencies not only test a theoretical rationale, but also revalidate, to some extent, the scales, the logic, the relationships, and the findings of earlier studies. Our focus on four quite different public sector agencies (a public energy firm, a public hospital, the police, and a local municipality) also adds to the knowledge in these fields. Moreover, the SEM technique applied here demonstrated its power in assessing competing models and hypotheses in public administration studies. Hence, despite its limitations, the chapter provides more solid, empirical support for the centrality of perceived performance in assessing the bureaucracy–democracy tango. It reconfirms that the bureaucratic realm and the democratic realm are distinctive but strongly related arenas with considerable effect on modern societies worldwide.

PART III

Strong Nations and Reconciliation of the Democratic–Bureaucratic Paradox: Several Alternatives

Can we bridge the gap between theoretically the bureaucratic and democratic ethos, both theoretically and practically? While some may argue that bridging these aspects of our life is already a reality (for example, modern democracies function under a bureaucratic system of administration and order), others will argue quite the opposite. The inherent paradox between the bureaucratic nature of governments and the democratic nature of our free societies creates many problems for both leaders and citizens. What seemed to be a reasonable solution in the twentieth century may be insufficient for the twenty-first century and beyond.

The goal of this closing part is to suggest several alternatives that can unite the odd couple. These alternatives are suggested in light of the previously citizens-oriented examination of public sector quality, performance, and democratic values and behaviors. It also considers the current dynamics in modern public administration, within the meaning of new citizenship, and in a globalizing world. I thus focus on three major tools and themes that, in my view, have the greatest potential benefit for "strong nations." These tools and mechanisms are: (1) collaboration with citizens and around them, (2) innovation by citizens and by governments, and (3) global reforms that work for citizens and for other stakeholders. I obviously see citizens of the modern state as the core element in any process of building strong nations. Strong nations are therefore comprised of knowledgeable citizens who are both willing and able to be part of performance improvement in governments. Governability, so it will be argued, is built on citizens' willing to share innovative ideas and care for their communities and states, even though this responsibility is traditionally expected from governments, politicians, and bureaucrats. These tools are useful both in the local and regional arena of any democracy, but also in the more global sense – as tools for creating productive, advanced, and liberal societies that add value to human kind and safeguard its existence and quality of life for the years to come.

Chapter 6
Strong Nations and Collaboration in Public Administration: A Myth or Necessity?[1]

Collaboration and reconciliation of the bureaucratic–democratic paradox

In this chapter, I will argue that collaboration is one very useful vehicle for resolving the bureaucratic–democratic paradox and the dilemmas it fosters. I will try to demonstrate why collaboration among sectors, divisions, individual citizens, and institutions at all levels is very much in keeping with the democratic ethos of freedom of voice and freedom of initiative. I will also argue that collaboration is a desirable goal for bureaucracy, for bureaucrats, for public officials, and public servants because none of them can function independently of the others. Lack of collaboration yields fewer and often poorer results than even the least successful collaborative effort. This contention may contradict some of the common wisdom about centralization and self-initiatives. However, what I am advocating here is the road to partnership, a road nations must travel if they want to become stronger in every sense of the word, be it institutionally, economically, politically, or socially.

Recent criticism of the responsiveness-oriented thinking of New Public Management has called for a theoretical and practical shift towards increased collaboration in and around public administration (Box et al., 2001; Vigoda, 2002b). One emerging view offers the alternative in which a market-based model of public administration needs to be assimilated into collaborative relationships between citizens and bureaucracies. Box et al. (2001) suggest that "this relationship is based on shared knowledge and decision-making rather than control pleasing and placating" and "assumes that citizens have the ability to self-govern, even in these complex and confusing times" (p. 616). Moreover, NPM breeds passivity among citizens as clients by overstating the idea of responsiveness (Vigoda, 2000a). Placing the citizen–client at the center sends a covert social message to the people saying, "Make your wish ... it is our goal to serve you." However, it adds, "But please don't bother us ... leave the professional work to us." In other words, NPM and the ethos of responsiveness put citizens as clients at the center by asking them

---

1 Some sections of this chapter are based on E. Vigoda-Gadot, *Managing Collaboration in Public Administration: The Promise of Alliance among Governance, Citizens, and Businesses*, Praeger Publishers (2003). Reproduced with permission of Greenwood Publishing Group, Inc., Westport, CT. Also E. Vigoda, "From responsiveness to collaboration: Governance, citizens, and the next generation of public administration," *Public Administration Review* (2002).

about their needs and demands. However, public administrators still ask citizens to keep their distance from the administrative work and the decision-making centers. The covert message is, "Bureaucracy needs to work for you, so keep away." Citizens' involvement is accepted only as passive client feedback to actions by the administration. Innovative methods of redefining goals and strategies are left in the hands of politicians or civic servants. Through this message, modern public administration wins the battle for responsiveness, but does not even try to fight the battle for collaboration.

Therefore, it seems essential that we turn towards more cross-sectoral collaboration and social orientation in the public sector. In many respects such a move bears a strong resemblance to any kind of administrative reform, one directed at the minds and hearts of policy makers, policy implementers, and other social players such as private entrepreneurs, third sector organizations, and citizens in general. Doing (good) administrative work *for the public* also means doing it *with the public*, as well as with all those who are concerned with the formation of modern, prosperous societies. Hence, despite some serious obstacles and difficulties, the idea of a "collaborative public administration" may be defined as reform in progress. It should promote the trust of citizens in government, enhance equality, and bring higher levels of citizens' participation and community involvement into our lives. It is a reform that has the potential to revise our conventional view of government by making government and public administration more willing to share ideas, knowledge, and power with others, not merely instruct citizens and patronize them.

Public administration is entering an era where there is a greater need for collaboration among various social players. However, quite ironically, but unsurprisingly, we have no way of knowing what lies ahead for our societies. In most of today's Western nations the free market doctrine is dominant in economic, social, and political affairs. Indeed, these nations have also woven an interesting and complex network of social constraints that are aimed at safeguarding human rights and providing minimum standards of living for their societies' less able citizens. Under the conventional title of "welfare states" or at least "caring states," the basic human needs of many are protected by central governments and by the law. Still, modern democracies of various types have encouraged a tradition of competition, conflict, and contest over resources. Based on the "Protestant Ethic" of Max Weber, competition has become a cornerstone of the ideology and philosophy of modern capitalist nations. "Competitive" jargon has been made commonplace by politicians, public sector officials, and businessmen alike. Consequently, this language has also become the most common terminology to explain public policy and governmental decision-making. In a world where competition is the "name of the game," governments are expected to respond better to citizens' demands by choosing the best of many options and reducing costs to a minimum. Hence, in recent decades we have seen the rise of new tools of privatization, outsourcing, or contracting-out, which represent a desire by policy makers to transform old-style bureaucracies into more flexible, responsive, effective, and efficient bodies.

While the contribution of these methods, actions, and reactions is not disputed, criticism has also been leveled against the "next step" in bureaucratic development. Are we moving towards the increased fragmentation of our societies and communities, or is there an alternative to the rising level of competition? In many respects, the term "competition" is the opposite of collaboration. In any situation where more than one person is involved, people may choose to compete or to collaborate in order to attain a certain goal or need. While patterns and strategies of competition in public affairs seem quite evident, the potential power of collaboration in this arena is still unclear. Collaboration has thus remained an underdeveloped area in managerial thinking, and the literature that has developed so far is scarce. In a world of dominant capitalistic values, competition takes the lead, and collaboration, at least as it pertains to the world of public affairs, is seen as less significant and more problematic.

Therefore, a gap must be filled in managerial writing and in public administration thinking. What does collaboration in the public sector arena actually mean? What does it imply in terms of managerial concepts? Is it a rational and reasonable solution to the various ills of our societies? If so, how can it be implemented wisely and what strategy should be used to guarantee success in this process? Where should we use collaborative ventures and who are the partners in this process? These are just a few of the questions I will raise in the chapter. However, the chapter may raise more questions than it answers.

Governability, public administration, and the September 11 effect

The simultaneous terrorist attacks on New York, Pennsylvania, and Washington D.C. on the morning of September 11 signaled the emergence of some striking changes in America and in the world. These events were in no way the reason for the writing of this book, which I had begun many weeks earlier, but their impact on my views about collaboration was remarkable. Perhaps one of the most interesting results of these terror actions was the sharp change in American public opinion about the role of government in day-to-day life, about its size, responsibilities, and challenges. As this book tries to demonstrate, one significant aftershock of the September 11 events may turn out to be our view and perception of the need for collaboration in modern society.

It was high-level collaboration among many terrorist organizations and states that support terror, such as Afghanistan, Iraq, Iran, and Syria, that made the attack on the United States so effective and successful. I believe that only a similar counter-process of collaboration among democratic nations can resist these threatening forces and safeguard the free world. In this conflict, as in other socially oriented conflicts, it is public administration that has the primary role and responsibility to provide answers to new needs. Today, more than ever before, its purpose is to enhance collaboration among various social players, and as all agree, to protect democracy through this mutual effort. We have always expected national and federal institutions to do this, and today they must become even more energetic and involved in such trends and developments.

There are several reasons for our ongoing heavy reliance on the government and its executive branches. First, we have no other institution or body to turn to when our basic rights and needs are endangered. Second, in the last century governments and the public sector have grown larger than at any other time in the past, increasing the public's dependence on the services and goods they provide. Third, the public sector and its administrative heads offer more services and goods than ever before, and they do so for larger populations with greater heterogeneity and expanding demands. In sum, we depend on governments and on public administration bodies because we believe that they hold the answers to our questions and the solutions to our needs. If they cannot do the right things for us, then who can?

Collaboration, bureaucracy, and the old style of public administration

For many years, conservative public administration and the conservative perception of the role of bureaucracy was actually non-collaborative by nature. According to the conventional political and administrative perspectives, governments are responsible for providing public services to the people. Governments rely heavily on the authoritative power of bureaucracy and on its patronage position towards other social players. Hence, the *state-level analysis* is elementary for the study of collaboration in public administration. No such process is possible unless governments and public administration are ready to initiate it, to commit resources and effort to it, and to recognize the enormous advantages that such a reform brings with it. Political support is no less important. While administrative officers are more likely to become engaged in such a change in mindset, the political realm is less likely to realize its advantages.

What are the foundations of this approach? The old type of public administration is identified with the very basic nature of classic bureaucracy with roots dating back thousands of years. The Bible mentions a variety of hierarchical and managerial structures that served as prototypes for the governance of growing populations. Ancient methods of public labor distribution were expanded by the Greeks and the Romans to control vast, conquered lands and many peoples. The Persian and Ottoman empires in the Middle East, like imperial China in the Far East, paved the way for public administration in the modern age, wherein European Christians, and later Christians of the New World, were in ascendance. All of these groups used a remarkably similar set of concepts, ideas, and methods for governing and administrating public goods, resources, and interests. They all employed professionals and experts from a variety of social fields. They all used authority and power as the cheapest control system for individuals, governmental institutions, and processes. All of them faced administrative problems similar in type and in nature to the problems of our own times: how to achieve better efficiency, effectiveness, and economy in government, how to satisfy the needs of the people, and how to maintain a stable political hegemony despite the divergent demands and needs of sectoral groups. Not surprisingly, all the above cultures and nations also used similar managerial tools and methods aimed at solving problems of this kind. They all applied division of labor, professionalism, centralization and decentralization mechanisms, accumulation of knowledge, coordination of jobs, complex staffing processes for employees, long-range planning, and controlling for performance in a fairly effective manner. Intuitively, one feels that nothing has really changed in the managerial and administrative process of public organizations for centuries, possibly millennia. But this feeling is, of course, exaggerated. Some major changes have taken place in recent centuries to create a totally different environment and new rules, to which rulers and citizens must adhere and by which they must adjust their operations. In fact, a new kind of governing game has taken shape in which public administration plays a central role.

Despite basic similarities, public administration in our time is an organism entirely different from public services in the past. It is *larger* than ever before, and it is still expanding. It is more *complex* than in the past, and becoming increasingly so by the day. It has many more *responsibilities* vis-à-vis its citizens, and it still has to cope with the increasing demands of the public. It is acquiring more *responsibilities*, but more than ever before it must restrain its operation and adhere to standards of equity, justice, social fairness, and especially accountability. Moreover, modern public administration is considered a social *science*, a classification that brings with it a certain measure of esteem but also firm obligations and rigid constraints. For many individuals who decide to become public servants, it is also a *profession and occupation* to which they dedicate their lives and careers. Most importantly, however, public administration is one of the highly *powerful institutions* in modern democracies. It wields considerable strength and influence in policy framing, policy-making, and policy implementation. Hence, it is subject to growing pressures from political players, social actors, and managerial professionals.

New Public Management reforms: Towards greater responsiveness to citizens

During the last two decades, many definitions have been suggested for NPM, and we reviewed several in earlier chapters. According to Lynn (1996: 38–9), six differences exist today between (old) public administration and (new) public management that make the former a new field of study and practice and, as far as we are concerned, make it a major factor in building strong nations. These are: (1) the use of general management functions such as planning, organizing, control, and evaluation in lieu of discussing social values and conflicts between bureaucracy and democracy; (2) an instrumental orientation favoring the criteria of economy and efficiency in lieu of equity, responsiveness, or political salience; (3) a pragmatic focus on mid-level managers in lieu of the perspective of political or policy elites; (4) a tendency to consider management as generic, or at least to minimize the differences between public and private sectors in lieu of accentuating them; (5) a singular focus on the organization, with external relations treated in the same rational manner as internal operations, in lieu of a focus on laws, institutions, and political bureaucratic processes; and (6) a strong philosophical link with the scientific management tradition in lieu of close ties to political science or sociology.

One important theme highlighted by the NPM approach has been the responsiveness of governments and public administration to citizens as clients. Vigoda (2000a) identified two possibly controversial but complementary approaches to understanding public administration's responsiveness. While offering distinct views of responsiveness, each approach contains checks and balances missing from the other. According to one approach, responsiveness is at best a necessary evil that appears to compromise professional effectiveness. At worst it is an indication of political expediency if not outright corruption (Rourke, 1992). According to this line of research, responsiveness contradicts the value of professionalism in governments and public administration because it forces public servants to satisfy citizens even when such actions run counter to the public's interests. In the name of democracy, professionals are almost obligated to satisfy demands that are often based on short-term considerations. Decisions are made based on their popularity, while other long-term issues receive little attention. In addition, there is the risk that powerful interests may dominate the discussion and pretend to represent the opinions of many when in fact they represent a small group with a partisan agenda. Such influences can result in a decision-making pattern that is undemocratic and may not represent the true voice of the majority. The other approach to responsiveness suggests that democracy requires administrators who are responsive to the popular will, at least through legislatures and politicians if not directly to the people (Stivers, 1994; Stewart and Ranson, 1994). This approach is more aware of the need to encourage a flexible, sensitive, and dynamic public sector. It fact, it argues that only by creating a market-derived environment can governments and public administration adopt the reforms needed to improve their performance, effectiveness, and efficiency.

While responsiveness is occasionally considered a problematic concept in public administration literature, it is undoubtedly critical for politicians, bureaucrats, and citizens alike. A responsive politician or bureaucrat must be reactive, sympathetic, sensitive, and capable of feeling the public's needs and opinions. Since the needs and demands of a heterogeneous society are dynamic, it is vital to develop systematic approaches to understanding it. Undoubtedly, this is one of the most important conditions for securing a fair social contract between citizens and governmental officials. Hence, scholars and practitioners suggest implementing performance indicators based on public opinion. The opinions of those receiving services must be considered good indicators of public policy outcomes (DHSS, 1979; National Consumer Council, 1986; Palfrey et al., 1992; Winkler, 1987). This information can help one to: (1) understand and establish public needs; (2) develop, communicate, and distribute public services; and (3) assess the degree of satisfaction with services (Palfrey et al., 1992: 128). Consequently, the NPM approach advocates the idea of treating citizens as clients, customers, and the main beneficiaries of the operations of the public sector (Thomas and Palfrey, 1996). In essence, the motivation to meet the demands of the public is equivalent to satisfying the needs of a regular customer in a regular neighborhood supermarket. According to this view, responsiveness in the public arena accords well with business-oriented statements such as "The customer is always right" and "Never argue with the clients' needs" that every salesperson memorizes from his/her first day at work.

But what does responsiveness actually mean? How can we define and operationalize it for dependable social research? In essence, responsiveness generally denotes the *speed* and *accuracy* with which a service provider responds to a request for action or for information. According to this definition, speed can refer to the waiting time between a citizen's request for action and the reply of the public agency or the public servant. Accuracy means the extent to which the provider's response meets the needs or wishes of the service user. However, while speed is a relatively simple factor to measure, accuracy is more complicated. Beyond the recent trends of analyzing public arenas in terms appropriate for the marketplace, public service accuracy must take into consideration social welfare, equity, equal opportunities, and the fair distribution of "public goods" to all citizens (Vigoda, 2000a). These values are additional to efficiency, effectiveness, and service that characterize market-driven processes (Palfrey et al., 1992; Rhodes, 1987). To test the accuracy of government and public administration endeavors, several methods may be applied:

1. Examining citizens' attitudes and feelings when consuming public services. This can be achieved by means of satisfaction measures indicating the outcomes of certain activities and the characterization of public administration actions as fruitful, beneficial, equally shared among a vast population, effective, fast, and responsive to public needs.
2. Examining the attitudes and perceptions of others who take part in the process of planning, producing, delivering, and evaluating public outcomes. These "others" include external private and nonprofit firms, suppliers, manufacturers, constructors, and so forth.
3. Comparing objective public outcomes with absolute criteria for speed, quality, and accuracy. The absolute criteria need to be determined in advance within a strategic process of setting performance indicators (PIs) (Pollitt, 1988). Such a comparison is even more effective when conducted over time, populations, cultures, geographical areas, and so on.
4. Comparing the distribution of services and goods with moral and ethical criteria as set forth by academics and professionals.

Responsiveness has a potentially positive effect on social welfare and improves the process of modernization in the public sector. Recent managerial positions such as the NPM approach also suggest that, as in the private sector, increasing external-related outcomes (such as responsiveness of governments and public administration to citizens' demands) will have a profound impact on internal control mechanisms (Smith, 1993). In other words, managers and public servants will become more sensitive to their duties and strongly committed to serving the people.

To increase responsiveness in public administration organizations, it is essential to constantly evaluate the perceptions of citizens–clients regarding various service providers (Vigoda, 2000a). However, responsiveness cannot be maintained unless these perceptions accord well with the expectations and perceptions of public administrators at all levels. Maintaining a certain level of fit between what clients expect and what public officials are ready, willing, or able to deliver is crucial. Vroom (1964) emphasized the meaning and importance of expectations inside the workplace. He argued that meeting employees' and managers' expectations is essential for obtaining proper individual outcomes and general organizational performance. In many ways, the theory of expectations may be applicable to the complex relationships between service providers and citizens as consumers. Supporters of the cognitive discipline (i.e., Lewin, 1936) have long argued that perceptions of reality, and not reality itself, determine peoples' behavior and attitudes towards other individuals and towards the environment. Therefore, the citizens' view of public service depends on their interpretation of reality and not on public administration actions per se. Likewise, it is difficult to measure responsiveness in absolute numbers. The "sense of responsiveness" matters differently in various administrative cultures and consequently should be treated as a relative rather than an absolute measure.

Collaboration: One step beyond responsiveness and a key to governability

Mounting interest in the idea of NPM has put serious pressure on state bureaucracies to become more responsive to citizens as clients. In many respects NPM has become the "religion" and responsiveness the "law." However, recently bureaucracies have also been urged or even forced to progress beyond responsiveness and extend their collaboration with other social players such as private businesses and third sector organizations as well as citizens. Without a doubt, these are important advances in contemporary public administration, which finds itself struggling in an ultra-dynamic marketplace arena. Some may even define the shift toward collaboration as an additional "law" in the "religion" of NPM. Like any other call for reform, it was built upon a necessary change in the minds and hearts of the players involved. In order to bring collaboration into the central halls of public administration, many old perceptions and attitudes need to be revised and re-framed.

Despite its envisaged benefits, the idea of collaboration also draws heavy fire from those who believe that it is merely a utopian idea with minimal impact on the administrative process. At most, opponents suggest that collaboration is a welcome change in theory building and in practical culture reconstruction, but they add that modern societies still confront a growth in the passivity of citizens, who tend to favor the easy chair of the customer over the sweat and turmoil of participatory involvement. Thus, the critics conclude, collaboration remains a utopian idea with only minimal impact on the nature of modern administration and on its activities.

A growing movement in contemporary public administration seeks to revitalize collaboration between citizens and administrative authorities through various strategies. In fact such trends are not so new. The need to foster certain levels of cooperation among political governmental institutions, professional agencies of public administration, and citizens as individuals or groups has been mentioned before, and has been advanced in several ways including through:

1. Increased cooperation with the third sector Gidron, Kramer and Salamon, 1992; Grubbs, 2000; Thompson et al., 2000).
2. Increased collaboration with the private sector and initiation of plans aimed at supporting communities through various services in the fields of internal security, transport, and education (Collin, 1998; Glaister, 1999; Schneider, 1999).
3. Encouragement of state and local municipality initiatives that foster values of democratic education, participation, and the involvement of citizens (e.g., the local democratic club established in Culver City, California, http://www. culvercityonline.com/accessed 25 June 2001). This pattern also coheres with the idea of a communitarian spirit that transfers some (but not all) responsibility for civic development from central government to local authorities in states and cities, as well as directly to individual citizens (Etzioni, 1994, 1995).
4. Innovation by citizen-initiated involvement through nonprofit civic organizations that help to establish a culture of participation and the practice of voice (see the examples of "citizens' conventions" in Europe: http://www. federaleurope.org/index.php?id=4121&L=3: Last accessed 9 June 2007).

Still, advocates of the NPM approach continue to claim that the main cure for poorly functioning governments and public administration systems is better responsiveness to citizens as clients or customers. According to this argument, which is rooted in political–economic rationality and social choice theory (Hughes, 1994; Kettl and Milward, 1996), only better compliance with people's wishes can steady the wobbly interface between citizens and rulers in contemporary democracies. However, is market-driven responsiveness really the best answer for crises in governance, or is it only an over simplification of broader problems in modern society?

Collaboration and strong nations: Back to the quest for hats and ladies

What are the advantages of citizens' being treated as clients/customers over the perception of them, and others, as equal partners in the process of governance? And what advantages does collaboration have for building strong nations? A metaphor of ladies and hats, previously mentioned in several of my essays, may prove useful here for examining two competing options. (1) There are two very distinct faces of government and public administration (two ladies), one that adopts the idea of responsiveness and one that favors collaboration. (2) The discipline of governance and public administration is more coherent (only one lady) than we might think, and at most it changes color over time (two hats).

Previously, I described two themes in current public administration research as separate and dissimilar perspectives. I argued that responsiveness is of the essence in NPM and further suggested that NPM seems detached from the idea of collaboration. Therefore, perhaps there are two different types of public administration; like the two ladies, one is attired by the supporters of responsiveness, the other by the supporters of collaboration. These two ladies differ substantially from one another because, as explained earlier, they advocate independent views of the roles of governments, public administration, and citizens in the process of running states and nations. However, I may in fact be suggesting only one lady with two hats. One hat, an older styled classic, is more oriented to bureaucratic tyranny and concentration of power in public agencies. It reflects a situation where public administration is the right hand of politicians and thus must preserve power through maximum centralization and control over decisions as well as resources. This hat/ attitude implies minimal concern about either responsiveness or collaboration because both mean depriving governments and public administration of their power. The other hat, however, is newer and more receptive and appreciative of de-centralized managerial ideas, such as better responsiveness and improved collaboration with citizens, which leads to a broader process of modernization. This second hat signals a continuous change in public administration systems, and, as it matures over time, implies increased participation of the people in the administrative process. The lady of public administration wearing the newer hat is less concerned about bureaucracy's losing power and control than she is about the sharing of responsibilities and the dialogue with citizens that may lead to cooperation and partnership on a higher level.

In addition, the "two ladies" version is a more classic approach to the understanding of responsiveness and collaboration in public arenas, so over the years it has received widespread scholarly attention. As noted earlier, one group of studies has concentrated on the first "lady" of public administration, namely the idea of responsiveness (e.g., Rourke, 1992; Stivers, 1994) while the other group has focused on the other lady, who represents the idea of collaboration and partnership (e.g., John et al., 1994; Nalbandian, 1999; Thompson et al., 2000). In fact, hardly any attempt has been made to try to integrate these views or to suggest that they may be better seen as stemming from one another. The "two hats for one lady" image is a step in the direction of this integration but it needs more extensive explanation and elaboration. According to this image, responsiveness and collaboration are inherently related. They describe different points on a continuum of a citizens–government/administration interaction that are constantly shifting and re-framed with time and social events. Thus, the framework of interaction with citizens is better presented here by one evolutionary continuum (one lady) of public administration. Along this continuum, responsiveness and collaboration are just different "hats" on one line.

Wise collaboration: Not new, not simple, not impossible

Strong nations should encourage collaboration among executive branches of government, as well as among the various other sectors in the society. In many respects, such a change brings with it all the typical symptoms of an additional administrative reform, one that is directed at the minds and the hearts of policy makers, policy implementers, and other social players such as private entrepreneurs, third sector organizations, and citizens in general. Doing (good) administrative work *for the public* also means doing it *with the public* as well as with all those who are concerned with the formation of modern, prosperous societies. Hence, despite some serious obstacles and difficulties, the idea of a "collaborative public administration" may be defined as a reform in progress. It is a reform that has the potential of revising our conventional way of looking at government by making government and public administration more willing to share ideas, knowledge, and power with others. While the theory underlying various recommended models of reform in public administration is equivocal, there are still two major models for such reforms that I mentioned in previous chapters: (1) bureaucracy-driven models, and (2) grassroots-driven models. Both of these models suggest an infusion of change in the public sector, but each one does it using a different starting point. Bureaucracy-driven models view governments and public administration as those who are responsible for the initiation of change and for making it work properly. The grassroots-driven models, on the other hand, put more demands on the people with the expectation that they, instead of governments and public administration, will make the first move towards reform. These models demonstrate how various reforms became successful when they begin as the response to the pressing needs of individuals, groups, or from spontaneous collective support of a grass-roots leader. Naturally, there is no *ideal* model for integrating both of these approaches in policy planning cycles. However, there may be an *ideal type* of model for collaborative reform. In the following chapters, I will try to explain the meaning of these theoretical models and to elaborate on their contribution to the creation of a "spirit of collaboration" in and around public administration. My core argument is thus that an ideal managerial type for collaboration should and can be portrayed.

Summary: Collaboration and strong nations: A look towards the future

The future of collaboration in public administration and its proposed contribution to building strong nations is rooted in the various social sciences, as described in the opening chapter. Political science and policy analysis have provided public administration with a core scientific terminology, a macro-conceptual framework, a research focus, and a politics-oriented agenda on which to base future developments. In most modern nations, public administration is considered mainly a blend of political and organizational knowledge that characterizes large bureaucracies. Sociology has contributed the cultural factors, which are relevant for cross-organizational and for cross-national studies (Hofstede, 1980). It also made possible the development of comparative studies and a better understanding of group dynamics and informal structures such as norms or values inside bureaucracies (Schein, 1985). The business approach has guided public administration through managerial considerations and individual behaviors in organizations. Traditional management science of the late 1800s and the concentration on the human side of organizations during the early 1900s exerted increasing influence on administrative thinking. A significant increase and extension of managerial influences on public administration thinking as a science and profession occurred during the mid-1980s with the evolution of NPM trends, which revitalized managerial theory in the public sector. Together, these three disciplines and their appropriate internal integration are essential for a better understanding of contemporary public services and are the cornerstones for building the theory and practice needed for strong nations.

At first glance, the collaboration of government and public administration with other social stakeholders seems to contradict the essence of bureaucracy. The ideal type of bureaucracy, as set out by Max Weber, has clearly defined organizational characteristics that have remained relevant over time. While public organizations have undergone many changes in the last century, they are still based on the Weberian legacy of a clear hierarchical order, concentration of power among senior officials, formal structures with strict rules and regulations, limited channels of communication, confined openness to innovation and change, and non-compliance with the option of being replaceable (Golembiewski and Vigoda, 2000). These ideas seem to be substantially different from the nature of collaboration, which means negotiation, participation, cooperation, free and unlimited flow of information, innovation, agreements based on compromises and mutual understanding, and a more equal distribution and redistribution of power and resources. According to this analysis, which some may find quite utopian, collaboration is an indispensable part of democracy. It means a partnership where authorities and state administrators accept the role of leaders who need to run citizens' lives better not because they are more powerful or superior but because this is a mission to which they are obligated. They must see themselves as committed to citizens who have agreed to be led or "governed" on condition that their lives continuously improve.

Still, the theory of collaboration and partnership sometimes fails to cohere with the complex realties around us. For example, Cloke et al. (2000) suggest that collaboration becomes an influential social tool only with the presence of massive citizenship involvement. However, only citizens and voluntary groups with proper resources and skills are likely to be able to discharge the responsibilities that collaboration and partnership entail (Murdoch and Abram, 1998). In addition, in certain ways, the continuous rise of experimental and often competitive partnership initiatives undermines the potential for policy and action from within the state, and at the same time achieves precious little in terms of establishing an effective alternative service delivery system (Bassett, 1996; Cloke et al., 2000: 113).

Hence, it sometimes seems odd to ask for genuine collaboration between those in power and those who delegated this power. Whereas collaboration is important for every nation, it may also contradict the natural instinct of governments and rulers to govern and rule with no "disruptions." In many respects, growing citizenry involvement by interest groups, political parties, courts, and other democratic institutions, as well as greater involvement by business firms and the private sector, may cause only bother for politicians in office and state administrators. In the eyes of elected politicians and appointed public officers, too broad an involvement may be perceived as interfering with their administrative work. This situation epitomizes the bureaucratic–democratic paradox.

The freedom of public voice is thus limited and obscured by the need of administrators and politicians to govern. Consequently, the public lacks sufficient freedom of voice and influence. While mechanisms of direct democracy are designed to show such impediments the door, modern representative democracy lets them back in through the window. Representative democracy frequently reduces the push for partnership with governance. Constitutions, legislatures, federal and local structures as well as electoral institutions are in slow but significant decline in many Western societies. They suffer from increasing alienation, distrust, and cynicism among citizens; they encourage passivity and raise barriers that limit individual involvement in state affairs (Berman, 1997; Eisinger, 2000). Thus, as a counter-revolutionary course of action, a growing element in contemporary public administration seeks to revitalize collaboration between citizens and administrative authorities through various strategies (Vigoda, 2002b).

The future of collaboration and its contribution to building strong and stronger nations is thus quite promising. I have stated in the opening chapters and elsewhere (Vigoda, 2002b) that during the last century modern societies have accomplished remarkable achievements in various fields, many of them thanks to an advanced public sector. Yet at the dawn of the new millennium, various new social problems still await the consideration and attention of the state and its administrative system. To overcome these problems and create effective remedies for new state ills, we must increase cooperation and collaboration and share information and knowledge among all parties in society. As this chapter demonstrates, a variety of models and opportunities for collaboration exist. Public administration bears the chief responsibility for making them work effectively and directing them well, if we want our nations to grow stronger.

As suggested by Kramer (1999) and King and Stivers (1998), building relationships among citizens, administrators, and politicians is a long-term and continuous project. For truly democratic government, administrators and citizens must engage each other directly on a regular basis in unrestricted public dialogue, with neither side holding back anything important. Democratic public administration involves an active citizenry and an active administration that uses discretionary authority to foster collaborative work with citizens. In sum, this chapter has proposed that there is something unique about the NPM approach that makes the incorporation of citizenship behavior especially important. Thus, the challenge for governance and new managerialism is a more comprehensive application of this valuable knowledge in public administration strategies.

Chapter 7

Strong Nations and Innovation in the Public Sector[1]

Public sector innovation and reconciliation of the bureaucratic-democratic paradox

Another potential remedy for the bureaucracy-democracy paradox and other pandemics of governability in the modern age is a continuous search for creativity and innovation in public sector organizations and among citizens. The concepts of "innovation" and "bureaucracy" seem to be almost mutually exclusive. Much of the criticism of bureaucracy is that it does not suffer innovation gladly. Bureaucracies of various types and in many cultures are more comfortable with conservative work patterns. They tend to follow strict rules and methods that have proven to work reasonably in the past and are reluctant to replace them with new, unconventional techniques and ideas that may seem risky or complicated. While this cautious attitude is true for almost every organization, bureaucracies need to overcome another hurdle on the road to effective renewal. This barrier is the mindset of public officials as policy makers and citizens as end-users. For many years, bureaucracies did not need to compete in the free market arena, and therefore no real pressure was put on them to update their services and become involved in the "reinvention game" (Thompson and Ingraham, 1996). Competition, which is the leading motivator for innovation in the private sector and in a free-market society, was perceived as less significant for old style bureaucracies. In addition, changes were stymied by the reluctance of the public sector leadership to become involved in extensive innovative projects.

Similarly, innovation is perceived as an engine for modernization. It increases competitiveness in large companies, smaller organizations, and even non-governmental organizations such as VNPOs (voluntary and not-for-profit organizations) by making them more flexible and responsive to market needs. However, innovation and bureaucracy seem to make an odd couple (Borins, 2001). In fact, many of the values I associate with bureaucracy – hierarchy, specialization, and impersonality – stand in sharp contrast to the flexibility, adaptability, creativity, and risk taking I associate with innovation in modern organizations. Nonetheless,

---

1 Some sections in this chapter are based on E. Vigoda-Gadot, N. Schwabski, A. Shoham, and A. Ruvio, "Public sector innovation for the managerial and the post-managerial era: Promises and realities in a globalizing public administration," *International Public Management Journal* (2005).

organizational innovation lies within the very fabric of modern societies. The development and improvement of public agencies is largely inspired by the willingness to make important changes at the right time and place (Rogers, 1983). Just as the private sector has recognized innovation as the driving force behind remaining competitive, so too, public sector organizations must realize that only through innovation can they continue to grow and develop.

Hence, it is quite surprisingly to find that the topic of innovation has played only a minor role in the discussion about the renewal of public administration. Moreover, the vast body of knowledge about innovation, entrepreneurship, and pro-activeness in business management has never been used extensively in public management. Thus, the prime goal of this chapter is to suggest a broader understanding for the study of innovation in modern bureaucracies and to point to some empirical efforts that may accelerate post public-managerial reforms. I believe that innovation in public administration is vital for building strong nations in a globalizing world.

After reviewing the current status of research in this arena, I will argue that innovation should be treated as another key element of the New Public Management doctrine and the reinventing government paradigm (Berry, 1994; Hood, 1991; Pollitt and Bouckaert, 2000). While theories about private sector innovation are extensive and well established, the same knowledge is not always transferred (or transferable) to modern bureaucracies. While in recent decades innovation has received some attention in public administration and public policy literature, it has not been fully integrated with the NPM approach. Therefore, its impact on current reforms is still marginal.

Our logic is based on the system-approach to organizations and its integration with political theories of bureaucracies, as well as with business approaches for managing these work sites (Damanpour, 1991). I will also present a detailed model of innovation in the public sector that builds on three elements: (a) conventional knowledge about public sector innovation and its characteristics, (b) antecedents of and preconditions to public sector innovation, and (c) consequences of innovation as previously encountered in the private business arena. In many ways, our strategy follows the call for "reinventing government" (Osborne and Gaebler, 1992) and the impressive efforts to reform the public sector that have been undertaken in the United States and across the globe using a business-oriented theory and methods. The chapter also analyzes current trends in NPM thinking in an attempt to pinpoint where new frontiers in this realm may arise. I argue that a more solid, systematic, and empirically oriented understanding of innovation can be used to reform our governmental structures and administrative processes, and by so doing, revitalize modern bureaucracies, communities, and societies.

Defining innovation in the dominion of democracy and bureaucracy

Rogers (1983: 11) defines innovation as "an idea, practice, or object that is perceived as new by an individual or another unit of adoption." In the context of nations, governments, and bureaucracies he further cites Benjamin Franklin (1781) who claimed that "to get the bad customs of a country changed and new ones, though better, introduced, it is necessary first to remove the prejudices of the people, enlighten their ignorance, and convince them that their interests will be promoted by the proposed changes; and this is not the work of a day."

In fact, most writings on the topic assume that innovation is by definition good and that increased innovation is better for organizations and society (Kimberly, 1981). Consequently, managers and politicians are usually urged to promote innovation in any possible way. However, other views dispute this assumption, arguing that some innovations have harmful effects that negate whatever benefits they bring. Bureaucrats usually warn against the "bad side of innovation" and prefer to maintain "tried but true" managerial mechanisms, tools, and processes. Indeed, the same innovation may be suitable for one adopter in one situation or arena, but unsuitable for another in a different situation or arena (Rogers, 1983) and many innovations become harmful only with the passage of time (Abrahamson, 1991; Kimberly and de Pouvourville, 1993). Thus, it is necessary to examine innovations in the proper environmental context, cultural landscape, and over a period of time. Moreover, the emergence of an *innovative idea* may differ substantially from the complete *innovative process*.

The evolution of a creative idea into a practical organizational change is usually classified as an *innovative process*. The ideal type of innovative process is characterized by the strong motivation of individuals, groups, and organizations to acquire new information and increase their sources of knowledge about a relevant problem in order to stabilize a turbulent social system. It also involves conceptual openness, pragmatism, and practical methods that can turn a promising idea into an ongoing productive change. Nonetheless, there are many valuable ideas, promising reforms, and change-seeking actions in public administration that fail to have any level of success. When such a process pits the "public good" against the conflicting interests of political players, the social cost of this unsuccessful innovation exceeds one's wildest imagination. Putting it other way, when we compare the consequences of ineffective innovation processes in the public sector with other ineffective innovations in the private sector, the costs of the former seem to exceed those of the latter.

Yet, what are the reasons for such failures? Can we provide reasonable explanations for the various shortcomings of public policy and management that stymied innovation when all the signs clearly indicated the desire for change? What are the theoretical tools that can enhance such understanding? Can these explanations contribute to better practical innovative dynamics for bureaucracies in the future? These questions are of the utmost importance for the field.

Analyzing innovation in the face of past bureaucratic experiences

Innovative ideas and policies in the public domain face a complex set of barriers and obstacles. Some examples may provide a clearer picture. The first, a relatively simple one, was presented by Rogers (1983), who referred to it as a classic example of public administration and policy. A lack of adaptability to clients' needs caused the failure of a two-year water-boiling campaign conducted in a Peruvian village. This campaign was aimed at creating a more hygienic environment and reducing the number of illnesses and diseases among the population. From the viewpoint of the public health agency, the task was simple. However, the results were very poor due to a lack of understanding about critical cultural factors. The villagers' local tradition links hot foods with illness. According to the village norms, water-boiling was used only to help the sick and the less able. The innovation agents complied with public organization procedures and routines, but their evaluation of the problem failed to take culture into account. In this illustration, cultural factors prevailed over the innovative process simply because the latter was not flexible. A rigid bureaucratic model of policy implementation was born to fail.

Other illustrations are even more explicit. Hobby (1985) shows how nearly two decades were needed to bring one of the most important discoveries of mankind, penicillin, to a successive finale. Penicillin was discovered in 1928 by Alexander Fleming, but it took until 1946 for it to become available for widespread clinical use. Beyond the influence on public health, can anyone imagine the loss in benefits for science, technology, and public health during these years? Historians, as well as public administration scientists agree today that much of this delay was due to the negativity of the scientific community whose skepticism and unwillingness to accept a major innovation hindered the widespread dissemination of this lifesaving drug. Obviously, a lack of adaptability to the environment and an over-reliance on bureaucratic tradition impeded a top priority innovation. A paradigmatic revolution (Kuhn, 1962), this time in the field of medicine, was delayed once more, with vast human and social consequences.

Another interesting example of innovation from the field of public health was the AIDS problem in the 1980s. Rogers (1991) analyzes this issue using the agenda-setting perspective and mass media model according to which an innovation process must diffuse over time. The innovation must diffuse, cross a socio-political firewall, and gain public recognition before finally resulting in a public policy that works. In this case, relative success in controlling AIDS was achieved, but not before a large population was exposed to excessive risks. The first published scientific account of a mysterious new disease was on 5 June 1981 (Centers for Disease Control, 1981). While the information about the disease was not complete, a relative consensus existed among experts that it was carried in the blood and could be transferred by it. However, it took four more years for the issue to receive major coverage by the American media, coverage that was prompted by the hospitalization and death of the movie star, Rock Hudson, from AIDS (July to October 1985). It was not until 4 February 1987 that a federal health official recommended widespread blood testing including mandatory testing for some cases (for example, all applicants for marriage licenses and everyone who was hospitalized). Again, conservatism, complaisance with current knowledge, and unresponsive bureaucratic mechanisms postponed vital measures that could have saved human lives.

Pandemics of innovation in the public sector

According to Rogers (1991), the core problem of innovation is, therefore, not creativity. Many good ideas are delayed or vanish due to their lack of adjustment to the environment. When public administration agencies are involved, bureaucracy and red tape become a barrier to innovation. Bureaucracy relies on old organizational models (tradition, vertical communication channels, compliance, order and control) rather than on new ones that represent creativity, commitment, the mixed flow of communication, autonomy, and responsibility. Successful innovation is self-defeated when grounded in the classic bureaucratic model (Golembiewski and Vigoda, 2000). Similarly, fostering innovation in public management requires the engagement of counter-bureaucratic activities to overcome traditional conservatism. As the next two sections illustrate, a system-based approach and new managerial thinking may provide the right tools with which to overcome such barriers.

The examples above of innovative processes illustrate the powerful conflicts between the "old" and the "new." The challenge of creating successful innovation in any organization, despite and regardless of many barriers, is immense. Public organizations, where wider social considerations are also involved, face even more complex tasks. Many obstacles must be removed before a creative idea realizes its full potential. Among these obstacles scholars emphasize cultural differences and red tape as the most significant and powerful ones (e.g., Kimberly and de Pouvourville, 1993). Individuals and organizations tend to oppose rapid changes that contradict their cultural orientations. In a public sector sphere, where the tradition of past knowledge, experience, and conservative institutional solutions strongly influence managers' decisions, such resistance to creativity and change is widespread.

Beyond such cultural barriers, bureaucracies are much less amenable to transformation and to innovation due to their complicated and inflexible organizational design and increasing red tape. The internal structure of classic public organizations is based on vertical communication channels that are ineffective, dogmatic decision-making mechanisms, and other rigid constructs that restrain the innovative process (Golembiewski and Vigoda, 2000). Therefore, the classic version of public administration is frequently incompatible with innovations.

Much support for these arguments can be found in a series of works by Borins (1998; 2000a; 2000b; 2001). According to his view, the traditional situation in the public sector prevents these bodies from becoming more innovative than they are.

A handful of reasons are presented to support this claim. For example, innovations developed by public servants are generally government property, public sector organizations are funded by legislative appropriations, there are no venture capitalists to fund public management innovations, there is no shared ownership, and the salary system is fixed with minimal linkage between productivity or innovation and compensation. Moreover, the consequences of unsuccessful innovations are grave. The level of criticism, by the media and by the political opposition, toward the government's failure to implement innovations is high. All of these reasons encourage a static bureaucracy that is much less innovative than similar organizations in the private sector.

The innovation process in public administration: Searching for remedies in the evolving system-based approach

One way of breaking through conservative views towards innovation in the public sector is by following a system-based approach. Figures 7.1 and 7.2 provide a general understanding of this approach not only in the broad context of organizations, but also in the classic public administration arena. This line of thinking has proved useful in studies of innovation in the business arena, and it coheres well with recent trends in NPM and neo-managerialsim in state agencies (Terry, 1998). Recently, Borins (2001) identified several criteria for successful innovations in the public sector and specifically recommended the system approach as a useful mechanism for studying the field (p. 312).

The system-based approach as presented in Figure 7.1 consists of three essential elements and a supplementary control one. The first three elements are (a) conventional knowledge about innovation, its characteristics and transformation, (b) antecedents of and preconditions to innovation, and (c) consequences of innovation as previously encountered in the private business arena. The additional element is feedback, learning, and innovation adjustment. In our globalizing and learning-oriented society, bureaucracies must improve the feedback element, as

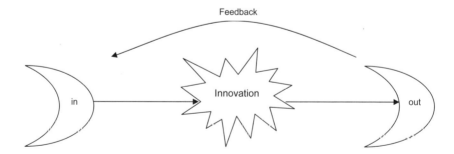

Figure 7.1   Basic system-approach to innovation

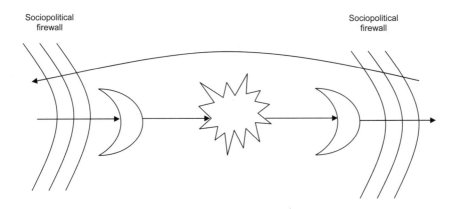

Figure 7.2   Innovation in classic public administration

it lays the groundwork for multilevel cooperation, cross-sectoral collaboration, cultural vitalization, and a change of attitude by leaders, innovators, and entrepreneurial public officials, and citizens alike.

Innovation in public administration: Characteristics and transformation

Figure 7.2 suggests that the implementation of the general system model of innovation in classic public administration involves breaking through serious socio-political firewalls. For many years, public sector agencies have not looked beyond policy problems of the past and have failed to predict future developments and the need to transition in a rapidly changing environment. Rogers (1983) suggested that the social and political barriers these agencies faced were overwhelming and led to the early collapse of any innovative effort. These barriers are comprised of old values and perceptions, along with a reliance on conservative managerial tools, methods, and political rules that appear to have produced reasonable outcomes in the past. In support of this view, a recent study by Peled (2001) defined public innovation as "a political process that propels organizations to launch a significant new public project that alters rules, roles, procedures, and structures that are related to the communication and exchange of information within the organization and between the organization and its surrounding environment" (p. 189). Thus, the innovation process in modern public domains is complex, as it is rooted in political decisions and considerations that strengthen the firewall against pro-activeness and creativity and smother promising potential services.

Figure 7.3 further suggests that modern societies need to adjust to multiple sources and preconditions for innovations as well as to their manifold consequences. A look into the world of modern innovations will reveal a multivariate picture based on antecedents to and outcomes of innovation, its multilevel analysis (individual, group, organizational, or inter-organizational), stages of innovations,

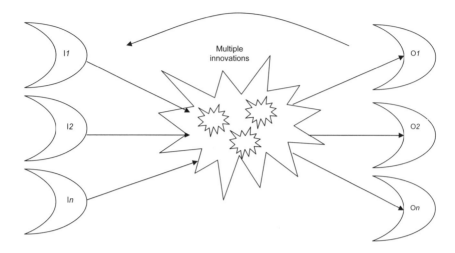

Figure 7.3   Innovation in the modern business arena

Notes: I1-n – Information generation and dissemination, responsiveness, and organizational learning capacity, internal communication, organizational conflict and politics, organizational structure, formalization, centralization and participation in decision-making, reward system, managers' attitudes towards change, top managers' support and vision.

O1-n – Individual factors (e.g., organizational commitment, esprit de corps, job satisfaction, job stress and burnout) and organizational/policy factors (e.g., organizational performance, policy outputs and outcomes, financial stability).

characteristics of innovators, types of innovations, and disciplinary focus of analysis (Peled, 2001). The theory of innovation in the business sector has contributed useful knowledge in this regard. Today, this theory covers a variety of possible antecedents and outcomes that are best reflected in the system-based model (i.e., Damanpour, 1991; Stewart and Roth, 2001). In the next sections, I argue for the solidity of the system-based model and its applicability to public domains. Our rationale is rooted in contemporary private sector knowledge that paved the way for the current NPM doctrine.

Antecedents to innovation in the public sector

The tradition in the business sciences views information management as the first determinant of innovativeness. Specifically, the theory deals with information generation, information dissemination, organizational responsiveness, and organizational learning (Deshpande, Farley, and Webster, 1997; Kohli and Jaworski, 1990; Narver and Slater, 1990). Information generation is defined as "organization-wide generation of market intelligence pertaining to present and future customer needs" (Jaworski and Kohli, 1993: 54). In the public sector domain, citizens-as-customers can be external or internal users of a given service. Information dissemination is the diffusion of intelligence across departments and individuals. Such dissemination refers to information's move through the organization with the support of managerial leadership (Borins, 2002). The third facet requires that organizations be responsive to the information generated and disseminated, where responsiveness is defined as two sets of activities: design (using information to develop plans) and implementation (executing the plans). Moreover, in light of the cultural firewall (Rogers, 1983, 1991), various studies suggest that the link between information management and organizational performance is not country-specific and should be studied in models that look at policy learning in a globalizing public sector, beyond cultures and regions (Levi-Faur and Vigoda-Gadot, 2004a, 2004b). Such learning is enhanced by an organization-wide shared interpretation of the acquired and disseminated information (Argyris, 1977; Senge, 1990). Consequently, the way organizations manage information can affect learning, and, through it, innovativeness (Slater and Narver, 1995).

Another important construct that may serve as an antecedent to innovation in the public sector is intra-organizational conflicts and politics. Organizational politics reflects both the level of conflicts and the use of power by organizational members in their efforts to influence others and secure interests, or, alternatively, to avoid negative outcomes within the organization (Vigoda-Gadot, 2003c). Studies that focused on workplace politics and conflicts (i.e., Cropanzano et al., 1997; Ferris, Russ, and Fandt, 1989; Kipnis et al., 1980) suggested that it strongly reflects fairness and justice in the organization. The findings of these studies supported the notion that politics, fairness, and justice have substantial negative impacts on organizational climate and outcomes (e.g., Ferris and Kacmar 1992; Folger et al., 1992; Kacmar and Ferris 1991; Vigoda, 2000b, 2000c, 2001). As such, organizational politics may potentially reduce innovativeness and creativity in any organization, including those of the public sector (Golembiewski and Vigoda, 2000). Moreover, inter-personal or inter-departmental communications may also be harmed by higher levels of conflict and politics in the organization. Public sector agencies are exposed to more conflicts and politics mainly due to the nexus between the professional cadre and the political cadre that too often have diverging interests and visions (Vigoda-Gadot and Kapun, 2005a). This antipathy may result in reduced information dissemination, lower levels of responsiveness to citizens' needs and demands (Ruekert and Walker, 1987), and decreased organizational innovativeness (Jaworski and Kohli, 1993).

Antecedents to innovation in the public sector must also look at the structure of the bureaucracy, especially at formalization, centralization, and participation in decision-making. The first two facets are expected to hinder innovativeness (Damanpour, 1991; Slater and Narver, 1995). Formalization and centralization conspire to reduce market orientation and, through it, to reduce innovativeness (e.g., Deshpande and Zaltman, 1982). In contrast, employees' participation in decision-making should affect public sector innovativeness positively. According to Muczyk and Reinmann (1987), high levels of employee participation in decision-making are typical for directive and permissive democratic leadership behavior, which combines participatory management with high and low levels of leadership direction, respectively. Permissive democratic leadership relates to innovativeness in that "it is appropriate when participation has informational and motivational value, when time permits group decision-making, when the employee group is capable of improving decision quality ..." (Dunham and Pierce, 1989: 560). These conditions appear to characterize the innovation context. Thus, participatory decision-making and employee empowerment should enhance innovation in modern bureaucracies, as it does in the business sector. Finally, in general, organizational reward systems should be tied to the desired end goal of the organization and to efforts exerted by public employees. Specifically, rewarding desirable organizational innovativeness should motivate public employees to become more innovative and creative (Selnes et. al., 1996).

Beyond these factors, top public management also plays an important role in instituting any organizational change (Moon, 1999). Management's attitude towards change and their willingness to take risks is one such facet that may affect innovativeness. The risk-adverse mindset that is so typical of many state-controlled agencies might reduce innovativeness, whereas a risk-oriented one might enhance it (Damanpour, 1991; Rose and Shoham, 2002; Shoham and Rose, 2001). In addition, top management's support has been identified as critical to the success of innovations (e.g., Jaworski and Kohli, 1993; Kohli and Jaworski, 1990; Selnes et al., 1996; Webster, 1988). The stronger the top managers' support, the better the chance that the innovation will be adopted. Finally, top management's vision in the public sector should stress innovativeness in order to make its importance apparent to all employees. Various studies in public administration have illustrated the importance of managerial vision and entrepreneurship in setting a clear policy strategy and implementing long range planning (Berry, 1994; Evans, 1996; Moon, 1999; Thompson and Ingraham, 1996). Just recently this view has been reiterated following the September 11th events in New York and Pennsylvania (Sloan, 2002).

Innovation and its consequences in the public sector

Compared to the vast number of theoretical models and empirical research on the antecedents of innovativeness in and around the public sector, the research on its consequences is relevantly scarce. Most of the existing research on this theme has focused on the effect of innovativeness and innovation adaptation on organizational performance (e.g., Frambach and Schillewaert, 2002). Research conducted from this perspective saw public sector innovation and innovativeness as an organizational strategy aimed at enhancing the organization's competitive advantage and performance. For example, Miles et al. (1978) have suggested that organization prospectors were conceptualized as having high levels of innovativeness, creativity, and aggressiveness. Thus, two types of outcomes are relevant for the public sector – the individual and the organizational.

The first type is largely behavioral and relies on attitudinal variables such as organizational commitment, esprit-de-corps, job satisfaction, job burnout, and other situational factors (i.e., Rose and Shoham, 2002; Shoham and Rose, 2001). As part of this individual level analysis, Jaworski and Kohli (1993) examined esprit-de-corps and organizational commitment as consequences of a competitive market orientation that gives rise to a unifying focus and vision, resulting in a sense of mission, belonging, and commitment to the organization or the public agency (Kohli and Jaworski, 1990). By extension, public sector innovativeness may also benefit esprit-de-corps and organizational commitment, as it makes modern public work sites more challenging and appealing to highly qualified staff and public servants. Moreover, innovation may lead to improved work conditions and benefits for public employees, either socially or psychologically. Public agencies that innovate may increase the levels of job satisfaction among employees and reduce their emotional exhaustion and burnout (Grandey, 2003). On the organizational/ policy level, studies have focused on organizational outputs and outcomes as reflected in their performance. Studies have shown that innovativeness enhances both innovation performance and the general performance or policy success of the organization (e.g., Deshpande, Farley, and Webster, 1997; Jaworski and Kohli, 1993; Narver, Jacobson, and Slater, 1993; Narver and Slater, 1990; Pelham and Wilson, 1996; Selnes et al., 1996).

Finally, as Figure 7.4 suggests, modern public agencies need to handle various types of innovative ideas and processes on a multi-level scale (for example, at the level of the individual, the unit, and the entire organization) simultaneously.

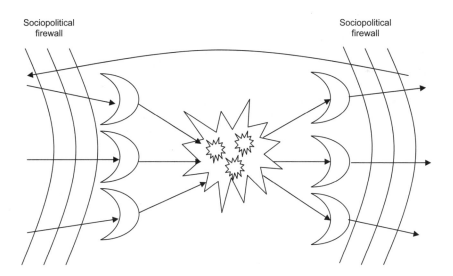

Figure 7.4   Innovation in New Public Management

Notes: The sociopolitical firewall – Intra- and extra-organizational culture (basic assumptions, norms, and values); national political agenda, socialization, technological development.

Multiple antecedents as presented above are influential as well, but they also need to break through a serious socio-political firewall (Rogers, 1983). This firewall is based on intra and extra organizational culture and political conditions. It draws its substance from the unwritten rules of bureaucratic culture, its basic assumptions, norms, values, and artifacts (Schein, 1985). Moreover, there are actually multiple "firewalls" and barriers in the shape of various interest groups, citizens as customers, third sector organizations, political parties, and the media (Dye, 1995). Therefore, innovation in the present managerial era of the public sector is far more complex than it was in the classical era of public administration. As will be explained hereafter, the future evolution of innovation in light of a maturing managerial and post-managerial vision is even more challenging.

Public sector innovation in light of managerial and post-managerial visions

Moving towards a globalizing world may create new realities and rules for innovation in the public sector (Carayannis and Gonzalez, 2003; Shavinina, 2003). As suggested in Figure 7.5, the single-nation system-based approach is rapidly changing into a global system-based movement where multiple innovations from multiple sources are simultaneously handled by public sector agencies around the globe (Farazmand, 1999).

In such a system there is no escape from higher levels of organizational learning, policy experience sharing, collaboration, and emulation of the best practices in management that have proved useful in other national locations. This trend of neo-managerialsim (Terry, 1998) or post-managerialism of public sector innovation is based on several studies. For example, Borins (2001) suggested the development of a holistic theory of innovation, one that consists of the following elements: (1) a higher level of inter-organization cooperation, (2) the creation of multiple services for individuals, (3) a re-engineering process, (4) the incorporation of information technology, and (5) the development of alternative service delivery mechanisms such as contracting out to business firms or partnering with the third sector. In fact, all these recommendations strongly echo the suggestions made by other studies in the context of New Public Management (i.e., Hood, 1991; Lyne, 1998; Pollitt and Bouckaert, 2000). They also adhere with the call for better collaboration among all three sectors as suggested by Vigoda-Gadot (2003a). Thus, in the post-managerial era, the meaning of innovation is somewhat different than the established one. In a globalizing world, policy renewal and other public sector innovations become even more significant because they can easily be imitated or emulated by bureaucracies in other countries. There is no need to "reinvent the wheel" in order to solve policy and managerial problems, as plenty of good ideas are available. The urgent need, however, is to improve the innovation process and its implementation. Under these new "rules of the game," the experience of other nations or organizations becomes of prime importance. The remaining but crucial obstacle is tailoring the style of the innovation to fit a specific cultural environment.

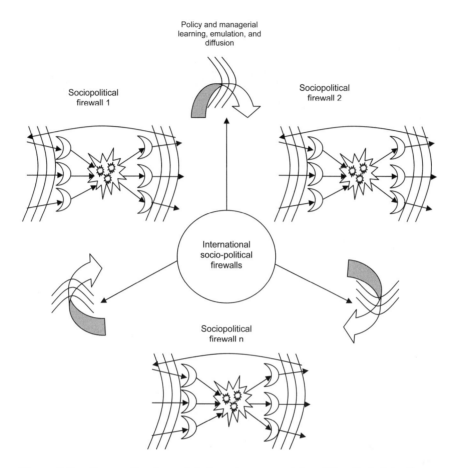

Figure 7.5   Innovation in a global post-managerial public administration

Notes: International sociopolitical firewalls – Cross-cultural barriers, international and foreign policy, global political agenda, globalization, cross-national knowledge diffusion.

As suggested in Table 7.1, over the years the evolution of the innovation process has changed across sectors and paradigms. The private sector has traditionally been the source of innovative ideas, and even today continues to facilitate the introduction of many new concepts and ideas (Model/Figures 7.1 and 7.3). However, the public sector, which has become more receptive to innovation in recent decades, has also made serious progress along the continuum. In moving from a classic bureaucratic structure (Model/Figure 7.2), through new managerial reforms (Model/Figure 4), towards a post-managerial era (Model/Figure 7.5), the literature has identified at least ten core questions about innovation that merit our attention.

Table 7.1   An evolutionary analysis of innovation in public administration: **Towards building strong nations**

Essential questions \ Evolution	The private sector origins	Classic public administration canons	New Public Management doctrine	Post-managerial Avenues: Towards building strong nations
Q1. What is innovation?	New ways to create economic added value	A threat to old reliable mechanisms	New ways to respond to citizens as clients and produce public goods	New ways to create social and psychological well-being, economic surpluses and political stability combined
Q2. Why do I need innovation?	Economic progress	Do I need it at all?	Improving managerial qualities in state owned bureaucracies to stabilize the welfare state	A good combination of managerial, social and democratic values
Q3. What are the disciplinary origins of innovation?	Economic and Business/ Engineering, Marketing	Engineering/Law/Political Sciences	Organizational and Managerial Sciences/Economics and Business/	A holistic view: Organizational and Managerial Sciences/ Political Sciences/Social Welfare/Information and Technology Systems
Q4. What are the primary goals of innovation?	Company profit, improved competitive skills	Maintaining the power of bureaucracy and its centrality in policy making and implementing processes	Improving the operative power of bureaucracy through better managerial skills and the triumph of professionalism over politization	Transforming the cultural sphere of public organizations, increasing global policy and management learning and emulation
Q5. Who are the key beneficiaries of innovation?	Company owners and clients	The private sector and social elites	Citizens as clients/customers	Citizens as owners and the global bank of policy and managerial knowledge, the community as a whole
Q6. How to portray the flow of innovative ideas?	Mostly bottom-up, initiated by front line employees	Ultimately top-down, and only when innovation serves political interests	First, top-down by professional managers who then empower a bottom-up channel	Top-down, bottom-up, and reliance on extra-organizational sources, learning and emulation processes

Table 7.1 continued   An evolutionary analysis of innovation in public administration: Towards building strong nations

Essential questions	Evolution / The private sector origins	Classic public administration canons	New Public Management doctrine	Post-managerial Avenues: Towards building strong nations
Q7. Primary players in the innovation process?	Mid-range managers and employees	Top managers, if at all	Managers and employees who improve their understanding of the needs of citizens as clients	Managers, employees, and extra-organizational players (i.e., the private sector, the third sector, transnational policy makers and academics)
Q8. How to achieve innovation?	Increased job autonomy, higher level of participation in decision-making, empowerment and entrepreneurial work culture	Almost no need; classic style bureaucracies don't really need innovation and see themselves as islands of stability and conservatism	Intensive contacts with the private sector and improved learning from successful innovators in business firms (PPPs – Public–Private Partnership)	Intensive global contacts with international innovators, benchmarking, learning and emulation of policy programs
Q9. How to evaluate innovation?	Emphasis on output measures and economic-focused assessments	Lack of formal tools and absence of standard criteria	Output and outcome measures and the development of performance indicators (PIs)	Output and outcome measures as well as input and process measures in a comparative international view
Q10. What are the moral justifications for innovation?	Utilitarianism and modernization	Higher standard of living for vast populations and better services for the less-able	Encouraging competition according to liberal ideological economy, increased efficiency and the saving of public money	Global human progress, policy learning, and more equal distribution of knowledge, practices, and goods across nations

Q1: On the meaning of innovation   In modern business management, innovation has always been a matter of competence and has represented new ways to create economic added value (King, 1990). In classic public administration, on the other hand, innovation represented a threat to old, reliable mechanisms that seemed to work reasonably well up to a certain point. In this view, innovation was not a matter of necessity, but more a desire to conform with emerging developments in the business/technological market (Golembiewski and Vigoda, 2000). NPM has changed these rules and identified innovation as an engine to spur reform (Pollitt and Bouckaert, 2000). Innovation was embraced as a tool with which the organization could create new ways to respond to citizens as clients and produce higher quality public goods (Osborne and Gaebler, 1992). It is expected that in public administration of the post-managerial era, innovation will explore new ways to create social and psychological well-being, along with a political stability that goes beyond mere economic surpluses.

Q2: On the need for innovation   The private sector seeks innovation as a basic condition for economic progress. According to this view, innovation is required in order to improve organizational performance and marketing orientations (Narver et al., 1993; Slater and Narver, 1994). In the face of this practical orientation, the classic public sector is dubious about the need for innovation, perhaps due to its potential turbulent impact and its image as a threat to administrative and political stability. However, in the new managerial era innovation is perceived as improving managerial quality in state owned bureaucracies and as exerting a stabilizing influence on the welfare state (Thompson and Ingraham, 1996). Looking towards post-managerialism in public administration, innovation, both in its individual and organizational/policy form, is expected to work on two additional levels – the managerial and the social. Hence, it should find better ways to combine new managerial tools and processes with the socio-democratic ethos and with the new, pro-citizen orientation of state agencies (Terry, 1998).

Q3: On the disciplinary origins of innovation   Historically, the private sector has based its knowledge about innovation on both the engineering sciences that have produced sophisticated technologies and the softer sciences such as economics, business management, and marketing that have brought managerial tools such as new approaches to marketing and financing processes to the fore (Shavinina, 2003). Generally speaking, classic public administration emulated the approaches of these latter disciplines when it came to areas such as legal requirements, regulatory issues, and the political implications of innovation, imitating scientific innovations only when necessary. However, New Public Management has again focused on the organizational and managerial sciences, on knowledge about organizational psychology, and on the economic, cost benefits of innovation (Borins, 1998, 2000a, 2000b). In the post-managerial era, innovation is also expected to be valued for its direct contribution to political institutions, to social and psychological well-being, and to increased avenues of access to public sector agencies (for example, e-governance and innovative ways to empower citizens and increase their democratic involvement in nation building). Much more attention is thus expected to be given to society-supported technology via sophisticated information systems that learn how to communicate with each other (Peled, 2001).

Q4: On the primary goals of innovation In the private sector, innovation is a desirable goal because it boosts the firm's profits and lays the groundwork for improving the competitive skills of individuals, groups, and the larger organizational machinery. In classic bureaucracies the goals of innovation, if any, are vague and torn between a general will to "do things better than before" and the stronger institutional paradigm of safeguarding the existing governmental structure and tradition. The general goal of classic public administration is to maintain the power of the bureaucracy and its centrality in the policy making and implementing processes. However, according to the NPM doctrine, innovation is perceived as a goal in and of itself that can lead to improving the operation of the bureaucracy through better managerial skills and the triumph of professionalism over politization (Hood, 1991). Moving towards post-managerialism brings with it additional goals such as transforming the cultural sphere of public organizations to become more supportive of grass-roots ideas, making innovation a value and norm that each public servant needs to seek in his/her career, and most importantly, developing a policy of global organizational learning and collaboration with other social players such as citizens' groups or third sector parties that contributes to the management learning and emulation dynamics (Levi-Faur and Vigoda-Gadot, 2004a, 2004b).

Q5: On the core benefits of innovation In the private sector, the key beneficiaries of an innovative idea are first, the company owners and secondarily, other clients. The rigid structure of classic bureaucracies views innovation as primarily beneficial to other players in the free market, namely to private sector firms. Classic public administration is suspicious of new innovations that may challenge the status quo. Innovations are feared because they bring with them changes in mindsets that may endanger bureaucrats' positions, power, and authority, and threaten "good old" working arrangements (Golembiewski and Vigoda, 2000). Thus, the private sector and specific social elites are perceived as potentially benefiting the most from new innovations, leaving ordinary citizens to struggle with old problems. The NPM approach, however, calls specifically for the movement towards such reforms of re-inventing government and reforming its basic apparatus and nature. According to the NPM approach, innovation is desirable because it has the power to improve services to citizens as clients or customers. Innovation is seen as an "engine" for development; its energy should be used in the same way it is used in the business sector (Lynn, 1998). Thus, according to a future post-managerial view, it is societies and communities, not merely individual citizens or citizens' groups, that will reap the rewards of innovation (Evans, 1996; Rogers, 1983). Innovation should be developed and diffused to citizens as the owners of public services and contributed to a global bank of policy and managerial knowledge (Farazmand, 1999).

Q6: On the flow of innovative ideas   The private sector generally sees innovation as a bottom-up phenomenon, rooted in the experience of front line employees. The quality circles method or other participatory initiatives in organizational behavior call for good, new ideas to come from front line employees, those who face the core problems and dilemmas of the organization (King, 1990). However, classic public administration treats innovation as a top-down process. Moreover, innovation is viewed as useful only in cases where it serves political interests. As the basic assumption is that innovation should be treated with caution and a great deal of skepticism, the old bureaucrats try to avoid it, if possible. Innovations will break through firewalls only when politicians and the administrative leadership have a direct interest in allowing them to grow (Borins, 2002). Alternatively, the NPM approach suggests that useful innovations are first top-down grounded. Professional managers must fuel them with the creativity and experience gained in the private sector. Only then can managers empower a bottom-up channel and offer a certain level of participation to other employees. Finally, as the post-managerial approach suggests, innovations are top-down and bottom-up at the same time. Moreover, they must rely on extra-organizational sources, emulating innovations successfully introduced in other societies, cultures, and nations (Schein, 1985; Selnes et al., 1996). Such replications must be tailored to the specific environment and not blindly imitated, as one innovation may be useful for one arena but not necessarily to the other (the contingency theory).

Q7: On primary players in the innovation process   The private sector views midrange managers and employees as those who represent the primary players in the innovative process. They are the source of most of these initiatives and are responsible for the diffusion process to other internal and external clients (Scott and Bruce, 1994). The classic bureaucratic approach, however, seeks no prime players in the innovation process and is ready to hand such responsibility, if at all, to top managers who can control the process in the most efficient manner. NPM sees both managers and employees as primary players in the innovation process and considers them as equal partners whose main task is to increase their understanding of the needs of citizens as clients. The post-managerial approach adds extra-organizational components to this list of players, components such as the private sector, the third sector, transnational policy makers, and academics who serve as the professional cadre from which state agencies can learn and grow (Farazmand, 1999).

Q8: On the way to achieve innovation   The business sector view is that innovation can be enhanced by increased job autonomy, a higher level of participation in decision-making, empowerment, and an entrepreneurial work culture (Kimberly, 1981; Kimberly and de Pouvourville, 1993). All of these factors contribute to a less formal and a more nurturing environment in which good ideas can thrive and a climate of renewal can flourish. Sharply contrasting with this view, classic public administration is frequently indifferent about the way to achieve innovation. Classic bureaucracies regard innovation as insignificant at best and time consuming and resource depleting at worst. This view considers bureaucracies as islands of stability and conservatism where the status quo should be maintained. This view leads to no substantive strategy by which innovation is promoted. However, the NPM approach believes that innovation is a necessity and that the best way to encourage it is by intensive contacts with other partners in the socio-political realm. Major partners are the private sector and the third sector, both of whom have benefited from learning about successful innovators in business firms (PPPs – Public–Private Partnerships) and in other voluntary and not-for-profit agencies (VNPO). Finally, according to the post-managerial view, the best way to achieve innovation is by intensive global contacts with international innovators, benchmarking, learning about and emulation of policy programs that have proved useful in other places (Vigoda-Gadot et al., 2005b).

Q9: On the way to evaluate innovation The private sector puts a great deal of emphasis on output measures and economic-focused assessments. Innovation is thus perceived as actions or processes that directly or indirectly contribute to organizational performance, profitability, and position in the market (Lumpkin and Dess, 1996). Standard criteria are encouraged to assess how many good ideas are being translated successfully into attractive outcomes, new products, or stimulating services for a large variety of customers. On the other hand, classic bureaucracies lack formal tools for the evaluation of innovation and suffer from an absence of standard criteria that benchmark creativity and renewal processes. The absence of such measurements may be due to the perception of innovation as threatening the stability of the old administrative order. The NPM approach has a completely different mindset in this area and focuses on output and outcome measures and the development of an impressive arsenal of performance indicators (PIs) that measure how well the bureaucracy is reforming itself (Pollitt and Bouckaert, 2000). In the post-managerial era, output and outcome measures are necessary but not sufficient. They must be accompanied by input and process measures in a comparative international view. That is, the evaluation process of innovation should be done in the light of the existing managerial and non-managerial innovations in other bureaucracies and in the face of the criticism against them.

Q10: On the moral justification for innovation The justification for innovation in the public sector comes from a utilitarian and modernization view. The very basic assumption by private firms is that society and markets are mutually dependent and that moving them forward requires a continuous search for better ways to create added value, for both the marketplace and for nations. Classic public administration, however, has developed no such understanding. It has not adapted to changes in its environment. The political firewall of such bureaucracies is complex and daunting and has stifled innovation (Rogers, 1983). The general theme of these institutions is a search for stability mixed with a suspicious aptitude towards any new policy or idea that could potentially shake commonly accepted wisdom. NPM, on the other hand, emphasizes the mutual responsibility of economics and citizenship in re-inventing government. The moral justification for innovation in modern bureaucracies is the idea that citizens deserve a higher standard of living and that this improvement should diffuse to vast populations who delegate political power to the government (Hood, 1991; Lyne, 1998). The NPM, however, neglects certain moral principles that are at risk when powerful market mechanisms are infused into government thinking. Safety nets for the weaker portions of the population and care for the less able may fall by the wayside when market concerns enter into bureaucratic thought. The encouragement of market forces through competition according to the dictates of a liberal, ideological economy and the quest for greater efficiency and cost saving measures may thus result in a dangerous moral indifference on the part of public administration. Hence, the post-managerial approach is to rely on a "third way" of governance and on a more ambitious, long-term ideology of global human progress, transnational policy learning, and a more equal distribution of knowledge, practices, and goods across nations and societies.

Summary: Building strong nations with innovation in public administration

In their review of innovation research in economics, sociology, and technology management, Gopalakrishnan and Damanpour (1997: 16) argued that "on the most basic level, innovation means 'something new,'" whether it is a new idea, product, method, or service. Thus, innovativeness is perceived in the literature as the adoption of many new ideas, methods, or services, which are its end "products," namely, actual innovations (Subramanian and Nilakanta, 1996). Stated differently, a highly innovative organization is one that adopts many innovations.

This chapter has dealt with the evolution of the fuzzy concept of innovation as a major theme in public administration theory. In addition, it has examined two ways in which the concept of innovation may prove valuable for the discipline. First, I have posited a comprehensive system-based model for the study of innovation. Second, I have tried to integrate this model into a dynamic managerial and post-managerial era, stressing the major roles of governments and citizens alike. As such, I suggest that innovation in modern public administration should be studied based on previous knowledge from the business sector, but also in relation to the evolution and development of the public management doctrine. This approach can make a valuable contribution to what I define as the globalizing public sector (Farazmand, 1999).

According to this view, innovation is a multi-dimensional construct that must break through powerful socio-political "firewalls" in order to take root. Hence, innovation in the current and future public arena must include several elements: (1) higher levels of creativity, (2) political wisdom, (3) risk-taking strategies, (4) tolerance for social differences, and (5) stronger emphasis on organizational responsiveness and adaptability.

Post-managerial creativity

Rosenfeld and Servo (1990: 252) see creativity as "the starting point for any innovation." Creativity can be defined as the generation of a new idea; thus, it serves as a fundamental facet of innovation. In order for creativity to lead to innovations, the idea must transform itself into a new product, technology, process, or service. However, it must be noted that not all new ideas are generated inside the focal organization. Some ideas are generated externally but are adopted by the organization (Damanpour and Gopalakrishnan, 1998). Thus, I extend the concept of creativity to include the adoption of a new idea.

Post-managerial political wisdom

In a study of 15 cases, Gow (1992) investigated the process of innovation in Canadian public agencies. His goal was to better understand the flow of innovative ideas in public administration. His findings indicated that many good, creative ideas were generated by committed public officials, but many of them were blocked due to a lack of political wisdom on the part of both the innovators and the entrepreneurs. In many cases, new ideas penetrated the organization on their own and without pre-existing political pressures to accommodate them. Thus, Gow concluded that despite the fact that the origins of new ideas in public organizations are non-political, many of them fail due to the "socio-political firewall." Various players such as political parties, interest and pressure groups, employee unions, or other interested parties decide to politicize the innovation and stop it in its tracks (Gow, 1992; Peled, 2001). Furthermore, Peled (2001) mentions the "agenda-setting" coalition that can use strong political patrons to put pressure on decision makers from within the organization to adopt a certain idea or creation. This pressure can come from influential individuals who hold formal positions in the public organization or from outsiders who have an external say in the organization, such as social leaders, the media, or the professional voice of academia.

Post-managerial risk-taking strategies

From the organization's perspective, risk is "the extent to which there is uncertainty about whether potential significant and/or disappointing outcomes of decisions will be realized" (Sitkin and Pablo, 1992: 10). It can be argued that the development or adoption of new ideas involves some degree of risk (Lumpkin and Dess, 1996), because there is no guarantee of valuable outcomes. The strategic management literature associates risk with novelty. An idea involving a high level of novelty is associated with a high degree of risk. For example, Stewart and Roth (2001) conducted a meta-analysis of risk propensity differences between entrepreneurs and managers. They reported that, "the risk propensity of entrepreneurs is greater than that of managers" (p. 145). By analogy, because innovativeness is inherently risky, risk-taking should be an important characteristic of high levels of innovation in public administration.

Post-managerial tolerance for social differences

Tolerance for differences allows diversity among members in the public organization to exist and flourish (Scott and Bruce, 1994; Siegel and Kaemmerer, 1978). Such diversity is essential and encourages bottom-up ideas that may generate successful innovations. Intolerant public organizations inhibit innovations by restricting employees to uniform menus of expected behaviors (King, 1990).

Post-managerial responsiveness to citizens and adaptability

This element relies on open-minded policy, learning orientations, and improved organizational connectedness. Alongside its bureaucratic structure, the post-managerial public sector must build close and informal relationships between individuals from different departments or units in the organization (Deshpande and Zaltman, 1982). Several research lines of thought suggest that "connectedness facilitates interaction and exchange of information, as well as the actual utilization of the information" (Jaworski and Kohli, 1993: 56). Thus, by allowing for a flow of information, such informal, cross-individual and cross-departmental communications should enhance public sector innovativeness (Kohli and Jaworski, 1990; Rose and Shoham, 2002; Shoham and Rose, 2001).

Finally, the path to strong and stronger nations builds on the assumption that the public sector, like the private sector, will seek better and more effective innovations in the coming generations. Yet, torn between the promise and the realities of innovation, the task of the public sector will remain more difficult, demanding, and complex. While increased globalization brings with it the spread of knowledge, it also raises socio-political firewalls and a resistance to change that is not confined to a single nation, but is cross-cultural as well. As suggested by Borins (2000a, 2000b), innovation and innovators are creatively solving public-sector problems and are usually pro-active, as they deal with problems before they escalate to crisis proportions. They build support for their ideas and then either cross or bypass the socio-political firewall by using personal tactics of persuasion or accommodation. Thus, I suggest that "innovative bureaucracy" is not necessarily a self-defeating concept. Bridging the gap between the promise and the realities of innovation has never been an easy task. Turning ideals into realities is still a major challenge facing public administration reform now and for the foreseeable future wherever people still have faith in a strong nation.

Chapter 8

Strong Nations and Global Reforms in Public Administration: A New, Borderless Public Policy[1]

Global reforms and reconciliation of the bureaucratic–democratic paradox

To build strong nations, we must engage in active and uncompromising progress towards global reforms in public administration. In making this statement, I do not want the reader to confuse this idea with reforms in the political arena. It is not my intention to discuss political issues such as voting systems, political order, or ideological debates about the nature of the specific state or region. Neither do I want to debate the political structure or the social constraints that permit (or inhibit) a nation from getting to where its people want it to be (and what does this mean, after all?). Instead, I am focusing on administrative reforms whose goal is to improve the life of the individual. The global administrative reforms to which I am referring are those that put the oil in the wheels of the democratic order and reinforce both the foundations of the free liberal world and governability *under* the conditions of a free and open society (Popper, 1991).

Modern societies are going global and in this process are redefining the boundaries between the domestic and the external. In a "shrinking world," policy lessons are increasingly learned on a cross-national basis rather than on specific national experience and are less and less constrained by cultural and geopolitical boundaries. The know-how of other nations is increasingly conceived as essential and relevant for the economic competitiveness of nations and for the welfare of their citizens. Epistemic communities, international organizations, and policy entrepreneurs transfer this know-how to domestic economic, political, and social settings that are often radically different from the original ones in which this knowledge was first learned. The benefits, costs, and implications of these policy transfers are the subject of this chapter. Specialists in public policy, public

---

1 Some sections in this chapter are based on D. Levi-Faur and E. Vigoda-Gadot, "The international transfer and diffusion of policy and management innovations: Some characteristics of a new order in the making," In D. Levi-Faur and E. Vigoda-Gadot, (eds), *International Public Policy and Management: Policy Learning Beyond Regional, Cultural, and Political Boundaries* (New York: Marcel Dekker, 2004), and "New public policy, new policy transfers: some characteristics of a new order in the making," *International Journal of Public Administration* (2006).

administration, and public management have joined together to explore the role of policy transfers in the promotion of more reflective and efficient public policies across the world. In doing so they aim to advance our knowledge about the new conditions of management, administration, and policy in a global world.

What I am trying to capture in this chapter is only partially new. Globalization of knowledge and international policy transfers were discussed in early political science literature. Take, for example, Ernest Barker's classic study of state expansion in Europe between 1660 and 1930. Barker's major attention was concentrated on the particular history of different countries but he was well aware of their interdependence and existence as a "social community:"

> When we consider the history of the Modern State ... we cannot but recognize the debt which all States owe to one another. Each country has developed according to its own genius; and each has produced its own fruit. But each has produced some institution, or some method of public service, which has served as an example to others; and each, in turn, has borrowed from each. There has been a rivalry of methods, but it has not been unfriendly; one country has studied, adopted, or tried to improve the methods of another; and all have combined, however unconsciously, to promote the growth of a common Europe standard of administration and public service (Barker, 1944: 93).

So policy transfers are an old phenomenon; yet what makes our era unique is the downsizing of geographical distance in general and national borders in particular, hence the increase in the quantity and arguably the quality of these policy transfers. I are more exposed than my predecessors to international ideas, and therefore, arguably, may learn more and might be able to go through the learning process with a somewhat better grip on the difficulties of innovating based on the experience of others. The issues at stake are increasingly documented and reflected in the literature of the social sciences at large and of organizational studies, law, politics, sociology, social psychology, and economics in particular (Vigoda, 2002c, 2003a). In all these disciplines, the issues discussed are subject to extensive scholarly debate. On one side stand the proponents of globalization, who advocate cross-national policy learning (and convergence) and believe it holds great promise for the advancement of management techniques, administrative controls, and policy effectiveness. On the other side are globalization's critics, who identify emulation, manipulation, and coercion as the major forces behind the changes that are widely evident across countries and policy spheres.

This debate, then, touches first on the meaning and origins of policy learning, on the necessary and sufficient conditions that propel it, on the autonomy and motives of the agents that promote it, and on the institutional and other constraints on the implementation of imported ideas in different contexts. We must also consider the question of the effects of transfer, and here I explore the suggestion that the dramatic expansion of policy transfers documented in this volume and in numerous others shapes a "new public policy." Perhaps the clearest statement to that effect was made by Ginadomenico Majone, who suggested that far-reaching ideological, political, and economic changes begun in the late 1970s brought about *"the transformations of the process and substance of policy making"* (Majone, 1996: 611). I hope that this volume, which looks at public policy beyond the nation state (though not without it), will add new insights into future work that tries to characterize this new public policy. Therefore, I built this chapter by setting out the common conceptual grounds for a discussion of the nature of cross-national and cross-cultural interaction with the help of two paradigms: policy transfer and policy diffusion. I will then explain how the idea of global reforms, policy transfer, and diffusion lead to the strengthening of nations, despite critics who may argue otherwise.

Public and management in a global world: Diffusion and policy transfer

Our point of departure is the supposition that cross-cultural and cross-national policy transfers and diffusion are reshaping the way public policy is formulated, expressed, and implemented. As suggested by Jacoby, (2000: 2):

> In scholarship on institutional change, imitation has become nearly invisible, relegated to the status of curiosity mentioned in historical footnotes or superficial prescriptive asides. I believe that imitation should in fact be acknowledged as crucial to many cases of institutional change. Surely, the idea that the fortunes of societies have no influence on choices beyond their own borders is implausible.

While these processes are not new, they seem to be on the increase to the extent that they remold the ways public policy is shaped, consolidated, and implemented. Social scientists often rely on two different paradigms to capture this process of change: the policy transfer and the policy diffusion paradigms (see Table 8.1). While the first is prevalent among political scientists and is methodologically oriented towards case analysis, the second is prevalent among sociologists and enjoys a rich tradition of quantitative research. Both paradigms fruitful and to some extent complementary, but we should clarify some of their strengths and weakness. Let us start with definitions. Policy transfers are concerned with "the process by which knowledge about how policies, administrative arrangements, institutions and ideas in one political setting (past or present) is used in the development of policies, administrative arrangements, institutions and ideas in another political setting" (Dolowitz and Marsh, 2000: 5). Diffusion is commonly defined as "the process by which an innovation is communicated through certain channels over time among members of social system. It is a special type of communication in that the messages are concerned with new ideas" (Rogers, 1995: 5). What differentiates these definitions is mainly the sociological emphasis of the diffusion paradigm. All other differences, including the methodological orientation, are marginal by comparison and there is no reason to believe that these two research traditions can *not* be brought together. In fact, it might well be that in the future the major differences with regard to central issues such as their rationality and the autonomy of actors will be within each of these paradigms rather than between them.

Table 8.1   Policy transfer and diffusion perspectives on policy change

Paradigm	Policy Transfer	Diffusion
Definition	"Policy transfer, emulation and lesson drawing all refer to the process by which knowledge about how policies, administrative arrangements, institutions and ideas in one political setting (past or present) is used in the development of policies, administrative arrangements, institutions and ideas in another political setting". (Dolowitz and Marsh, 2000, 5)	"The process by which an innovation is communicated through certain channels over time among members of social system. It is a special type of communication in that the messages are concerned with new ideas". (Rogers, 1995, 5)
Dominance	Among political scientists and analysts of public policy and public management.	Among sociologists, but increasingly utilized by political scientists.
Methodological Orientation	Case studies and Comparative Analysis.	Quantitative.
Major terms and concepts	Policy learning, lesson drawing, Bayesian learning.	Contagion, bandwagoning, herding, isomorphism.
Major assumption	The process of change is political in the sense that policy learning is filtered by political institutions.	The process of change occurs in social networks.
Mechanisms of policy change	Varies between coercive and voluntary; e.g., emulation, elite network, harmonization through international regime and penetration by external actors and interests. (Bennett, 1991)	Isomorphism, culture, international norms, best-practices.
Outcomes	Bias towards convergence.	Strong bias towards convergence.
Focus in regard to the policy process	Comprehensive: focus on policy goals, content, instruments, outcomes, styles.	Selective: focus on policy goals and content.

Source: Levi-Faur and Vigoda-Gadot (2004a, 2004b).

The paradigm of diffusion, especially formulations grounded in sociological institutionalism, has three advantages. First, sociology has an impressive tradition of diffusion analysis at the national (Rogers, 1995) and international level (Meyer et al., 1997), which does not have any equivalent in political science and the policy transfer literature. Note, however, that the pioneering work on diffusion research across the American states (Gray, 1973; Walker, 1969) is an exception. It is only with the policy learning/policy transfer literature of the 1990s that the issue again became a major focus of research in the discipline.

Second, the emphasis on transfer among members of the social system in the diffusion literature seems to allow us to look at the process outside the hierarchies of the top-down and bottom-up approaches to change. This emphasis figures clearly in the literature on policy networks (Rhodes and Marsh, 1992; van Waarden, 1992) and on governance (Rhodes, 1997), which emphasizes the fragmentation of political structures and the volatility of power. It connects naturally to the notions of epistemic communities (Haas, 1992), webs of influence (Braithwaite and Drahos, 2000) and transnational policy communities (Stone, 2003) as "channels of policy transfer" across nations.

Finally, I see some value in the "contagious" aspect of the diffusion perspective, that is, in the willingness of scholars within this research tradition to look beyond the structural aspects of the process to its internal dynamics (this does not mean, however, that all diffusion analysis pays attention to the contagious aspects of the process). Contagious-focused research examines how prior adoption of a trait, policy, institution, or practice in a population alters the probability of adoption for any remaining non-adopters (Strang, 1991: 325). Diffusion scholars often treat the process as organic and invoke the idea of contagion as a major source of change. Causality is not external but internal to the population in question. Unlike structuralists, who look at "independent observations" and treat interdependency as a problem of control (the Galton problem), diffusion studies perceive the evidence of interdependence as a major theoretical focus of study. This distinction between structural and contagious causes has notable implications for the way I conceive causality in the social and political system. It may suggest that variations and similarities are explained not by structural factors such as the configuration of actors' interests and relative power but by the solutions and models that are shaped by former events:

> Hence, in Australia we have laws criminalizing rape not because of any titanic struggle between a women's movement (or some other actor) which demanded rape laws and others who resisted them; rather, we acquired them without debate from British criminal law. Having occurred, it is now nearly impossible for any actors with any amount of political power to argue for a way of dealing with rape that disposes of the criminal-law model in favor of a radically different strategy (Braithwaite and Drahos, 2000: 582).

While the "policy transfer" approach is open to the idea that "emulation" or "copying" might be a distinct and independent source of change, there is no effort to look at it as a contagious, dynamic process of change. The policy transfer literature is essentially structuralist in its causal imagination. While the diffusion perspective offers these two advantages, it is often criticized as being politically neutral or uninformed. As diffusion analysis often focuses on broad historical, spatial, and socio-economic causes for a *pattern* of policy adoption, it neglects the political dynamics involved (Jacoby, 2000: 8; Peters, 1997: 76; Stone, 2003: 4). Here the policy transfer literature that distinguishes between coercive and voluntary mechanisms of transfer seems to have the upper hand. Power in the "sociological–institutional" diffusion perspective is confined almost solely to the power of ideas, norms, and symbols. Yet these "ideational" forms of power are hardly coercive and interest-driven, and frequently are not the major focus of the diffusion analysts.

Policy analysis is to be enriched from both perspectives, and it is possible to demonstrate how these two approaches may inform each other. This is evident in the work of Diana Stone, who suggests that global policy networks make a major impact on the way policy is shaped on the global as well as national level. She distinguishes three models that combine the assertions about the power of ideas and knowledge with the network approach: the epistemic community approach, the embedded knowledge networks framework, and the transnational discourse community approach (Stone, 2003). She then places her "knowledge actors" in a framework of analysis that combines the policy network approach and the policy transfer literature, and in doing so opens up a new frontier for policy analysts. The move to the global level repeatedly raises the question about the centrality of the state vis-à-vis international organizations, nongovernmental organizations, corporations, and cities in these networks of power. Scholars diverge on this point, as do the two paradigms of diffusion and policy transfer. In general, policy transfer seems to reflect the dominance of the nation state in political science while the diffusion perspective reflects the notion that states are recipients of a normative order that is created outside them, and they are, therefore, secondary in importance to international norms.

One major issue in the policy transfer and diffusion literature touches on the degrees and types of rationality that are involved in the process of change. Some versions of the policy transfer literature, such as lesson-drawing (Rose, 1993) and social learning (Hall, 1993), seem to perceive the process of transfer as a learning process. In this literature, the emphasis is on cognition and the redefinition of interests on the basis of new knowledge that affects the fundamental beliefs and ideas behind the policy. In some way related, though more demanding, are models of Bayesian learning (Meseguer, 2003). By contrast, sociological interpretations of the process of change emphasize a group's norms rather than individual rationality. See, for example, Marta Finnemore's argument about the notion of "state interests:"

> State interests are defined in the context of internationally held norms and understandings about what is good and appropriate. That normative context also changes over time, and as internationally held norms and values change, they create coordinated shifts in state interests and behavior across the system … states' redefinitions of interest are often not the result of external threats or demands by domestic groups. Rather thy are shaped by internally shared norms and values that structure and give meaning to international political life (Finnemore, 1996: 2–3).

This emphasis on the normative side of supposedly rational action suggests that emulation may be of some importance as a mechanism of policy change. It also necessitates a distinction between "learning" and "emulation" as major features of the process of policy transfer. The distinction between the two may be based on the scope of information involved in the decision-making process. Policy learning is defined as the redefinition of one's interest and behavior on the basis of newly acquired knowledge, after watching *the actions* of others and the *outcomes* of these actions. Policy emulation, by contrast, is the redefinition of one's interest and behavior on the basis of newly acquired knowledge and after watching only *the actions* of others (Jordana and Levi-Faur, 2003). I distinguish between the learners and the emulators by the extent to which adaptation to new behavior involves information not only about the actions of others but also about the consequences of those actions. The crucial difference is that the learner processes a greater amount of information than the emulator and is therefore less dependent and more autonomous.

Finally, the outcomes of policy transfers and diffusion are often presented through the expectation of convergence. Convergence theories postulate that growing international integration will have direct (for example, a change in the domestic distribution of political power) and indirect (for example, an influence on government policy) implications for domestic policy that will lead to similar policies and institutions. This is usually contrasted with divergence theories that suggest that growing international integration will not deflect states from their historically rooted trajectories, so that not convergence, but constant and perhaps even increasing variations will be the result for policies and institutions. The expectation of convergence in diffusion theory reflects a scholarly bias that is not necessary implied and embedded in the theories of transfer and diffusion (Jacoby, 2000: 8). Indeed, Gabriel Tarde, one of the founding fathers of sociology and author of the Laws of Imitation, describes the process of diffusion as one in which agents simultaneously converge on a fashion and distinguish themselves from others (It might well be that we all wear jeans to work, but we will make an effort to distinguish ourselves from others either by the sort of jeans we use or by adding accessories to them. We want to be similar to others and at the same time different). The process of change may involve convergencies and divergencies at the same time. The bias inherent in some of the diffusion and policy transfer literature towards a sort of "convergence" might best be balanced by a notion of change that takes both convergence and divergence as important dimensions.

The internationalization of public policy and public management

One of the most important debates in the social sciences in the last decade has focused on the future of the nation-state (Marsh and Smith, 2004; Weiss, 2003). Various scholars argue from different points of view that the power of the state is expected to decline and that new types of actors and political organization are gradually taking over responsibilities and policy capacities that were once the exclusive domain of the nation state (Ohame, 1995; Strange, 1996). A forceful argument to that effect was made recently by Braithwaite and Drahos (2000), who argue that most states outside Europe and the US "have become rule-takers rather than rule-makers:"

> the extent to which states have become rule-takers rather than rule-makers is greater than most citizens think, largely because when governments announce new regulatory laws they are somewhat embarrassed to disclose that the national legislature voted for those laws without having any say in shaping them ... for years some of Australia's air safety standards have been written by the Boeing Corporation in Seattle, or if not by that corporation, by the US Federal Aviation Administration in Washington. Australia's ship safety laws have been written by the International Maritime Organization in London, its motor vehicle safety standards by Working Party 29 of the Economic Commission for Europe and its food standards by the Codex Alimentarius Commission in Rome. Many of Australia's pharmaceuticals standards have been set by a joint collaboration of the Japanese, European and US industries and their regulators, called the International Conference on Harmonization. Its telecommunications standards have been substantially set in Geneva by the ITU. The Chair (and often the Vice-Chair) of most of the expert committees that effectively set those standards in Geneva are Americans ... (Braithwaite and Drahos, 2000: 3–4).

Summary: Strong nations in a global village

Building strong nations in a shrinking global village relies on adaptation to different rules and principles, rules that were not as pivotal for previous generations. The world as a global village means that none of the existing world nations can play as freely and independently as it used to in the past. Rapid communications and knowledge transfer, accompanied by free markets systems and greater collaboration among manifold stakeholders and global parties, imply that building strong nations is dependent upon breaking new ground for interface between bureaucratic and democratic systems. When one country's bureaucracy is at the same time learning from some bureaucracies and serving as a model for others, there is no recipe for the "right formula" or "right answer" that can resolve the bureaucratic–democratic dilemma. The answers depend on culture and values.

Nonetheless, the more elegant global policy transfer, emulation, and diffusion of knowledge, innovation, and experiences speed up processes that used to take decades or even centuries. Mass technology and communications allow leaders, politicians, civil servants, and citizens to benchmark and learn from both successful and less successful lessons of other nations. Thus, for resolving the bureaucratic–democratic paradox, the knowledge and experience that is shared in the international arena is precious and irreplaceable. As national units become increasingly similar to one another, we will see the development of new of best practices that many nations can emulate successfully. After all, building one strong nation is not necessarily at the expense of other nation, because the game is more one of win–win rather than win–lose.

Chapter 9

Building Strong Nations by Effective Governability in a Democratic Cosmos

Epilogue

How can we integrate all this knowledge and experience into better ways for building strong nations? There are at least two potential directions worthy of consideration in this epilogue: safeguarding democracy and regaining citizens' trust in governments that deserve this trust, and at the same time, strengthening governability by not fearing a strong bureaucracy. Moreover, and as demonstrated in the previous chapters, steps taken in this direction must be accompanied by an increase in cross-sectoral collaboration, innovation in public service, and an ongoing search for global reforms that can put public service at the front and center of the state's priorities.

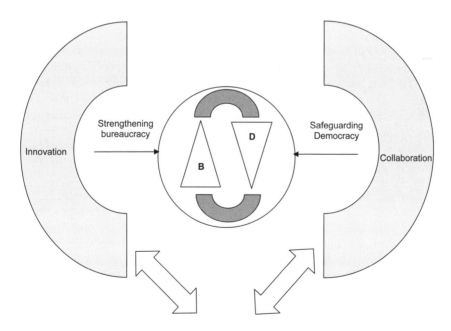

Figure 9.1   Building strong nations by reconciliation of the democratic–bureaucratic paradox

In this concluding chapter, I will try to explain why these tracks of mutual protection of democracy and bureaucracy do not contradict one another. Despite the democracy–bureaucracy paradox, there are a handful of options for reconciling the dilemmas that these social structures bring with them into our lives.

Safeguarding democracy: Rebuilding citizenship and values in the modern age

If democracies are here to stay, much more effort must be made, both in academia and in politics and public affairs, to safeguard democracy, regain citizen's trust in government, and empower communities in the liberal state. According to Van de Walle et al. (2005), citizens' trust in government and in the public sector has taken center stage in the public sector reform discourse. Participants in the debate often take low levels of public satisfaction with service delivery and a continual decline in citizens' trust in the public sector for granted. Where sufficient data is available, evidence of such a decline is disputed, and more often, data is simply not available for mapping reliable trends. Like me, Van de Walle and his colleagues believe that the performance of public agencies is often seen as a major factor in the perceived decline of trust. Yet, they continue, evidence about evolutions in public sector performance is inconclusive. A causal relation between government performance and citizens' trust is far from obvious. Nonetheless, our empirical findings in Chapter 5 try to solve some of the mystery surrounding this relationship by suggesting that the effect of satisfaction on trust seems more robust than vice versa. Still, I concur that the road towards regaining citizens' trust in government and in public administration, worldwide, is only partially explained by improvement of services to the people and by increasing satisfaction. Trust can also be regained by improving the managerial quality of the public sector, by enhancing moral and ethical values, by improving and developing the professional cadres of public servants and by other mechanisms such as collaboration, innovation, and global reform and learning from other cultures. As the earlier chapters of this book have demonstrated, empirical examinations, cross-national comparisons, and longitudinal analysis over time and locations are the road that must be followed to clarify the enigma of relationships between bureaucracy and democracy, if knowledge on building strong nations is there to be explored.

Hence, there are several promising paths on the roadmap to regaining citizens' trust in government. They all stem from the recognition that the problem is not merely due to weaknesses in the democratic system. They are due to the complex task of bringing together democracy and bureaucracy, in a village-size world where citizens are much more aware and demanding than they used to be even thirty or forty years ago. Thus, the remedies for mistrust are: safeguarding democracy, strengthening bureaucracy, and most importantly, understanding and resolving the "black box" where bureaucracy and democracy interface with one another.

As we travel this road, special attention must be paid to a triple arsenal of principles for safeguarding democracy: a massive enrichment of values, morality, ethics, and integrity for all players who act on the national stage; rethinking citizenship and citizenship behavior in order to build new types of democracy; and making these changes relevant for the age of technology and mass communication.

Enrichment of values: Putting morality and integrity first

Perhaps the most challenging task facing modern nations is the goal of education, enrichment of values, and enhancement of ethics and morality in and around the public sector. Richardson (1997), in an attempt to link governability, citizenship, and values suggests that:

> A principle function of the (Greek) *polis* (a term that encompassed far more than our contemporary *state* or *government* and is imperfectly rendered by our word regime) was to nurture or inculcate the distinctive traits that it valued – say, a love of honor, wealth, moderation, political courage – into the citizenry … According to Aristotle, this nurturing could occur successfully only within the polis or regime, and the very best of these regimes attempted to promote the highest possible character, that which pursued the *advantageous and just* while avoiding the *harmful and unjust*. Indeed, the nurturing of these traits was most decidedly a political act, one that decisively liked *ethics* and politics (p. 105).

Thus, building strong nations must rely on the enrichment of values among public servants, who are expected to be disinterested and avoid the harmful consequences of political behavior and of organizational politics. The classic call of Woodrow Wilson in his seminal essay *Study of Administration* to separate politics and administration is a blunt reflection of the struggle for administrative ethics and higher standards of morality. Putting morality and integrity first means clearer borders between the elected politicians and their professional civil servants, but still leaving enough room for coupling the work of democracy and bureaucracy. Those who still believe that a total separation is possible are as wrong as those who argue that these spheres should not be separated. The solution is, after all, a loose coupling where democracy functions independently and has the sovereignty to voice the peoples' wishes, but bureaucracy decides on the correct ways to implement these wishes and demands and where ethics, morality, character, and principles of fairness and justice underpin all governmental and administrative decisions. Thus, the reconciliation of bureaucracy and democracy can materialize only where the black box of interface draws sustenance from similar values and principles of morality and ethics. Otherwise, no coupling or decoupling is relevant, effective, or useful.

Rethinking citizenship and building new models of democracy[1]

In a previous section, I discussed the nexus between citizenship and management in the public sector. Several questions were highlighted including (1) Why should we study the meaning and interrelations of citizenship in public organizations and in the bureaucratic landscape? (2) What layers of citizenship can be identified and how can they be related with modern worksites? (3) What are the theoretical and conceptual foundations of the citizenship–management integration, and how useful is it for a better understanding of our modern administrative systems, governance, and quality of life in democratic cultures? and (4) What, if any, are the practical implications of these relationships at multiple levels – the individual, group, organizational, system, and even state levels?

Our interest is hardly unique. Indeed, the general topic has long been on the minds of many observers, in both public as well as business management. Although many contemporary writers may imply that new discoveries have been made, organizational citizenship and democracy can be traced to seminal lines of work (e.g., Pateman, 1970, among others); and this core is connected to a long series of milestones marking other progress (e.g., Bernstein, 1980; Elden, 1977; Golembiewski, 1989, 1990). Recently, and advertised as "special topics" (Harrison and Freeman, 2004), related themes have received fulsome space and been accorded prominent status in the literature.

Rethinking the heritage of citizenship and bureaucracy   The general perspective is that citizenship and bureaucracy influence one another, a belief that contributes to both the theory and the practice of business and public administration. Defining the meaning, boundaries, and implications of the term "citizenship" is a complex task. Citizenship has multiple meanings in the judicial, statutory, national, psychological, and social senses. It frequently denotes the official status of individuals in a national environment, where they also hold a variety of rights and duties, privileges and obligations, liberties and responsibilities.

Indeed, the roots of the term "citizenship" date back to antiquity and appear in various cultural contexts. Citizenship was probably first recognized by the ancient Greeks who also introduced the related concepts of "civic virtue," "good citizenship," and "civic duties." At the very least, major authorities see the matter in similar terms. For example, Aristotle argued that citizenship was born in Greek city-states, small enough to give their members the chance to "know one another's character" (Aristotle, 1948: 1326b). He identified as citizens "all who share in the ... life of ruling and being ruled in turn" (p. 1283b), but emphasized the importance of participation through which citizens could influence their leaders and the governance

---

1 Some sections of this chapter are based on E. Vigoda-Gadot and R.T. Golembiewski, "Rethinking citizenship in public administration: one more look in a series," In M.A. Rahim and R.T. Golembiewski, eds., *Current Topics in Management* (New Brunswick, Transaction, 2005).

process, thereby affecting their environment as well as their day-to-day life. Centuries later, Machiavelli used the term "civic virtue" to describe the obligations a citizen has toward a state and a community. These obligations should be learned through education, religion, and a healthy fear of the consequences following the dereliction of civic duty (Oliver and Heater, 1994: 14). While Machiavelli pointed out the coercive role of the state in shaping citizens' obedience, he did not ignore altruistic and voluntary behavior adopted by citizens of their own free will and aimed at improving the welfare and prosperity of the state or community.

Like Locke and others, later variations also reflected this central core of ideas. In the seventeenth century, like Locke and others, Hobbes promoted the idea that people and governments should share a kind of mutual agreement, later known as a social contract. This contract requires people's obedience and loyalty to the government in return for the government's commitment to provide the people with certain basic "natural" rights. It advocates bi-directional transactions of human resources promoting the mutual interests of citizens, states, nations, and societies. Similarly, Montesquieu in *The Spirit of the Laws* argued that unlike other forms of government, a state based upon popular participation depends for its stability on the civic virtue of its *good* citizens. Rousseau emphasized the importance of citizens' freedom, political participation, and a "general will," which calls for an altruistic contribution to the governing and administrative process made solely with the thought of advancing the common interest. The liberal tradition of citizenship expanded with American independence as well as with the French Revolution in the late eighteenth century. Subsequently, democratic values were embraced in many other European countries during the nineteenth century. They emphasized the contribution that the citizens' voluntary political action made to the creation of the common good and a prosperous society (e.g., Golembiewski, 1989, 1990).

Compared to citizenship, bureaucracy represents what seems to be an entirely different set of values and principles. While citizenship is based mainly on a balanced view of the rights and duties of the individual, bureaucracy is basically uninterested in the individual as such and emphasizes the power of administrative institutions, which frequently have quite a negative valence. This negative image stands in sharp contrast to the favorable image of (good) citizenship behavior. As suggested by Goodsell (1983) in *The Case for Bureaucracy*, we all tend to hate bureaucrats and bureaucracy. Bureaucracy is attacked in the press, in popular magazines, and in best-sellers. It is denounced by the political right as well as the left. It is assaulted by molders of culture and professors of academia. It is castigated by most economists, sociologists, policy analysts, political scientists, organizational theorists, and social psychologists. In addition, it is charged with a wide array of crimes, which I group under several heads – failure to perform; abuse of political power; and the repression of employees, citizens as clients, and other individuals. These failures bring in their wake cynical attitudes toward bureaucracy that are commonplace and widespread. The difficulties modern nations have found in serving the public's needs have turned bureaucracies into a faulted icon of red tape, ineffectiveness, ineptitude, and heavy-handedness.

However, like citizenship, bureaucracy also reflects two main domains in our lives. It represents our social institutions and the formal mechanisms of the administrative state (Richardson, 1997). For most scholars in the political sciences and in public administration, for example, bureaucracy is the most essential instrument of nation building. It is the tool through which the state discharges its obligations to serve and govern its people. Bureaucracy means the power to govern by state officials, by public professionals, and by experts in policy implementation. Despite its popular, negative image, bureaucracy is necessary in our lives. It becomes even more essential as time goes on and citizens' needs and demands increase, as Wilson (1987) has perhaps argued most persuasively. Hence, for good or ill, there exists a clear theoretical linkage between citizenship and bureaucracy in modern democracies. Citizens are an essential part of the bureaucratic state and play an increasing role in modern democracies (Vigoda, 2002a). By applying various kinds of "citizenship behavior" in various areas and at various levels, one can influence the actions and decisions of bureaucrats and bureaucracy. Western democracies have made remarkable progress in terms of managing the state. Perhaps the most impressive milestone is that people in democratic nations are encouraged to become more and more involved in community action through individual enterprises or via third sector organizations, and the evidence suggests they and their institutions profit from such enrichment (e.g., Golembiewski, 1989, 1990). In recent decades, the third sector has become a grass-roots platform of citizen action that is energized increasingly by the people and for the people, above and beyond the governmental umbrella. Some would even say that these actions are a necessary tonic for the growing impotencies of bureaucracy.

Conventional wisdom implies that modern welfare states cannot and should not take responsibilities away from the people in order to make their lives better. Citizens themselves should bear some of the direct social burden. Consequently, citizenship behavior is recognized today as an essential tool for the effective functioning of every social institution. The "good soldier syndrome" (OCB – Organizational Citizenship Behavior), as presented by Organ (1988), is a powerful reflection of civic virtue that is and should be widely encouraged inside and outside all organizations. There seems little doubt that its actual and potential impact on public organizations is great, and only our wit can inhibit that potential from becoming immense.

Extending this look at individual citizenship and bureaucracy   What can be added to this view? To begin with, individual citizenship behavior refers to the very basic construct of personal actions and reactions by individual citizens. These are spontaneous and usually altruistic deeds of "unorganized" persons aimed at enhancing the prosperity and development of their environment. Citizens may show compassion for other citizens, contribute time, money, and other resources to help the less capable, provide assistance for others whenever the situation requires and without seeking any personal advantage or compensation (e.g., Conover, Crewe, and Searing, 1993; Monroe, 1994; Piliavin and Charng, 1990). Moreover, inside public organizations, citizens–employees may exert additional efforts to help fellow employees in fulfilling their duties and in serving the public without explicitly seeking any personal rewards.

As mentioned earlier, the general management literature has defined these enterprises as OCB, or Organizational Citizenship Behavior, which reflects an informal contribution that participants can choose to withhold without regard to sanctions or formal incentives. As noted in many studies (e.g., Organ, 1988; Organ and Konovsky, 1989; Podsakof and MacKenzie, 1997), when these contributions are aggregated over time and persons, they considerably enhance organizational efficiency and effectiveness of operations. Further studies concluded that working under multiple pressures, public organizations are well-advised to make a better effort at understanding the relationship between citizenship behavior inside and outside the workplace, management, and organizational outcomes (Cohen and Vigoda, 1998, 2000; Graham, 1991). Hence, I propose that encouragement of citizenship behavior in and around public agencies may contribute to organizational productivity, competence, as well as success, and hence also to society in general.

Citizenship, public administration, and the added value of collaboration   Better incorporation of the idea of citizenship into new managerial thinking is essential, then. So far, I have demonstrated that citizenship behavior has many faces. However, it has only one source, namely the people and their willingness to engage in constructive action. Building strong nations relies on a spirit of new managerialism in which citizens take the lead. It means bringing the citizens closer to their ideal role as more active participants in the administrative process. An added value is necessary for turning simple bureaucracies and stagnated public services into more flexible, responsive, and vital entities upon whose broad shoulders modern societies can safely rest. While the body of relevant research in this field is limited, we can briefly examine several ideas for moving forward in this direction.

First, Figure 9.2 provides a graphic view of the types of citizenship and possible paths for building citizenship-oriented behaviors and spirits. Table 9.1 provides more details about theoretical and empirical findings of the types of citizenship profiles. The two types depicted in Table 9.1 suggest promising aspects of citizenship such as: characteristics; probable antecedents; probable outcomes; and mutual relationships, elaborated by "loops" or "feedbacks" among the types of citizenship. As shown in Table 9.1, some empirical work has demonstrated the usefulness of the collaborative analytical approach for bringing together various ideas about the nature and meaning of citizenship. For example, the *horizontal loop* in Table 9.1 can be illustrated in two ways. The seminal works of Almond and Verba (1963) and others that followed, like Verba et al. (1995), have dealt with Type 1 citizenship – that is, political participation and involvement at the national and communal levels. In addition, Organ (1988) and Organ and Ryan (1995) focused on Type 2 citizenship when they developed the idea of Organizational Citizenship Behavior (OCB).

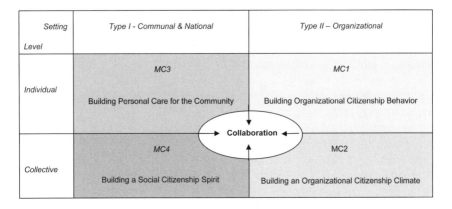

Figure 9.2   Collaboration and citizenship for strong nations

Source: E. Vigoda-Gadot and R.T. Golembiewski (2005), "Rethinking citizenship in public administration: One more look in a series".

A *vertical loop* in Table 9.1, in contrast, tries to relate Type I citizenship with Type II citizenship. This relationship was suggested by Cohen and Vigoda (1998: 2000), as well as by Graham (1991) and Peterson (1990) who focused on the relationship between good citizenship at the national/communal level and organizational citizenship behavior such as OCB. Similarly, Near, Rice, and Hunt (1987) examined satisfaction with one's life and job satisfaction as probable outcomes of good citizenship. Vigoda (2002a) related democratic values and productivity in organizations. Finally, Sobel (1993) examined the relationship between political participation at the national level and job involvement and voice activities at the organizational level.

The significant relationships that were reported in most of these studies support our contention that much more work is needed to uncover the vertical loops between Type I and Type II citizenship. Finally, several studies have also tested diagonal loops where, for example, obedience and participation at the national/communal levels may relate to organizational performance and to job satisfaction (Cohen and Vigoda, 2000; Vigoda, 2002a). In addition, Organ (1994) related personal and personality factors with organizational commitment and extra-role behaviors that are typical of good organizational citizens. To a similar end, Golembiewski et al. (1996) discussed burnout as reflecting a global pandemic that seems to affect citizens and citizenship worldwide. This review of research could be extended, but the basic conclusion is evident. This research all points to the need to study citizenship as a complex variable that has many facets, which eventually will be shown to be mutually related.

Table 9.1   Building strong nations with two types of citizenship profiles and possible interrelationships

Citizenship type	Characteristics (A)	Probable antecedents (B)	Probable outcomes (C)	Empirical examination of loops (examples)
Type I National and Communal Citizenship (Individual and Collective)	A1. Obedience A2. Loyalty A3. Participation	B1. Socialization B2. Educational B3. Personal and Personality	C1. Democratic values C2. Political stability C3. Social health and welfare C4. Economic efficiency C5. Satisfaction with life C6. Ethical government	*Horizontal Loop:* *Type 1:* Almond and Verba (1963); Verba et al. (1995) *Type 2:* Organ (1988), Organ and Ryan (1995) Direction of emphasis: ↔
Type II Organizational Citizenship (Individual and Collective)	A4. Intra-role behavior A5. Commitment A6. Extra-role behavior A7. Voice activities and Job Involvement	B4. Exchange B5. Org.Development B6. Fairness B7. Personal and Personality	C7. Productivity and performance C8. Intentions to leave C9. Job satisfaction C10. Stress and Strain C11. Burnout C12. Ethical employees and management	*Vertical Loop:* A1-A3 vs. A4-A6: Cohen and Vigoda (1998; 2000), Graham (1991); Peterson (1990) C5 vs. C9: Near, Rice and Hunt (1987) C1 vs. C7: Vigoda (2002a) A3 vs.A7: Sobel (1993) Direction of emphasis: ↕ *Diagonal Loop:* A1-A3 vs. C7,C9: Cohen and Vigoda (2000), Vigoda (2002a) B3 vs. A4-A6: Organ (1994) C10-C11 vs. B1-B3: Golembiewski et al. (1996) Direction of emphasis: ↗

Source: E. Vigoda-Gadot and R.T. Golembiewski (2005): *Rethinking citizenship in public administration: One more look in a series.*

Empowering democracy in an age of technology

How can we empower democracy in an age of technology and mass communications? Studies have been struggling with this question over the last decades. No doubt that a reform is needed in the meaning of citizenship. Innovative ideas and creative mechanisms should be encouraged to reinforce authentic citizenship involvement, community care, and collaboration among players in the process of governance. In fact, citizens' participation has been one of the most studied concepts in political science. In their extensive work *Voice and Equality: Civic Voluntarism in American Politics*, Verba, Schlozman, and Brady (1995) argue that "citizen participation is at the heart of democracy" and that "democracy is unthinkable without the ability of citizens to participate freely in the governing process" (p. 1). As suggested by Barner and Rosenwein (1985), "... Democratic values are in essence participatory values. At the heart of democratic theory is the notion that people should get involved in the process of governing themselves ..." (p. 59). Those who do not participate politically are likely to have a very undemocratic view of the world (Guyton, 1988; Knutson, 1972).

Not surprisingly, a large amount of research has been conducted in an attempt to understand the forms and determinants of political participation and citizens' involvement in states, communities, and organizations (Vigoda and Golembiewski, 2000). However, only recently have researchers become more interested in the practical essence of citizens' participation, the forms of involvement in administrative actions and in the process of nation building and policy making or implementation. Whereas political participation has a long heritage of being a most influential element in the research of modern democracy, investigation into administrative participation is in its early stages of evolution and recognition. In an era of e-government and a search for new forms of effective democratic mechanisms, participation and involvement have regained their central role in our societies.

Buss et al. (2006) present a varied collection of essays on citizens' participation in modern democracy in the age of information and technology. They try to point to the nexus between those who make and implement public policy and those affected by it. The era of technology mandates changes in policy agenda designed to increase citizens' participation; community learning and collaboration; strategies for greater accountability in developing countries; new methods for improving participation, such as focus groups, surveys, workshops, e-governance and other technology-supported ideas for citizens' involvement; simulation and decision support technologies for citizens' engagement in policy making and in policy implementation. A variety of players and stakeholders struggle with new demands for the authentic involvement of citizens in forming the institutions that affect their lives and their quality of life. The echo of this trend is heard in many fields such as environmental projects, transportation, planning and development, welfare policies, healthcare, crime prevention, and other governmental initiatives that may benefit from input by the public prior to implementation or even planning.

However, when we consider democratic changes in the era of technology, we must pay more attention to the role of modern lifestyles in our societies. Our modern lifestyles hinder many efforts to increase participation. For example, even with highly sophisticated technology, computer-based voting systems, and advanced techniques for involving citizens in policy making, the average individual will still avoid involvement when other, more pressing issues exist. Our modern lifestyle urges us to devote more time to personal issues such as providing for our families and saving time and energy for leisure activities. In a marketplace society where welfare networks are weakening and solidarity arises only in the face of governments' inability to govern and provide services to the people, why would the average person devote time to saving the government from its own self-defeating decisions? This interesting question should be mentioned, even if it is not answered in the discourse about participation and involvement in modern society. In many respects, not much has changed in the "civic society" of fifty years ago (i.e., Almond and Verba, 1963). However, enough has changed to conclude that we all have less time to invest in collective efforts targeted at making our life better. This is an ironic conclusion but one that certainly seems to be true. Thus, in some respects, the good will of active citizenship, by individuals and by government, is frequently diminished in the face of mass media, instant information, and the generally hectic lifestyle of the twenty-first century (Vigoda and Golembiewski, 2001).

Finally, citizens' participation in political and administrative dynamics is a cornerstone of democracy, even in times of global changes and transformations in management style, technology, and knowledge structures. Whereas such participation may be classified as part of the idea of civism (i.e., Box, 1998; Fredrickson, 1982; King and Stivers, 1998), I believe it better suits what Fox and Miller (1996) describe as the "discourse theory" of public administration. This theory seeks to mediate the two conventional doctrines of public administration: institutionalism/constitutionalism and communitarianism/civism. It is a third voice, one that adheres well with the seminal works of Giddens (1984, 1990) about the third way of governance. It emphasizes the authentic contribution of citizens to their states, communities, and fellow-citizens that will endure in the years to come, even if its form and structure change. At the same time it urges governments to develop a direct link to communities and to develop an effective "discourse" with citizens. Just as democracy is dynamic and changes its face over time, so too do the types and methods of participation constantly transform and reinvent themselves through the actions of both citizens and governments. Therefore, people's attitudes and behaviors in a democracy must be studied with the best tools that science can offer. Using T.H. Marshall's (1950) typology, participation is the less obvious role of citizens in modern democracies. Beyond obedience and loyalty, participation is the active part of citizenship and definitely a major component of good citizenship behavior. The discourse approach also calls for innovative mechanisms that can bring the public closer to decision-making processes and encourage the genuine involvement of individuals in setting the policies and strategies of states and nations.

Strengthening governability: Why (not to) fear strong bureaucracy

Despite the "bad name" and "bad reputation" of bureaucracy as the paradigm of inflexible rules and red tape, I argue that strengthening formal institutions and procedures of governance is more than essential in our times of uncertainty and instability. Governments, social structures, and the shrinking world village put bureaucracy in an almost impossible situation where it is expected to function, but has few effective tools at is disposal and is under growing pressure to become overly flexible at times. Trends in liberal democracy, the free flow of knowledge and information, and growing public criticism (justified and unjustified) sometimes make it impossible for governments to rule. The world courtyard of governance is narrowing as the number of (knowledgeable) stakeholders grows rapidly and each one promotes its individual interests more aggressively. Thus, safeguarding governability and promoting effective bureaucracy are major milestones on the road to building strong nations. I believe that in our changing environment, we should not fear strong bureaucracies, as long as they are formed wisely and see the protection of democracy as the cornerstone of their activity. Naturally, reforms must ensure that older patterns of slow and ineffective procedures of government agencies bogged down by red tape are swept aside. Here again, a triple agenda of principles must dominate the discourse: governments need to rule, reduce red tape, and foster higher levels of professionalism and learning.

Governments need to rule

There is no effective way to ask for our nations to grow stronger unless the legitimate cadre of politicians and administrators are allowed to rule. Obviously, ruling effectively is predicated upon a reasonable level of trust in democracy and the commitment of those who attain the power to serve the people. Beyond the elementary need for the multiple contributions of many stakeholders to the public debate, a problem facing many modern democracies is the too heavy burden of what used to be effective "checks and balances" in politics. Governments need to rule and must have access to all the resources that allow them to rule effectively. This need does not contradict the need to maintain and safeguard the system of checks and balances. As in many other areas, the question arises when such checks and balances become a barrier to policy making and the implementation of good ideas.

How can we allow governments to rule in a free society where almost every citizen, as an individual or in a collective effort, systematically challenges this desire by leaders and the bureaucracy to rule? The advocates of the institutional theory suggest that the power of bureaucracy is so strong and so dominant that in fact, there is no need to make it easier on governments to rule: their basic source of power, so say supporters of institutionalism, is the legitimate and collective power of the bureaucracy where decisions are taken and implemented impersonally and according to a clear (and hopefully fair) procedure. However, in a modern society this should not be taken for granted.

Reducing red tape

Effective governability can be attained only when red type is minimized. Raising formal barriers that impede the smooth functioning of administrators and bureaucrats is a recipe for getting incurring citizens' mistrust and creating a lack of confidence. Bureaucracy, as a rule and as a tool, is not inherently negative or evil. It is only when bureaucracy is awkward and ineffective that it resorts to red tape. The fine line between what must remain firmly in the hands of public officers and what can be delegated to citizens, to third sector parties, or to the free market players is subtle, but not impossible to define. Strong nations have the right and authority to do what other parties in the society cannot or will not do. Strong nations should maintain under their control only those services that are essential for running citizens' daily life. All other functions that are less essential for maintaining security, safety, or the protection of vital interests should be privatized and left for the free market and for other players in the civic society. Obviously, reducing red tape means becoming more flexible but at the same time implies a certain degree of caution in the face of the tyranny of the markets. Thus, strong nations try to sweep away all those regulations and procedures that eliminate innovation, competitiveness, and continuous national growth. Naturally, the specific choices in this area will vary according to the norms and values of a given culture and its people. In nations that maintain satisfactory standards and function in accordance with norms of ethics, morality, care for community, and collective prosperity, governability can be improved by reducing red tape. However, in those nations where a minimal level of these values and standards has not been reached, the formality of rules and procedures safeguards bureaucracy and allows democracy to function. The alternative in such cases would be a slippery slide into anarchy.

Increased professionalism and learning

Finally, an urgent need is to make sure that the quality of public servants improves, hand in hand with the demands and expectations of citizens and other stakeholders in the public sphere. In the face of growing pressures and the ultra-complicated environment of public agencies, the process of learning and professional excellence must reach a variety of audiences. The technological era of mass information is a facilitator for learning (witness the sharp rise in distance learning programs in universities across the globe or the growing number of start-ups that focus of the transference of data, the creation of databases of knowledge, and the sharing and dissemination of information among various audiences across the globe). However, it can also become a barrier (witness the tendency of many public servants to become experts in their own field of knowledge, via sophisticated technologies and advanced tools, while at the same time knowing almost nothing about what is going on in related fields outside their area of expertise). Nonetheless, technology offers many options and alternatives for learning. Good models are out there, but the experts must determine what type of case or experience is useful and what type may prove less useful for a certain culture, nation, or social structure. Science can make effective comparisons but experience is also valuable because it can help us avoid pitfalls and dead ends.

Summary: Towards a happy marriage?

As I demonstrated in the previous parts of this book, relating managerial quality, performance, and trust in government is an ambitious task. It involves knowledge from several related but separate disciplines such as political science, political psychology, policy analysis, management, and public administration. Similarly, there are at least two different approaches to the study of the citizens' role in society. The first approach treats citizens as political creatures who act as voters, protesters, or members of political institutions (e.g., Nye, Zelikow, and King, 1997; Verba, Schlozeman, and Brady, 1995). The second approach views citizens as clients of governments, as part of the emerging businesslike public environment, or as those who act like customers in the marketplace of the state (e.g., Osborne and Gaebler, 1992; Pollitt, 1988). According to Hirschman (1970) the political orientations of citizens can be defined as "voice" activities, while their business orientation is more of an "exit" activity in that it allows the citizen-as-customer to make rational choices and move freely among service providers.

As the vast majority of the political science literature points out, most citizens are not willing to take an active part in political life or in political decision-making. This observation is very indicative of the administrative arena and the willingness to become engaged in administrative decisions, at the national or even communal level of neighborhoods and more intimate social groups. Citizens have a varying level of knowledge about and interest in politics, bureaucracy, and democracy. The knowledge of the average citizen about commonplace public issues is rather low. Consequently, researchers agree that involvement in politics and in administrative decisions that shape the life of many occupy a very small part of the majority of most citizens' daily routine (Almond and Verba, 1963; Berelson, Lazarsfeld, and McPhee, 1954; Campbell et al., 1960; Hibbing and Theiss-Morse, 2002; Milbrath, 1981; Miller and Shanks, 1996).

However, citizens of modern nations live in a highly political environment. Furthermore, the echo of the political environment is amplified by modern media and communication channels. Therefore, it is practically impossible for citizens to ignore the service aspect of running a strong, modern nation. They must become more engaged and not leave the decisions in the hands of politicians or even professional bureaucrats. Governments are politically created entities whose essential duty is as much to safeguard the lives of their citizens as it is to provide them with various public goods and services. Thus, the tension between the political demands on the state and the pressures on it to function in a businesslike manner, elsewhere defined as a democratic–bureaucratic conflict (i.e., Thompson, 1983), is one of the most interesting and provocative issues in contemporary social debate.

Practically, citizens tend to leave the process of political decision-making and its implementation in the hands of the government and the public servants. This hands-off approach is particularly remarkable because it is the citizens who finance the government and its programs. Citizens are also those who expect to profit from "good decisions" and pay for "bad decisions." Therefore, citizens hope for public services that are flexible and responsive to their different and varied needs (Chi, 1999) but they still do too little to influence these decisions. Even at this late stage in the book, the question remains regarding the order in which these developments occur. Does the political order of democracy impact the administrative/economic realm of bureaucracy or does the latter dictate the format of the former? This is a paradox that remains and must be considered in future studies. It leaves us with questions but also with the understanding that the marriage of democracy and bureaucracy is essential for building string nations. It is a fascinating arena for research, practice, and analysis that can produce knowledge, innovation, collaboration and culturally sensitive reforms for making modern societies safer and healthier than ever. A possible solution to the enigmatic tension between democracy and bureaucracy is suggested in this book. For such an experiment to succeed, citizens and the meaning of citizenship must be changed but at the same time, the actions of government and governance must be transformed as well. Collaboration among those players is a third condition for creating strong and strong

Appendix
The Questionnaire

Dear Citizen

This questionnaire is part of a project which focuses on citizens' attitudes to and perceptions of the public sector and public administration. It is aimed at acquiring information about your satisfaction with public services, and your trust in governmental organizations and civil servants, as well as about general prospects for the activities and orientations of public administration.

The information you are asked to provide is of great value and will be kept confidential. The estimated time needed for completing the questionnaire is 15 to 20 minutes. Please try to answer all the questions, including those concerning personal details. There are no right or wrong answers as we are only interested in your personal opinions.

Please remember that much effort has been invested in this project and your personal participation is most appreciated. We thank you in advance and trust we shall have the benefit of your cooperation, which is invaluable for research purposes and for the general improvement of public services.

Thank you,

Prof. Eran Vigoda-Gadot
Dr. Shlomo Mizrahi

University of Haifa, Division of Public Administration and Policy, School of Political Sciences, Mount Carmel Haifa 31095, ISRAEL Tel: 972-4-8240709
Fax: 972-4-8257785

Below is a list of public institutions and organizations that deliver various services to citizens. Please circle the number from 1 to 5 that best reflects *your satisfaction* with their services. If you have not used a certain service recently, please try to express a general impression that most closely reflects your opinion.

Citizens' Satisfaction (ST)	Very dissatisfied	Somewhat dissatisfied	Neither satisfied nor dissatisfied	Somewhat satisfied	Very satisfied
1. Hospitals and public clinics	1	2	3	4	5
2. Public schools	1	2	3	4	5
3. Courts	1	2	3	4	5
4. Ministry of Interior	1	2	3	4	5
5. Labor ministry and employment services	1	2	3	4	5
6. Police	1	2	3	4	5
7. Transportation ministry	1	2	3	4	5
Public transport					
8. Buses	1	2	3	4	5
9. Rails	1	2	3	4	5
10. El-Al (Israel Airlines)	1	2	3	4	5
11. Airport authority	1	2	3	4	5
12. Public postal system	1	2	3	4	5
13. Local municipality	1	2	3	4	5
14. Electricity company	1	2	3	4	5
15. Religious services system	1	2	3	4	5
16. Welfare system and national security	1	2	3	4	5
17. Bezeq (Israel telecommunication services)	1	2	3	4	5
18. Income tax system	1	2	3	4	5

In the following section you will find a list of various *agencies and organizations, most of which belong to the Israeli public sector.* Please circle the number from 1 to 5 that best reflects the level of *trust* you have in each of them.

Trust (Institutions) – (TRST1)	Very low trust	Low trust	Neither trust or distrust	High trust	Very high trust
19. Ministry of Health	1	2	3	4	5
20. Public hospitals	1	2	3	4	5
21. Public clinics	1	2	3	4	5
22. Kindergartens and schools	1	2	3	4	5
23. Higher education (colleges and universities)	1	2	3	4	5
24. Judiciary system	1	2	3	4	5
25. Israel Defense Forces	1	2	3	4	5
26. Secret security services	1	2	3	4	5
27. Police and prisons	1	2	3	4	5
28. Public broadcasting system in general	1	2	3	4	5
29. Public broadcasting in Arabic	1	2	3	4	5
30. Israeli newspapers	1	2	3	4	5
31. Ministry of Transportation	1	2	3	4	5
32. Ministry of National Infrastructures (management of water system and national lands)	1	2	3	4	5
33. Ministry of Environment	1	2	3	4	5
34. State comptroller's office	1	2	3	4	5
35. Religious services system	1	2	3	4	5
36. State treasury and tax system	1	2	3	4	5
37. The Central Bank (Bank of Israel)	1	2	3	4	5
38. Israeli political parties	1	2	3	4	5
39. The Knesset (parliament)	1	2	3	4	5

In the following section you will find a list of various *public servants by field of occupation*. Please circle the number from 1 to 5 that best reflects the level of *trust* you have towards each of the groups.

Trust (Individuals) – (TRST2)	Very low trust	Low trust	Neither trust or distrust	High trust	Very high trust
40. Medical doctors	1	2	3	4	5
41. Managers and supervisors of the health system	1	2	3	4	5
42. Public teachers	1	2	3	4	5
43. Lecturers and researchers at universities	1	2	3	4	5
44. Judges	1	2	3	4	5
45. State attorneys	1	2	3	4	5
46. Other lawyers	1	2	3	4	5
47. IDF soldiers	1	2	3	4	5
48. IDF officers and commanders	1	2	3	4	5
49. Military judges	1	2	3	4	5
50. IDF spokesmen	1	2	3	4	5
51. IDF radio	1	2	3	4	5
52. Operatives of the general security service	1	2	3	4	5
53. Operatives of the "Mossad"	1	2	3	4	5
54. Policemen	1	2	3	4	5
55. Prison wardens	1	2	3	4	5
56. Reporters on TV Channel 1 and the Voice of Israel (public broadcasting)	1	2	3	4	5
57. Reporters on TV Channel 2 and 10	1	2	3	4	5
58. Newspaper reporters	1	2	3	4	5
59. Administrators of the water resources	1	2	3	4	5
60. Employees of local municipalities	1	2	3	4	5
61. Elected officials in local government	1	2	3	4	5

Trust (Individuals) – (TRST2)	Very low trust	Low trust	Neither trust or distrust	High trust	Very high trust
62. State comptroller	1	2	3	4	5
63. General ombudsman	1	2	3	4	5
64. Chief rabbis	1	2	3	4	5
65. City rabbis	1	2	3	4	5
66. Employees of the religion services	1	2	3	4	5
67. Employees of the welfare system	1	2	3	4	5
68. Employees of the treasury system	1	2	3	4	5
69. Employees of the tax system	1	2	3	4	5
70. Employees of the Bank of Israel	1	2	3	4	5
71. Members of Knesset	1	2	3	4	5
72. Cabinet members	1	2	3	4	5

The next items refer to your evaluation of various aspects of the Israeli public sector. Please circle the number from 1 to 5 that best indicates your personal agreement with the following sentences.

	Strongly disagree	Disagree	Neither agree nor disagree	Agree	Strongly agree
Internal/Organizational Politics (IP/OP)					
73. Favoritism rather than merit determines who gets ahead in the public sector.	1	2	3	4	5
74. There have always been influential groups in the public sector environment that no one ever crosses.	1	2	3	4	5
75. Public sector employees usually don't speak up for fear of retaliation by others.	1	2	3	4	5
76. Many public sector employees attempt to build themselves up by tearing others down.	1	2	3	4	5

	Strongly disagree	Disagree	Neither agree nor disagree	Agree	Strongly agree
77. The actions of public administration serve the purposes of only a few individuals, not the public system or the public interest.	1	2	3	4	5
78. Generally speaking, public administration operates appropriately and is not affected by political pressures.	1	2	3	4	5
Image and Reputation (Additional) 79. If I had the right opportunity, I would be interested in joining public service.	1	2	3	4	5
80. Many of my acquaintances think that a job in the public sector is a respectable and good one.	1	2	3	4	5
81. I would advise my friends and family members to look for a job in public service.	1	2	3	4	5
82. The image of Israeli public administration has improved in recent years.	1	2	3	4	5
83. I think that Israeli public administration has a positive image.	1	2	3	4	5
84. Compared with other countries, Israel's public administration has a good reputation.	1	2	3	4	5
Stress (Additional) 85. Whenever I go to government offices or other public institutions for some purpose, I feel tense and anxious.	1	2	3	4	5
86. For me, contacting public agencies is an irritating chore.	1	2	3	4	5

	Strongly disagree	Disagree	Neither agree nor disagree	Agree	Strongly agree
87. When I need to talk to a public officer I generally feel ill at ease.	1	2	3	4	5
Professionalism (HQ1) 88. Employees in public service are professionals and highly qualified.	1	2	3	4	5
89. Employees in public service show understanding, care, and willingness to serve the citizens.	1	2	3	4	5
90. The Israeli public service employs only high quality individuals.	1	2	3	4	5
Leadership (HQ2) 91. Public leadership and senior management in the Israeli public service are well qualified and have high professional standards.	1	2	3	4	5
92. The Israeli public service is managed appropriately and is in good order.	1	2	3	4	5
93. The leaders of the Israeli public service have a clear vision and a long range view as to where we are going.	1	2	3	4	5
Accountability and Transparency (TA) 94. Israeli public administration takes public criticism and suggestions for improvement seriously.	1	2	3	4	5
95. Today, more than ever before, the public system is willing to be exposed to the public and to the media.	1	2	3	4	5
96. Public administration treats shortcomings found by the state comptroller seriously.	1	2	3	4	5

	Strongly disagree	Disagree	Neither agree nor disagree	Agree	Strongly agree
97. Public administration sees criticism as an important tool for future service improvement.	1	2	3	4	5
98. Israeli public administration encourages public employees to accept criticism and use it to improve services for citizens.	1	2	3	4	5
Responsiveness (RS) 99. Israeli public administration responds to public requests quickly.	1	2	3	4	5
100. Israeli public administration is efficient and provides quality solutions for public needs.	1	2	3	4	5
101. Israeli public administration is sensitive to public opinions and makes a sincere effort to support those citizens who need help.	1	2	3	4	5
102. Citizens' appeals to public agencies are treated properly, effectively, and within a reasonable period of time.	1	2	3	4	5
Innovation and Creativity (IC) 103. Israeli public administration formulates promising new ideas that improve citizens' quality of life.	1	2	3	4	5
104. Compared with other countries, Israel occupies a leading position in developing useful projects for the public.	1	2	3	4	5
105. Advanced technology is involved in improving quality of service in this country.	1	2	3	4	5

	Strongly disagree	Disagree	Neither agree nor disagree	Agree	Strongly agree
Ethics and Morality (EM) 106. In Israeli public administration, most civil servants are impartial and honest.	1	2	3	4	5
107. Citizens of this country receive equal and fair treatment from public officials.	1	2	3	4	5
108. In Israeli public administration, deviations from moral norms are rare.	1	2	3	4	5
Social Orientation (Additional) 109. Israeli government ministries really try to help the weak and the unfortunate.	1	2	3	4	5
110. The state invests more in areas that need development and promotion than in other, stronger areas.	1	2	3	4	5
111. The state shares taxes equally between the rich and the poor.	1	2	3	4	5
112. The burden of reserve military duty is shared equally by all citizens.	1	2	3	4	5
113. Generally speaking, social justice considerations are more important for the public administration than financial and economic considerations.	1	2	3	4	5
Business Orientation (additional) 114. Israeli public administration is more concerned about financial matters than about helping the less fortunate.	1	2	3	4	5

	Strongly disagree	Disagree	Neither agree nor disagree	Agree	Strongly agree
115. For the Israeli public administration, economic efficiency is the most important goal, while the citizens are those who must pay the price.	1	2	3	4	5
Communication Channels (Additional) 116. When a problem arises that must be dealt with by the public sector, I know exactly who to turn to.	1	2	3	4	5
117. I think that the Israeli public administration develops reasonable ways to keep in touch with the public.	1	2	3	4	5
118. If you really want to find solution to a problem you can always turn to the public administrator who is in charge and ask for his/her help.	1	2	3	4	5
Participation in Decision-making (PDM) 119. The public administration is interested in involving the public in important decision-making processes.	1	2	3	4	5
120. The public administration treats citizens as a central partner in decision-making processes aimed at improved public performance and efficiency.	1	2	3	4	5
Political Efficacy (PE) 121. The public has a great deal of control over what public servants do in office.	1	2	3	4	5
122. The average person can make a difference by talking to public officials.	1	2	3	4	5

	Strongly disagree	Disagree	Neither agree nor disagree	Agree	Strongly agree
123. The average citizen has considerable influence over state affairs and governmental policy.	1	2	3	4	5
124. State leaders are usually sensitive to public opinion.	1	2	3	4	5
125. The average person has much to say about running local government.	1	2	3	4	5

The next items refer to your behaviour in the national and communal sphere. Please circle the number from 1 to 3 that best indicates the frequency of your involvement in these political activities on a three-point scale: 1 (never been active), 2 (was active in the past but not today), 3 (active today).

	Never been active	Was active in the past	Was or wasn't active in the past and active today
Political Participation (PP) 126. Being a member of a political party.	1	2	3
127. Keeping informed about politics.	1	2	3
128. Voting regularly in general elections.	1	2	3
129. Sending support/protest letters to politicians or to different newspapers.	1	2	3
130. Being an active member of a public organization (public committee, political party etc.)	1	2	3
131. Taking part in demonstrations or political meetings.	1	2	3
132. Engaging in political discussions.	1	2	3
133. Being a candidate for public office; signing petitions on political issues.	1	2	3

	Never been active	Was active in the past	Was or wasn't active in the past and active today
Community Involvement (CI) 134. Being a member of a voluntary organization in the community.	1	2	3
135. Being a member of a tenants' committee.	1	2	3
136. Being a member of a parents' school committee.	1	2	3
137. Taking part in community cultural activities.	1	2	3
138. Writing letters to the mayor or to other local officials about different issues	1	2	3
139. Writing letters to the local newspaper regarding community affairs.	1	2	3

Finally, the following questions request some personal details. All details will be kept confidential. Please circle the appropriate answer or clearly print where necessary.

1. Gender

    (0) Male   (1) Female

2. Marital Status

    (0) Married   (1) Not married

3. Age

    What is your age? _____

4. Number of children

    How many children under 18 do you have? _____

5. Education

    (0) Academic   (1) High education or partially academic
    (2) High school   (3) Partially high school or elementary

6. Where were you born?

    (0) Israel   (1) Other state: Please write: _____

7. Religion

    (0) Jewish   (1) Christian   (2) Moslem   (3) Other _____

8. Where do you live?

    Please write clearly the name of city or town: _____

9. Do you work as a public sector employee?

    (0) No   (1) Yes: Please indicate where exactly? _____

10. My net salary per month is

    (0) Up to NIS4000   (1) NIS5000–4001   (2) NIS6000–5001
    (3) NIS7000–6001   (4) NIS8000–7001   (5) Above NIS8000

Bibliography

Abrahamson, E. (1991). Managerial fads and fashion: The diffusion and rejection of innovations. *Academy of Management Review, 16*, 586–612.

Adams, M. and Lennon, M.J. (1992). Canadians, too, fault their political institutions and leaders. *The Public Perspective, 3*, 19.

Aiken, M. and Hage, J. (1966). Organizational alienation. *American Sociological Review, 31*, 497–507.

Almond, G.A. and Verba, S. (1963). *The Civic Culture: Political Attitudes and Democracy in Five Nations: An Analytic Study*. Boston: Little Brown.

Anderson, C. (1995). *Blaming the Government: Citizens and the Economy in Five European Democracies*. Armonk, NY: ME Sharpe.

Argyris, C. (1977). Double loop learning in organizations. *Harvard Business Review, 55*, 115–25.

Aristotle (1948). *Politics*. Translated by E. Barker. Oxford: Clarendon.

Aucoin, P. (1995). *The New Public Management: Canada in Comparative Perspective*. Montreal, Quebec: IRPP, Ashgate Publishing Ltd.

Avolio, B.J. and Bass, B.M. (1991). *The Full-range of Leadership Development*. Binghamton, NY: Center for Leadership Studies.

Baker, T.L. (1998). *Doing Social Research*. Boston: McGraw Hill.

Balk, W.K. (1985). Productivity improvement in government agencies: An ethical perspective. *Policy Studies Review, 4*, 475–83.

Barber, B. (1984). *Strong Democracy: Participatory Politics for a New Age*. Berkeley: University of California Press.

Barker, E. (1944). *The Development of Public Services in Western Europe, 1660–1930*. Oxford University Press: London.

Barner, C. and Rosenwein, R.E. (1985). *Psychological Perspectives on Politics*. Englewood Cliffs, NJ: Prentice Hall.

Baron, R.M. and Kenny, D.A. (1986). The moderator–mediator variable distinction in social psychological research: Conceptual, strategic, and statistical considerations. *Journal of Personality and Social Psychology, 6*, 1173–82.

Bass, B.M. (1985). *Leadership and Performance Beyond Expectations*. New York: Free Press.

Bennett, C. (1991). What is policy convergence and what causes it? *British Journal of Political Science, 21*, 215–33.

Bentler, P.M. (1990). Comparative fit indexes in structural models. *Psychological Bulletin, 107*, 238–46.

Bentler, P.M. and Bonett, D.G. (1980). Significance tests and goodness-of-fit in the analysis of covariance structures. *Psychological Bulletin, 88*, 588–606.

Berelson, B.R., Lazarsfeld, P.F., and McPhee, W.N. (1954). *Voting: A study of Opinion Formation in a Presidential Campaign*. Chicago: University of Chicago Press.

Berman, E.M. and West, J.P. (1994). Values management in local government. *Review of Public Personnel Administration, 14*, 6–21.

Berman, E.M. (1995). Empowering employees in state agencies: A survey of recent progress. *International Journal of Public Administration, 18*, 833–50.

Berman, E.M. (1997). Dealing with cynical citizens. *Public Administration Review 57*, 105–112.

Bernstein, P. (1980). *Workplace Democratization*. New Brunswick, NJ: Transaction Publishers.

Berry, F.S. (1994). Innovation of public management – the adoption of strategic planning. *Public Administration Review, 54*, 322–30.

Block, P. (1988). *The Empowered Manager: Positive Political Skills at Work*. San Francisco: Jossey Bass.

Bollen, K.A. (1989). *Structural Equation with Latent Variables*. New York: Wiley.

Borins, S. (1998). *Innovation with Integrity*. Washington D.C.: Georgetown University Press.

Borins, S. (2000a). Loose cannons and rule breakers, or enterprising leaders? Some evidence about innovative managers. *Public Administration Review, 60*, 490–99.

Borins, S. (2000b). What border? Public management innovation in the United States and Canada. *Journal of Policy Analysis and Management, 19*, 46–74.

Borins, S. (2001). Encouraging innovation in the public sector. *Journal of Intellectual Capital, 2*, 310–19.

Borins, S. (2002). Leadership and innovation in the public sector. *Leadership and Organization Development Journal, 23*, 467–76.

Borre, O. (2000). Critical issues and political alienation in Denmark. *Scandinavian Political Studies, 23*, 285–309.

Bouckaert, G. and Van de Walle, S. (2001). *Government Performance and Trust in Government*. Paper presented at the annual meeting of the European Group of Public Administration, Vaasa, Finland.

Bouckaert, G., Van de Walle, S., Maddens, B., and Kampen, J.K. (2002). *Identity vs. Performance: An Overview of Theories Explaining Trust in Government*. Second Report. Public Management Institute, Leuven.

Bouckaert, G. and Van de Walle, S. (2003). Quality of public service delivery and trust in government. In A. Salminen (Ed.), *Governing Networks: EGPA Yearbook* (pp. 299–318). Amsterdam: IOS Press.

Box, R.C. (1998). *Citizen Governance: Leading American Communities into the 21st Century*. Thousand Oaks, CA: Sage.

Box, R.C. (1999). Running governments like a business: Implications for public administration theory and practice. *American Review of Public Administration, 29*, 19–43.

Box, R., Marshall, G.S., Reed, B.J., and Reed, C.M. (2001). New public management and substantive democracy. *Public Administration Review*, *61*, 608–619.

Bozeman, B. (1993). *Public Management*. San Francisco: Jossey Bass.

Bozeman, D.P., Perrewe, P.L., Kacmar, K.M., Hochwarter, W.A., and Brymer, R.A. (1996). *An Examination of Reactions to Perceptions of Organizational Politics*. Paper presented at the Southern Management Association Meeting, New Orleans, LA.

Brady, H.E. (1999). Political participation. In J.P. Robinson, P.R. Shaver, and L.S. Wrightsman (Eds), *Measures of Political Attitudes* (pp. 737–801). San Diego: Academic Press.

Braithwaite, J. and Drahos, P. (2000). *Global Business Regulation*. Cambridge: Cambridge University Press.

Brief, A.P. and Motowidlo, S.J. (1986). Prosocial organizational behaviors. *Academy of Management Review*, *11*, 710–25.

Brinton, M.H. (1994). Nonprofit contracting and the hollow state. *Public Administration Review*, *54*, 73–7.

Brudney, J.L. (1990). *Fostering Volunteer Programs in the Public Sector: Planning, Initiating, and Managing Voluntary Activities*. San Francisco: Jossey Bass.

Brudney, J.L. and Duncombe, W.D. (1992). An economic evaluation of paid, volunteer, and mixed staffing options for public services. *Public Administration Review*, *52*, 474–81.

Buss, T.F., Stevens Redburn, F., and Guo, K. (Eds) (2006). *Modernizing Democracy: Innovations in Citizen Participation*. Armonk, NY: M.E. Sharpe.

Caiden, G. and Caiden, N. (2002). Toward more democratic governance: Modernizing the administrative state in Australia, Canada, the United Kingdom, and the United States. In E. Vigoda (Ed.), *Public administration: An Interdisciplinary Critical Analysis* (pp. 37–61). New York: Marcel Dekker.

Callahan, K. and Holzer, M. (1994). Rethinking governmental change: New ideas, new partnership. *Public Productivity and Management Review*, *17*, 201–214.

Campbell, A., Converse, P.E., Miller, W.E., and Stokes, D.E. (1960). *The American Voter*. New York: Wiley.

Carayannis, E.G. and Gonzalez, E. (2003). Creativity and innovation = competitiveness? When, how, and why. In L.V. Shavinina (Ed.), *The Handbook of Innovation* (pp. 587–606). Oxford: Pergamon.

Carnis, I. (2005). *The Economic Theory of Bureaucracy: Mainstream Approach versus Austrian Developments*. 2nd Mises Seminar. http://brunoleoni. servingfreedom.net/WP/051007_Mises_WP_Carnis.pdf.

Carter, N. (1989). Performance indicators: "Backseat driving" or "hands off" control? *Policy and Politics*, *17*, 131–8.

Centers for Disease Control (1981). Pheunocystis pneumonia: Los Angeles, *Morbidity and Mortality Weekly Report*, *30*, 250.

Chanley, V.A. and Rahn, T.J. (2000). Quality of public service and trust in government. *Public Opinion Quarterly*, *64*, 239–56.

Chi, K.S. (1999). Improving responsiveness. *Public Administration Review, 59,* 278–80.

Chisholm, R. (1998). *Developing Network Organization.* Reading, MA: Addison-Wesley.

Christensen, T. and Laegreid, P. (1999). New public management – design, resistance, or transformation? A study of how modern reforms are received in a civil service system. *Public Productivity and Management Review, 23,* 169–93.

Citrin, J. (1974). Comment: The political relevance of trust in government. *American Political Science Review, 68,* 973–88.

Citrin, J. and Luks, S. (2001). Political trust revisited: Déjà vu all over again? In J.R. Hibbing and E. Theiss-Morse (Eds), *What is it About Government that Americans Dislike?* (pp. 9–28). Cambridge, MA: Cambridge University Press.

Citrin, J. and Muste, C. (1999). Trust in government. In J.P. Robinson, P.R. Shaver, and L.S. Wrightsman (Eds), *Measures of Political Attitudes* (pp. 465–532). San Diego: Academic Press.

Coble, R. (1999). The nonprofit sector and state governments: Public policy issues facing nonprofit in North Carolina and other states. *Nonprofit Management and Leadership, 9,* 293–313.

Cohen, A. (2003). *Multiple Commitments in the Workplace: An Integrative Approach.* Mahwah, NJ: Lawrence Erlbaum Associates.

Cohen, A. and Vigoda, E. (1998). The growth value of good citizenship: An examination of the relationship between civic behavior and involvement in the job. *Applied Psychology: An International Review, 47,* 559–70.

Cohen, A. and Vigoda, E. (1999). Politics and the workplace: An empirical examination of the relationship between political behavior and work outcomes. *Public Productivity and Management Review, 22,* 389–406.

Cohen, A. and Vigoda, E. (2000). Do good citizens make good organizational citizens? An empirical examination of the effects of citizenship behavior and orientations on organizational citizenship behavior. *Administration and Society, 32,* 506–624.

Cohen, J. (1988). *Statistical Power Analysis for the Behavioral Sciences (2nd edn).* Hillsdale, NJ: Lawrence Erlbaum Associates.

Collin, S.O. (1998). In the twilight zone: A survey of public–private partnership in Sweden. *Public Productivity and Management Review, 21,* 272–83.

Conover, P.J., Crewe, I., and Searing, D.D. (1993). *Citizen Identities in the Liberal State.* Paper prepared for the annual meeting of the American Political Science Association.

Cotton, J.L., Vollrath, D.A., Froggat, K.L., Lengnick-Hall, M.L., and Jennings, K.R. (1988). Employee participation: Diverse forms and different outcomes. *Academy of Management Review, 13,* 8–22.

Coulson, A. (1998). Trust and contract in public sector management. In A. Coulson (Ed.), *Trust and Contracts: Relationships in Local Government, Health and Public Services* (pp. 9–34). Bristol: The Policy Press.

Cropanzano, R., Howes, J.C., Grandey, A.A., and Toth, P. (1997). The relationship of organizational politics and support to work behaviors, attitudes, and stress. *Journal of Organizational Behavior, 18*, 159–80.

Crozier, M. and Friedberg, E. (1980). *Actors and Systems.* Chicago: University of Chicago Press.

Dahl, R.A. (1971). *Polyarchy, Participation and Opposition.* New Haven: Yale University Press.

Damanpour, F. (1991). Organizational innovation: a meta-analysis of effects of determinants and moderators. *Academy of Management Journal, 34*, 555–90.

Damanpour, F. and Gopalakrishnan, S. (1998). Theories of organizational structure and innovation adoption: The role of environmental changes. *Journal of Engineering and Technology Management, 15*, 1–24.

DeLeon, L. (1996). Ethics and entrepreneurship. *Policy Studies Journal, 24*, 495–510.

Deshpande, R., Farley, J.U., and Webster, F.E., Jr. (1997). *Factors Affecting Organizational Performance: A Five-country Comparison.* Marketing Science Institute Working Paper Report, 97–108; Cambridge, MA: Marketing Science Institute.

Deshpande, R. and Zaltman, G. (1982). Factors affecting the use of market research information: A path analysis. *Journal of Marketing Research, 19*, 14–31.

DHSS (1979). *Patients First.* HMSO, London.

Dolowitz, D. and Marsh, D. (1996). Who learns what from whom: A review of the policy transfer literature. *Political Studies, 44*, 343–57.

Dolowitz, D. and Marsh, D. (2000). Learning from abroad: The role of policy transfer in contemporary policy-making. *Governance, 13*, 5–24.

Drory, A. (1993). Perceived political climate and job attitudes. *Organizational Studies, 14*, 59–71.

Drucker, P. (1966). *The Practice of Management.* New York: Harper and Row.

Drucker, P. (1974). *Management: Tasks, Responsibilities, Practices.* New York: Harper and Row.

Dunham, R.B. and Pierce, J.L. (1989). *Management.* Glenview, IL: Scott, Foresman and Co.

Dye, T. (1995). *Understanding Public Policy (8th edn),* Englewood Cliffs, NJ: Prentice Hall.

Eisinger, R.M. (2000). Questioning cynicism. *Society, 37*, 55–60.

Elden, M. (1977). *Political Efficacy at Work.* Paper presented for Seminar on Social Change and Organizational Development, Inter-University Center for Graduate Studies. Dubrovnik, Yugoslavia (December).

Erber, R. and Lau, R.R. (1990). Political cynicism revisited: An information-processing reconciliation of policy-based and incumbency-based interpretations of changes in trust in government. *American Journal of Political Science*, *34*, 236–53.

Erez, M., Earley, C.P., and Hulin, L.C. (1985). The impact of participation on goal acceptance and performance: A two-step model. *Academy of Management Journal*, *28*, 50–66.

Erez, M. and Rim, Y. (1982). The relationship between goals, influence tactics and personal and organizational variables. *Human Relations*, *35*, 877–8.

Esman, M.J. (1997). Public administration, ethnic conflict, and economic development. *Public Administration Review*, *57*, 527–33.

Etzioni, A. (1994). *The Spirit of Community*. New York: Touchstone.

Etzioni, A. (1995). *New Communitarian Thinking: Persons, Virtues, Institutions, and Communities*. Charlottesville: Virginia University Press.

Etzioni-Halevy, E. (1983). *Bureaucracy and Democracy: A Political Dilemma*. Boston: Routledge and Kegan Paul.

Evans, K.G. (1996). Managing chaos and complexity in government: A new paradigm of managing change, innovation, and organizational renewal. *Public Administration Review*, *56*, 491–4.

Farazmand, A. (1999). Globalization and public administration. *Public Administration Review*, *59*, 509–522.

Farh, J., Podsakoff, P.M., and Organ, D.W. (1990). Accounting for organizational citizenship behavior: Leader fairness and task scope versus satisfaction. *Journal of Management*, *16*, 705–721.

Ferlie, E., Hartley, J., and Martin, S. (2003). Changing public service organizations: Current perspectives and future prospects. *British Journal of Management*, *14*, 1–14.

Ferris, G.R., Frink, D.D., Galang, M.C., Zhou, J., Kacmar, M.K., and Howard, J.L. (1996). Perceptions of organizational politics: Prediction, stress-related implications, and outcomes. *Human Relations*, *49*, 233–66.

Ferris, G.R. and Kacmar, K.M. (1992). Perceptions of organizational politics. *Journal of Management*, *18*, 93–116.

Ferris, G.R., Russ, G.S., and Fandt, P.M. (1989). Politics in organizations. In R.A. Giacalone and P. Rosenfeld (Eds), *Impression Management in the Organization* (pp. 143–70). Hillsdale, NJ: Lawrence Erlbaum.

Finkel, S.E., Sigelman, L., and Humphries, S. (1999). Democratic values and political tolerance. In J.P. Robinson, P.R. Shaver, and L.S. Wrightsman (Eds), *Measures of Political Attitudes* (pp. 203–296). San Diego: Academic Press.

Finkelstein, N.D. (Ed.) (2000). *Transparency in Public Policy: Great Britain and the United States*. London: Macmillan Press.

Finnemore, M. (1996). *National Interests in International Society*. Ithaca, NY: Cornell University Press.

Folger, R., Konovsky, M.A., and Cropanzano, R. (1992). A due process metaphor for performance appraisal. In L.L. Cummings and B.M. Staw (Eds), *Research in Organizational Behavior, 14 (*pp. 129–77). Greenwich, CT: JAI Press.

Fomburn, C.J. (1996). *Reputation: Realizing Value from the Corporate Image.* Boston: Harvard Business School Press.

Fombrun, C. and Shanley, M. (1990). What's in a name? Reputation building and corporate strategy. *Academy of Management Journal. 33*, 233–58.

Fornell, C., Anderson, E.W., Cha, J., and Bryant, B.E. (1996). The American Customer Satisfaction Index: nature, purpose and findings. *Journal of Marketing, 60*, 7–18.

Fox, C.J. and Miller, H.T. (1996). *Postmodern Public Administration; Toward Discourse.* London: Sage.

Fox, C.J. and Miller, H.T. (1997). The depreciating public policy discourse. *American Behavioral Scientist, 41*, 64–89.

Frambach R.T. and Schillewaert, N. (2002). Organizational innovation adoption – A multi-level framework of determinants and opportunities for future research. *Journal of Business Research, 55*, 163–76.

Frederickson, G.H. (1982). The recovery of civism in public administration. *Public Administration Review, 42*, 501–509.

Frederickson, G.H. (1997). *The Spirit of Public Administration.* San Francisco: Jossey Bass.

Gandz, J. and Murray, V.V. (1980). The experience of workplace politics. *Academy of Management Journal, 23*, 237–51.

Garson, G.D. and Overman, E.S. (1983). *Public Management Research in the United States.* New York: Praeger.

Gawthrop, L.C. (1976). Administrative responsibility: Public policy and the Wilsonian Legacy. *Policy Studies Journal, 5*, 108–113.

Gawthrop, L.C. (1997). Democracy, bureaucracy, and hypocrisy redux: A search for the sympathy and compassion. *Public Administration Review, 57*, 205–210.

Gawthrop, L.C. (1998). *Public Service and Democracy: Ethical Imperatives for the 21st Century.* New York: Chatham House.

Giddens, A. (1984). *The Constitution of Society: Outline of the Theory of Structuration.* Berkeley: University of California Press.

Giddens, A. (1990). *The Consequences of Modernity.* Stanford, CA: Stanford University Press.

Gidron, B. and Kramer, R.M. (1992). *Governments and the Third Sector: Emerging Relationships in Welfare States.* San Francisco: Jossey Bass.

Glaister, S. (1999). Past abuses and future uses of private finance and public–private partnership in transport. *Public Money and Management, 19*, 29–36.

Glaser, M.A. and Hildreth, B.W. (1999). Service delivery satisfaction and willingness to pay taxes. *Public Productivity and Management Review, 23*, 48–67.

Goldoff, A.C. (1996). The public interest standard and deregulation. The impact of the fairness doctrine. *International Journal of Public Administration, 19,* 51–74.

Golembiewski, R.T. (1989). Toward a positive and practical public management: Organizational research supporting a fourth critical citizenship. *Administration and Society, 21,* 200–227.

Golembiewski, R.T. (1990). A bit further ... *Administration and Society, 21,* 493–500.

Golembiewski, R.T. (1995). *Practical Public Management.* New York: Marcel Dekker.

Golembiewski, R.T., Boudreau, R.A., Munzenrider, R.F. and Luo, H. (1996). *Global Burnout: A Worldwide Pandemic Explored by the Phase Model.* Greenwich, CT: JAI Press.

Golembiewski, R.T. and Vigoda, E. (2000). Organizational innovation and the science/craft of management. In M.A. Rahim, R.T. Golembiewski, and K.D. Mackenzie (Eds), *Current Topics in Management* (vol. 5 pp. 263–80). Greenwich, CT: JAI Press.

Goodsell, C.T. (1983). *The Case for Bureaucracy: A Public Administration Polemic.* Chatham, NJ: Chatham House Publishers.

Gopalakrishnan, S. and Damanpour, F. (1997). A review of innovation research in economics, sociology, and technology management, *Omega-International Journal of Management Science, 25,* 15–28.

Gow, J.I. (1992). Diffusion of administrative innovations in Canadian public administrations, *Administration and Society, 23,* 430–54.

Graham, J.W. (1991). An Essay on Organizational Citizenship Behavior. *Employee Responsibilities and Rights Journal, 4,* 249–270.

Grandey, A. (2003). When "the show must go on": surface acting and deep acting as determinants of emotional exhaustion and peer-rated service delivery. *Academy of Management Journal, 46,* 86–96.

Gray, V. (1973). Innovation in the states: A diffusion study. *American Political Science Review, 67,* 1174–85.

Grubbs, J.W. (2000). Can agencies work together? Collaboration in public and nonprofit organizations, *Public Administration Review, 60,* 275–80.

Haas, M.P. (1992). Introduction: Epistemic communities and international policy coordination. *International Organization, 46,* 1–36.

Halachmi, A. (2002). Who gets what when and how: Performance measures for accountability? For improved performance? *International Review of Public Administration, 7,* 1–11.

Hall, A.P. (1993). Policy paradigms, social learning and the state. *Comparative Politics,* 25: 275–96.

Harris, K.J. and Kacmar, K.M. (2005). Easing the strain: The buffer role of supervisors in the perceptions of politics-strain relationship. *Journal of Occupational and Organizational Psychology, 78,* 337–54.

Harrison, J.B. and Freeman, R.E. (Eds) (2004). Democracy in and around organizations. *Exchange, 18*, 49–98.

Hart, D. (1997). A partnership in virtue among all citizens: The public service and the civic humanist tradition. *International Journal of Public Administration, 20*, 967–80.

Hart, D.K. and Grant, N.K. (1989). A partnership in virtue among all citizens: The public service and civic humanism; response to David Kirk Hart. *Public Administration Review, 49*, 101–107.

Hibbing, J.R. and Theiss-Morse, E. (2001). Process preferences and American politics: What the people want government to be. *American Political Science Review, 95*, 145–53.

Hibbing, J.R. and Theiss-Morse, E. (2002). *Stealth Democracy: Americans' Beliefs about how Government should Work.* Cambridge, MA: Cambridge University Press.

Hill, C.J. (2005). Is hierarchical governance in decline? Evidence from empirical research; [1]. *Journal of Public Administration Research and Theory, 15*, 173–96.

Hirschman, A.O. (1970). *Exit, Voice and Loyalty.* Cambridge, MA: Harvard University Press.

Hobby, G.L. (1985). *Penicillin: Meeting the challenge.* London: Yale University Press.

Holzer, M. (1989). Public service: Present problems, future prospects. *International Journal of Public Administration, 12*, 585–93.

Holzer, M. and Rabin, J. (1987). Public service: Problems, professionalism, and policy recommendations. *Public Productivity Review, 43*, 3–12.

Hood, C. (1991). A public management for all seasons? *Public Administration, 69*, 3–19.

Hood, C. (1998). *The Art of the State. Culture, Rhetoric, and Public Management.* Oxford, Clarendon Press.

Hurd, D. (1989). Freedom will flourish where citizens accept responsibility. *The Independent*, 13 September.

Irvin, R.A. and Stansbury, J. (2004). Citizen participation in decision-making: Is it worth the effort? *Public Administration Review, 64*, 55–65.

Jacoby, W. (2000) *Imitation and Politics: Redesigning Modern Germany.* Ithaca: Cornell University Press.

Janoski, T. and Wilson, J. (1995). Pathways to voluntarism: Family socialization and status transmission model. *Social Forces, 74*, 271–92.

Jaworski, B.J. and Kohli, A.K. (1993). Market orientation: Antecedents and consequences. *Journal of Marketing, 57*, 3, 53–70.

John, D., Kettl, D.F., Dyer, B., and Lovan, W.R. (1994). What will new governance mean for the federal government? *Public Administration Review, 54*, 170–76.

Johnston-Conover, P., Serring, D., and Crewe, I. (2004). The elusive ideal model of equal citizenship: Political theory and political psychology. *Journal of Politics, 66*, 1036–1068.

Jordan, A., Wurzel, R., and Zito, A. (2005). The rise of "new" policy instruments in comparative perspective: Has governance eclipsed government? *Political Studies*, *53*, 477–96.

Jordana, J. and Levi-Faur, D. (2003). *The Rise of the Regulatory State in Latin America*. Presented at the American Political Science Association Annual Meeting, Philadelphia, 28–31 August.

Joreskog, K.G. (1977). Structural equation models in the social sciences: Specifications, estimation and testing. In P.R. Krishnaiah (Ed.), *Application of Statistics* (pp. 265–87). Amsterdam: North Holland.

Joreskog, K. and Sorbom, D. (1994). *Structural Equation Modeling with the SIMPLIS Command Language*. Chicago: Scientific Software International.

Joreskog, K.G. and Van Thillo, M. (1973). *LISREL – A General Computer Program for Estimating a Linear Structural Equation System involving Multiple Indicators of Unmeasured Variables*. Research Report 73–5, Department of Statistics, Uppsala University, Sweden.

Joyce, M.S. (1994). Citizenship in the 21st century: Individual self-government. In D.E. Eberly (Ed.), *Building a Community of Citizens* (pp. 3–10). Lanham, MD: University Press of America.

Kaase, M. and Marsh, A. (1979). Political action: A theoretical perspective. In S.H. Barnes, M. Kaase, et al., (Eds), *Political Action: Mass Participation in Five Western Democracies* (pp. 27–56). Beverly Hills, CA: Sage.

Kacmar, K.M., Bozeman, D.P., Carlson, D.S., and Anthony, W.P. (1999). An examination of the perceptions of organizational politics model: Replication and extension. *Human Relations*, *52*, 383–416.

Kacmar, K.M. and Carlson, D.S. (1994). *Further Validation of the Perceptions of Politics Scale (POPS): A Multiple Sample Investigation*. Paper presented at Academy of Management Meeting, Dallas, Texas.

Kacmar, K.M. and Ferris, G.R. (1991). Perceptions of organizational politics scale (POPS): Development and construct validation. *Educational and Psychological Measurement*, *51*, 193–205.

Kahn, L.M. (1993). Managerial quality, team success, and individual player performance in major league baseball. *Industrial and Labor Relations Review*, *46*, 531–47.

Katz, D. and Kahn, R.L. (1966). *The Social Psychology of Organizations*. New York: Wiley.

Keller, R.T. (1997). Job involvement and organizational commitment as longitudinal predictors of job performance: A study of scientists and engineers. *Journal of Applied Psychology*, *82*, 539–45.

Kelly, M.R. (1998). An inclusive democratic polity, representative bureaucracies, and the New Public Management. *Public Administration Review*, *58*, 201–208.

Kenny, D.A., Kashy, D.A., and Bolder, N. (1998). Data analysis in social psychology. In D.T. Gilbert, S.T. Fiske, and G. Lindzey (Eds), *The Handbook of Social Psychology*, 4th edn, (vol. 1, pp. 233–65). New York: Oxford University Press.

Keon, S.C. (1999). Improving responsiveness. *Public Administration Review, 59,* 278–80.

Kimberly, J.R. (1981). Managerial innovation. In P.C. Nystrom and W.H. Starbuck (Eds), *Handbook of Organizational Design* (vol. 1, pp. 81–109). New York: Oxford University Press.

Kimberly, J.R. and de Pouvourville, G. (1993). *The Migration of Managerial Innovation.* San Francisco: Jossey Bass.

King, C., Feltey, K.M., and Susel, B.O. (1998). The question of participation: Toward authentic public participation in public administration. *Public Administration Review, 58,* 317–26.

King, C. and Stivers, C. (1998). *Government is Us: Public Administration in an Anti-government Era.* Thousand Oaks, CA: Sage.

King, D. (1997). The polarization of American parties and mistrust of government. In J.S. Nye, P.D. Zelikow, and D.C. King (Eds), *Why People don't Trust Government* (pp. 155–78). Cambridge, MA: Harvard University Press.

King N. (1990). Innovation at work: the research literature. In M.A. West and J.L. Farr (Eds), *Innovation and Creativity at Work* (pp. 15–59). England: Wiley.

Kipnis, D. and Schmidt, S.M. (1982). *Profile of Organizational Influence Strategies.* San Diego: University Associates.

Kipnis, D. and Schmidt, S.M. (1983). An influence perspective on bargaining. In M. Bazerman and R. Lewicki (Eds), *Negotiating in Organizations (*pp. 303–319). Beverly Hills, CA: Sage.

Kipnis, D. and Schmidt, S.M. (1988). Upward influence styles: Relationship with performance evaluations, salary, and stress. *Administrative Science Quarterly, 33,* 528–42.

Kipnis, D., Schmidt, S.M., and Wilkinson, I. (1980). Intraorganizational influence tactics: Exploration in getting one's way. *Journal of Applied Psychology, 65,* 440–52.

Koch, J. and Cabula, R.J. (1994). In search of excellent management. *The Journal of Management Studies, 31,* 681–99.

Kock, M.H. de (1974). *Central banking (4th edn).* London: Crosby, Lockwood, Staples.

Kohli, A.K. and Jaworski, B.J. (1990). Market orientation: The construct, research propositions, and managerial implications. *Journal of Marketing, 54,* 1–18.

Kramer, R. (1999). Weaving the public into public administration. *Public Administration Review, 59,* 89–92.

Kuhn, T.S. (1962). *The Structure of Scientific Revolutions.* Chicago: University of Chicago Press.

Lane, R. (1965). The politics of consensus in an age of affluence. *American Political Science Review, 59,* 874–95.

Levi-Faur, D. (2002). *Herding Towards a New Convention: On Herds, Shepherds, and Lost Sheep in the Liberalization of the Telecommunications and Electricity Industries.* Politics Papers Series (Nuffield College, University of Oxford), W6.

Levi-Faur, D. (2004). Comparative research design in the study of regulation: How to increase the number of cases without compromising the strengths of case-oriented analysis. In J. Jordana and D. Levi-Faur (Eds), *The Politics of Regulation* (pp. 177–99). Manchester: Elgar and the Centre on Regulation and Competition, University of Manchester.

Levi-Faur, D. and Vigoda-Gadot, E. (Eds) (2004a). *International Public Policy and Management: Policy Learning beyond Regional, Cultural and Political Boundaries*. New York: Marcel Dekker.

Levi-Faur, D. and Vigoda-Gadot, E. (2004b). The international transfer and diffusion of policy and management innovations: Some characteristics of a new order in the making. In D. Levi-Faur and E. Vigoda-Gadot (Eds), *International Public Policy and Management: Policy Learning beyond Regional, Cultural, and Political Boundaries* (pp. 1–24). New York: Marcel Dekker.

Levi-Faur, D. and Vigoda-Gadot, E. (2006). New public policy, new policy transfers: some characteristics of a new order in the making. *International Journal of Public Administration*, *29*, (4,5,6), 247–62.

Lewin, K. (1936). *Principles of Topological Psychology*. New York: McGraw Hill.

Luhmann, N. (1988). Familiarity, confidence, trust: Problems and alternatives. In D. Gambetta (Ed.).*Trust Making and Breaking Cooperative Relations* (pp. 94–107). Oxford: Basil Blackwell.

Lui, T.T. and Cooper, T.L. (1997). Values in flux: Administrative ethics and the Hong Kong public servant. *Administration and Society*, *29*, 301–324.

Lum, L., Kervin, J, Clark, K., Reied, F., and Sirola, W. (1998). Explaining nursing turnover intent: Job satisfaction, pay satisfaction, or organizational commitment? *Journal of Organizational Behavior*, *19*, 305–320.

Lumpkin, G.T. and Dess, G.G (1996). Clarifying the entrepreneurial orientation construct and linking it to performance. *Academy of Management Journal, 21*, 135–72.

Lynn, L.E. (1996). *Public Management as Art, Science, and Profession*. Chatham, NJ: Chatham House Publishers.

Lynn, L.E. (1998). The new public management: How to transform a theme into a legacy. *Public Administration Review*, *58*, 231–7.

Madison, L.M., Allen, R.W., Porter, L.W., Renwick, P.A., and Mayes, B.T. (1980). Organizational politics: An exploration of managers' perceptions. *Human Relations*, *33*, 79–100.

Majone, G. (1996). Public policy and administration: Ideas, interests and institutions. In Goodin, E. Robert, and Klingemann, Hans-Dieter (Eds), *A New Handbook of Political Science* (pp. 610–27). Oxford: Oxford University Press.

Marsh, D. and Smith, J.N. (2004). *Globalization, The Discourse of Globalization and the Hollowing Out of the Nation State*. Unpublished manuscript.

Marshall, D. (1990). The restorative qualities of citizenship. *Public Administration Review*, *50*, 21–5.

Marshall, T.H. (1950). *Citizenship and Social Class and Other Essays*. Cambridge: Cambridge University Press.

Marshall, T.H. (1965). *Class, Citizenship and Social Development*. Garden City, NY: Anchor.

McKevitt, D. (1998). *Managing Core Public Services*. Oxford: Blackwell.

McPherson, J.M. and Rotolo, T. (1996). Testing a dynamic model of social composition: Diversity and change in voluntary groups. *American Sociological Review*, *61*, 179–202.

Medsker, G.J., Williams, L.J., and Holahan, P.J. (1994). A review of current practices for evaluating causal models in organizational behavior and human resources management research. *Journal of Management*, *20*, 239–64.

Meseguer, C. (2003). *The Diffusion of Privatisation in Industrial and Latin American Countries: What Role for Learning?* Prepared for delivery at the workshop on the Internationalization of Regulatory Reforms: The Interaction of Policy Learning and Policy Emulation in Diffusion Processes, Berkeley, 24–25 April.

Meyer, J.W., Boli, J.T., George M., and Ramirez, F.O. (1997). World society and the nation-state. *American Journal of Sociology*, *103*: 144–81.

Michael, H. (1981). Youth, voluntary associations and political socialization. *Social Forces*, *60*, 211–23.

Milbrath, L.W. (1981). Political participation. In S.L. Long (Ed.), *The Handbook of Political Behavior* (vol. 4, pp. 197–237). New York: Plenum.

Milbrath, L.W. and Goel, M.L. (1977). *Political participation (2nd edn)*. Chicago: Rand McNally and Company.

Miles, R.E., Snow, C.C., Meyer, A.D., and Coleman, H.J. (1978). Organization strategy, structure, and process, *Academy of Management Review*, *3*, 546–62.

Miller, A.H. and Listhoug, O. (1990). Political parties and confidence in government: A comparison of Norway, Sweden and the United States. *British Journal of Political Science*, *20*, 357–86.

Miller, A.H. and Listhoug, O. (1998). Policy preferences and political distrust: A comparison of Norway, Sweden and the United States. *Scandinavian Political Studies*, *21*, 161–87.

Miller, W.E. and Shanks, J.M. (1996). *The New American Voter*. Cambridge, MA: Harvard University Press.

Mintzberg, H. (1983). *Power In and Around Organizations*. Englewood Cliffs, NJ: Prentice Hall.

Mises, L. (von) (1939). Le calcul économique en régime collectiviste. In N.G. Pierson, Ludwig von Mises, G. Halm, E. Barone and F.A. von Hayek (Eds), *L'économie dirigée en régime collectiviste, Etudes critiques sur les possibilités du socialisme* (pp. 93–132). Librairie de *Médicis*.

Mises L. (von) (1983 [1969] [1944]). *Bureaucracy*. The Libertarian Press.

Mises, L. (von) (1990 [1920]). *Economic Calculation in the Socialist Commonwealth*. Auburn, AL: Ludwig von Mises Institute.

Mishler, W. and Rose, R. (1997). Trust, distrust and skepticism: Popular evaluation of civil and political institutions in post-communist societies. *Journal of Politics*, *59*, 418–51.

Mizrahi, S. (2002). Workers' participation in decision-making processes and firm stability. *British Journal of Industrial Relations, 40*, 689–707.

Molm, L.D. (1997). *Coercive Power in Social Exchange*. Cambridge: Cambridge University Press.

Monroe, K.R. (1994). A fat lady in a corset: Altruism and social theory. *American Journal of Political Science*, *38*, 861–93.

Moon, M.J. (1999). The pursuit of managerial entrepreneurship: Does organization matter? *Public Administration Review*, *59*, 31–43.

Morrison, E.W. (1996). Organizational citizenship behavior as a critical link between HRM practices and service quality. *Human Resource Management*, *35*, 493–512.

Mosher, F. (1982). *Democracy and the Public Service*. (2nd edn) New York: Oxford University Press.

Muczyk, J.P. and Reinmann, B.C. (1987). The case for directive leadership. *Academy of Management Executive*, *1*, 301–311.

Mueller, R.O. (1996). *Basic Principles of Structural Equation Modeling*. New York: Springer.

Nagel, J.H. (1987). *Participation*. Englewood Cliffs, NJ: Prentice Hall.

Nalbandian, J. (1980). The bureaucrat. *New Brunswick*, *9*, 38.

Nalbandian, J. (1999). Facilitating community, enabling democracy: New roles for local government managers. *Public Administration Review*, *59*, 187–97.

Narver, J.C., Jacobson, R., and Slater, S.F. (1993). *Market Orientation and Business performance: An Analysis of Panel Data*. Marketing Science Institute Working Paper Report Number, 93–121. Cambridge, MA: Marketing Science Institute.

Narver, J.C. and Slater, S.F. (1990). The effect of a market orientation on business profitability. *Journal of Marketing*, *54*, 20–35.

National Consumer Council (1986). *Measuring Up: Consumer Assessment of Local Authority Services*. London.

Near, J.P., Rice, R.W., and Hunt, R.G. (1987). Job satisfaction and life satisfaction: A profile analysis. *Social Indicators Research*, *19*, 383–401.

Niehoff, B.P. and Moorman, R.H. (1993). Justice as a mediator of the relationship between methods of monitoring and organizational citizenship behavior. *Academy of Management Journal*, *36*, 527–56.

Niemi, R.G., Craig, S.C. and Mattei, F. (1991). Measuring internal political efficacy in the 1988 National Election Study. *American Political Science Review*, *85*, 1407–1413.

Niskanen, W.N. (1968). The peculiar economics of bureaucracy. *American Economic Review, Papers and Proceedings of the Eightieth Annual Meeting of the American Economic Association*, *58(*2) 293–305.

Niskanen, W.N. (1994). *Bureaucracy and Public Economics*. The Locke Institute.

Nowrot, K. (1999). Legal consequences of globalization: The status of non-governmental organizations under international law. *Indiana Journal of Global Legal Studies*, 6(2), 579–645.

Nye, J.S., Zelikow, P.D., and King, D.C. (Eds) (1997). *Why People Don't Trust Government*. Cambridge, MA: Harvard University Press.

Nyhan, R.C. (1995). Performance measurement in the public sector: Challenges and opportunities. *Public Productivity and Management Review*, *18*, 333–48.

O'Connell, B. (1989). What voluntary activity can and cannot do for America. *Public Administration Review*, *49*, 486–91.

Ohame, K. (1995). *The End of the Nation State*. London: Collins.

Oliver, D. and Heater, D. (1994). *The Foundation of Citizenship*. London: Harvester Wheatsheaf.

Organ, D.W. (1988). *O.C.B.: The Good Soldier Syndrome*. Lexington, MA: Lexington Books.

Organ, D.W. (1994). Personality and organizational citizenship behavior. *Journal of Management*, *20*, 465–78.

Organ, D.W. and Konovsky, M. (1989). Cognitive versus affective determinants of organizational citizenship behavior. *Journal of Applied Psychology*, *74*, 157–64.

Organ, D.W. and Ryan, K. (1995). A meta-analytic review of attitudinal and dispositional predictors of organizational citizenship behavior. *Personnel Psychology*, *48*, 775–802.

Osborne, D. and Gaebler, T. (1992). *Reinventing Government*. New York: Plume.

Osterman, P. (1999). *Securing Prosperity*. Princeton: Princeton University Press.

Ostrom, E. (1993). A communitarian approach to local governance. *National Civic Review* (Summer), 226–33.

Palfrey, C., Phillips, C., Thomas, P., and Edward, D. (1992). *Policy Evaluation in the Public Sector*. Hants: Avenbury.

Parry, K.W. (2003). Leadership, culture and performance: The case of the New Zealand public sector. *Journal of Change Management*, *4*, 376–99.

Pateman, C. (1970). *Participation and Democratic Theory*. London: Cambridge University Press.

Peled, A. (2001). Network, coalition and institution: the politics of technological innovation in the public sector. *Information Technology and People*, *14*, 184–205.

Pelham, A.M. and Wilson, D.T. (1996). A longitudinal study of the impact of market structure, firm structure, strategy, and market orientation culture on dimensions of small-firm performance. *Journal of the Academy of Marketing Science*, *24*, 27–43.

Perry, J.L. and Kraemer, K. (1983). *Public Management: Public and Private Perspectives*. Palo Alto, CA: Mayfield.

Peters, G. (1997). Policy transfers between governments: The case of administrative reforms. *West European Politics*, *20*(4), 71–88.

Peters, G. (2000). Government and comparative politics. In J. Pierre (Ed.), *Debating Governance* (pp. 36–53). Oxford: Oxford University Press.

Peters, G. (2001). *The Politics of Bureaucracy*. London: Sage.

Peterson, S.A. (1990). *Political Behavior*. Thousand Oaks, CA: Sage.

Pfeffer, J. (1992). *Management with Power*. Boston: Harvard Business School Press.

Pharr, S.J. (1997). Public trust and democracy. In J.S. Nye, P.D. Zelikow, and D.C. King (Eds), *Why People Don't Trust Government*. Cambridge, MA: Harvard University Press.

Pierre, J. (1999). Models of urban governance: The institutional dimension of urban politics. *Urban Affairs Review, 34*, 372–96.

Piliavin, J.A. and Charng, H.W. (1990). Altruism: A review of recent theory and research. *Annual Review of Sociology, 16*, 27–65.

Podsakoff, P.M. and MacKenzie, S.B. (1997). Impact of Organizational Citizenship Behavior on Organizational Performance: A review and suggestions for future research. *Human Performance, 10*, 133–51.

Poister, T.H. and Henry, G.T. (1994). Citizen ratings of public and private service quality: A comparative perspective. *Public Administration Review, 54*, 155–60.

Pollitt, C. (1988). Bringing consumers into performance measurement. *Policy and Politics, 16*, 77–87.

Pollitt, C. and Bouckaert, G. (2000). *Public Management Reform*. Oxford: Oxford University Press.

Pollitt, C., Girre, X., Lonsdale, J., Mul, R., Summa, H., and Waerness, M. (1999). *Performance or Compliance?* Oxford: Oxford University Press.

Popper, K.R. (1991). *The Open Society and its Enemies*. London: Routledge.

Porter, L.W., Steers, R.M., Mowday, R.T., and Boulian, P.V. (1974). Organizational commitment, job satisfaction and turnover among psychiatric technicians. *Journal of Applied Psychology, 59*, 603–609.

Powell, M.A. (Ed.) (1999). *New Labor, New Welfare State: The "Third Way" in British Social Policy*. The Policy Press.

Putnam, R. (1993). *Making Democracy Work: Civic Traditions in Modern Italy*. Princeton, NJ: Princeton University Press.

Rainey, H. (1990). Public management: recent development and current prospects. In N.B. Lynn and A. Wildavsky (Eds), *Public Administration: The State of the Discipline* (pp. 157–84). Chatham, NJ: Chatham House.

Rhodes, R.A.W. (1987). Developing the public service orientation, or, let's add a soupcon of political theory. *Local Government Studies, May–June*, 63–73.

Rhodes, R.A.W. (1997). *Understanding Governance: Policy Networks, Governance, Reflexivity and Accountability*. Open University Press.

Rhodes, R.A.W. and Marsh, D. (1992). New directions in the study of policy networks. *European Journal of Political Research, 21*, 181–205.

Richardson, W.D. (1997). *Democracy, Bureaucracy, and Charter: Founding Thought*. Lawrence, KS: University Press of Kansas.

Richardson, W.D. and Nigro, L.G. (1991). The constitution and administrative ethics in America. *Administration and Society*, *23*, 275–87.

Ridder, H.G., Bruns, H.J. and Spier, F. (2005). Analysis of public management change processes: The case of local government accounting reforms in Germany. *Public Administration*, *83*, 443–71.

Rimmerman, C.A. (1997). *The New Citizenship: Unconventional Politics, Activism, and Service*. Boulder, CO: Westview Press.

Rogers, E.M. (1995). *The Diffusion of Innovations* (5th edn). New York: Free Press.

Rogers, E.M., Dearing, J.W., and Chang, S. (1991). AIDS in the 1980s: The agenda-setting process for a public issue. *Journalism Monographs*, *126*, April, 1–47.

Romm, T. and Drory, A. (1988). Political behavior in organizations: A cross-cultural comparison. *International Journal of Value Based Management*, *1*, 97–113.

Rose, G.M. and Shoham, A. (2002). Export performance and market orientation: establishing an empirical link. *Journal of Business Research*, *55*, 217–25.

Rose, L. (1999). Citizen (re)orientations in the welfare state: From private to public citizens? In J. Bussemaker (Ed.), *Citizenship and Welfare State Reform in Europe* (pp. 131–48). London: Routledge.

Rose, R. (1993). *Lesson Drawing in Public Policy*. New Jersey: Chatham House.

Rosenfeld, R. and Servo, J.C. (1990). Facilitating innovations in large organizations. In M.A. West and J.L. Farr (Eds), *Innovation and Creativity at Work* (pp. 28–33). England: Wiley.

Rourke, F.E. (1992). Responsiveness and neutral competence in American bureaucracy. *Public Administration Review*, *52,* 539–46.

Ruekert, R.W. and Walker, O.C. Jr. (1987). Marketing's interaction with other functional units: A conceptual framework and empirical evidence. *Journal of Marketing*, *51*, 1–19.

Ruhil, A.V.S. (2000). New ethical imperatives. *Journal of Public Administration Research and Theory, 10*, 831–4.

Ruscio, K.P. (1997). Trust in the administrative state. *Public Administration Review*, *57*, 454–8.

Saris, W. and Stronkhorst, H. (1984). *Causal Modeling in Non-experimental Research: An Introduction to the LISREL Approach*. Amsterdam: Sociometric Research Foundation.

Schachter, H.L. (1997). *Reinventing Government or Reinventing Ourselves*. Albany: State University of New York Press.

Schall, E. (1997). Public-sector succession: A strategic approach to sustaining innovation. *Public Administration Review*, *57*, 4–10.

Schedler, J.L. and Wade, K.S.W. (1997). *International Perspectives on New Public Management*. Greenwich, CT: JAI Press.

Schein, E.H. (1985). *Organizational Culture and Leadership*. San Francisco, CA: Jossey Bass.

Schnake, M. (1991). Organizational citizenship: A review, proposed model, and research agenda. *Human Relations*, *44*, 735–59.

Schneider, A.L. (1999). Public-private partnerships in the U.S. prison system. *The American Behavioral Scientist*, *43*, 192–208.

Schwartz, R. (2001). Managing government-third sector collaboration: Accountability, ambiguity, and politics. *International Journal of Public Administration*, *24*, 1161–89.

Scott, S.G. and Bruce, R.A. (1994). Determinates of innovative behavior: A path model of individual innovation in the workplace. *Academy of Management Journal, 37*, 580–607.

Selnes, F., Jaworski, B.J., and Kohli, A.K. (1996). Market orientation in United States and Scandinavian companies: A cross-cultural study. *Scandinavian Journal of Management*, *12*, 139–57.

Senge, P.M. (1990). *The Fifth Discipline.* New York: Doubleday.

Shavinina, L.V. (2003). *The Handbook of Innovation.* Oxford: Pergamon.

Shoham, A. and Rose, G.M. (2001). Marketing orientation: A replication and extension. *Journal of Global Marketing*, *14*(4), 2–25.

Siegel, S.M. and Kaemmerer, W.F. (1978). Measuring the perceived support for innovation in organizations. *Journal of Applied Psychology*, *63*, 553–95.

Simonsen, W. and Robbins, M.D. (2000). *Citizen Participation in Resource Allocation.* Boulder, CO: Westview.

Sitkin, R.B. and Pablo, A.L. (1992). Reconceptualizing the determinants of risk behavior. *Academy of Management Review*, *17*, 9–38.

Skarlicki, D.P. and Latham, G.L. (1996). Increasing citizenship behavior within a labor union: A test of organizational justice theory. *Journal of Applied Psychology*, *81*, 161–9.

Slater, S.F. and Narver, J.C. (1995). Does competitive environment moderate the market orientation–performance relationship? *Journal of Marketing*, *58*, 1, 46–55.

Sloan, S. (2002). Organizing for national security: The challenge of bureaucratic innovation in the war against terrorism. *Public Administration Review*, *62*, 124–5.

Smith, C.A., Organ, D.W., and Near, J.P. (1983). Organizational citizenship behavior: Its nature and antecedents. *Journal of Applied Psychology*, *68*, 653–63.

Smith, P. (1993). Outcome-related performance indicators and organizational control in the public sector. *British Journal of Management*, *4*, 135–51.

Smith, S.R. and Lipsky, M. (1993). *Non-Profits for Hire: The Welfare State in the Age of Contracting.* Cambridge, MA: Harvard University Press.

Sobel, R. (1993). From occupational involvement to political participation: An exploratory analysis. *Political Behavior, 15*, 339–53.

Soss, J. (1999). Lessons of welfare: Policy design, political learning, and political action. *American Political Science Review*, *93*, 363–80.

Staats, E.B. (1988). Public service and public interest. *Public Administration Review*, *48*, 601–605.

Stewart, J. and Ranson, R. (1994). Management in the public domain. In D. McKevitt and A. Lawton (Eds), *Public Sector Management* (pp. 54–70). London: Sage.

Stewart, W.H. and Roth, P.L. (2001). Risk propensity differences between entrepreneurs and managers: A meta-analytic review. *Journal of Applied Psychology*, *86*, 145–53.

Stipak, B. (1979). Citizen satisfaction with urban services: Potential misuse as a performance indicator. *Public Administration Review*, *39*, 46–52.

Stipak, B. (1980). Local governments' use of citizen surveys. *Public Administration Review*, *40*, 521–5.

Stivers, C. (1994). *Gender Images in Public Administration: Legitimacy and the Administrative State*. Thousand Oaks, CA: Sage.

Stivers, C. (2001). *Democracy, Bureaucracy and the Study of Administration*. Boulder, CO: Westview Press.

Stone, D. (2003). The "knowledge bank" and the global development network. *Global Governance*, *9*, 43–61.

Strang, D. (1991). Adding social structure to diffusion models: An event-history framework. *Sociological Methods and Research*, *19*: 324–53.

Strange, S. (1996). *Retreat of the State*. Cambridge: Cambridge University Press.

Subramanian, A. and Nilakanta, S. (1996). Organizational innovativeness: Exploring the relationship between organizational determinants of innovation, types of innovations, and measures of organizational performance. *Omega-International Journal of Management Science*, *24*, 631–47.

Suzuki, P.T. (1995). Public sector ethics in comparative perspective. *Annals of the American Academy of Political and Social Science*, *537*, 173–83.

Swindell, D. and Kelly, J.M. (2000). Linking citizen satisfaction data to performance measures: A preliminary examination. *Public Performance and Management Review*, *24*, 30–52.

Terry, L.D. (1998). Administrative leadership, neo-managerialism, and the public management movement. *Public Administration Review*, *58,* 194–200.

Terry, L.D. (2005). The thinning of administrative institutions in the hollow state, *Administration and Society*, *37*, 426–44.

Thomas, J.C. (1999). Bringing the public into public administration: The struggle continues. *Public Administration Review*, *59*, 83–8.

Thomas, P. and Palfrey, C. (1996). Evaluation: Stakeholder-focused criteria. *Social Policy and Administration*, *30*,125–42.

Thompson, A.A., Tancredi, F.B., and Kisil, M. (2000). New partnership for social development: Business and the third sector. *International Journal of Public Administration*, *23*, 1359–85.

Thompson, D. (1983). Bureaucracy and democracy. In G. Duncan (Ed.), *Democratic Theory and Practice* (pp. 235–50). Cambridge: Cambridge University Press.

Thompson, J.L. (1990). *Strategic Management: Awareness and Change.* London: Chapman and Hall.

Thompson, J.R. and Ingraham, P.W. (1996). The reinvention game. *Public Administration Review*, *56*, 291–8.

Ulbig, S.G. (2002). Policies, procedures, and people: Sources of support for government. *Social Science Quarterly*, *83*, 789–809.

Van de Walle, S. and Bouckaert, G. (2003). Public service performance and trust in government: The problem of causality. *International Journal of Public Administration*, (Forthcoming).

Van de Walle, S., Van Roosbroek, S., and Bouckaert, G. (2005). *Strengthening Trust in Government: What Role for Government in the 21st Century: Annex: Data on Trust in the Public Sector.* Analytical annex prepared for the OECD meeting of the Public Governance Committee at ministerial level, Rotterdam, 27–28 November 2005. Paris: OECD.

Van Dyne, L., Graham, J.W., and Dienesch, R.M. (1994). Organizational Citizenship Behavior: Construct redefinition, measurement, and validation. *Academy of Management Journal*, *37*, 765–802.

Van Ryzin, G.G. (2004). The measurement of overall citizen satisfaction. *Public Performance and Management Review*, *27*, 9–28.

Van Ryzin, G.G. (2005). Testing the expectancy disconfirmation model of citizens satisfaction with local government. *Journal of Public Administration Research and Theory*, *16*, 599–611.

Van Ryzin, G.G. and Freeman, E.W. (1997). Viewing organizations as customers of government services. *Public Productivity and Management Review*, *20*, 419–31.

Van Ryzin, G.G., Muzzio, D., Immerwahr, S., Gulick, L., and Martinez, E. (2004a). Drivers and consequences of citizen satisfaction: An application of the American Customer Satisfaction Index model to New York City. *Public Administration Review*, *64*, 331–41.

Van Ryzin, G.G., Muzzio, D., and Immerwahr, S. (2004b). Explaining the race gap in satisfaction with urban services. *Urban Affairs Review*, *39*, 613–32.

Van Waarden, F. (1992). Dimension and types of policy networks. *European Journal of Political Research*, *21*, 29–52.

Vardi, Y. and Wiener, Y. (1996). Misbehavior in organizations: A motivational framework. *Organization Study*, *7*, 151–65.

Verba, S. and Nie, N.H. (1972). *Participation in America: Social Equality and Political Democracy.* New York: Harper and Row.

Verba, S., Schlozman, K.L., and Brady, H. (1995). *Voice and Equality: Civic Voluntarism in American Politics.* London: Harvard University Press.

Vigoda, E. (2000a). Are you being served? The responsiveness of public administration to citizens' demands: An empirical examination in Israel. *Public Administration, 78*, 165–91.

Vigoda, E. (2000b). Internal politics in public administration systems: An empirical examination of its relationship with job congruence, organizational citizenship behavior and in-role performances. *Public Personnel Management, 29,* 185–210.

Vigoda, E. (2000c). The relationship between organizational politics, job attitudes, and work outcomes: Exploration and implications for the public sector. *Journal of Vocational Behavior, 57,* 326–47.

Vigoda, E. (2001). Reactions to organizational politics: A cross-cultural examination in Israel and Britain, *Human Relations, 54,* 1483–518.

Vigoda, E. (2002a). Administrative agents of democracy? A Structural Equation Modeling (SEM) of the relationship between public sector performance and citizenship involvement. *Journal of Public Administration Research and Theory, 12,* 241–72.

Vigoda, E. (2002b). From responsiveness to collaboration: Governance, citizens, and the next generation of public administration. *Public Administration Review, 62,* 527–40.

Vigoda, E. (Ed.) (2002c). *Public Administration: An Interdisciplinary Critical Analysis.* New York: Marcel Dekker.

Vigoda, E. (2002d). Stress-related aftermaths to workplace politics: An empirical assessment of the relationship among organizational politics, job stress, burnout, and aggressive behavior. *Journal of Organizational Behavior, 23,* 571–91.

Vigoda-Gadot, E. (2003a). *Managing Collaboration in Public Administration: Governance, Businesses, and Citizens in the Service of Modern Society.* Westport, CT: Praeger.

Vigoda-Gadot, E. (2003b). New public management. In J. Rabin (Ed.), *Encyclopedia of Public Administration and Public Policy* (pp. 812–16). New York: Marcel Dekker.

Vigoda-Gadot, E. (2003c). *Developments in Organizational Politics: How Political Dynamics Affect Employee Performance in Modern Work Sites.* Cheltenham: Edward Elgar.

Vigoda-Gadot, E. (2007). Citizens' perceptions of organizational politics and ethics in public administration: A five-year study of their relationship to satisfaction with services, trust in governance, and voice orientations. *Journal of Public Administration Research and Theory, 17,* 285–305.

Vigoda-Gadot, E. and Cohen, A. (2004). *Citizenship and Management in Public Administration: Integrating Behavioral Theories and Managerial Thinking.* Cheltenham: Edward Elgar.

Vigoda-Gadot, E. and Drory, A. (Eds) (2006). *Handbook of Organizational Politics.* Cheltenham: Edward Elgar.

Vigoda, E. and Golembiewski, R.T. (2001). Citizenship behavior and the spirit of new managerialism: A theoretical framework and challenge for governance. *American Review of Public Administration, 31,* 273–95.

Vigoda-Gadot, E. and Golembiewski, R.T. (2005). Rethinking citizenship in public administration: One more look in a series. In M.A. Rahim and R.T. Golembiewski (Eds). *Current Topics in Management* (vol. 10, pp. 241–62). New Brunswick, Transaction.

Vigoda-Gadot, E. and Kapoon, D. (2005a). Perceptions of politics and performance in public and private organizations: A test of one model across two sectors. *Policy and Politics*, *33*, 251–76.

Vigoda-Gadot, E. and Mizrahi, S. (2007). Public sector management and the democratic ethos: A longitudinal study of key relationships in Israel. *Journal of Public Administration Research and Theory*, (Forthcoming).

Vigoda-Gadot, E., Schwabski, N., Shoham, A., and Ruvio, A. (2005b). Public sector innovation for the managerial and the post-managerial era: Promises and realities in a globalizing public administration. *International Public Management Journal*, *8*, 57–81.

Vigoda-Gadot, E. and Yuval, F. (2003a). Managerial quality, administrative performance, and trust in government: Can we point to causality? *Australian Journal of Public Administration*, *62*, 12–25.

Vigoda-Gadot, E. and Yuval, F. (2003b). Managerial quality, administrative performance, and trust in governance revisited: A follow-up study of causality. *International Journal of Public Sector Management*, *16*, 502–522.

Vigoda-Gadot, E. and Yuval, F. (2004). The state of bureaucracy: Public opinion about the performance of government agencies in Israel and the role of socioeconomic and demographic variables. *International Journal of Public Opinion Research*, *16*, 1, 63–80.

Vroom, V.H. (1964). *Work and Motivation*. New York: Wiley.

Waldo, D. (1977). *Democracy, Bureaucracy, and Hypocrisy*. A Royer Lecture. Berkeley, CA: Institute of Governmental Studies, University of California.

Walker, J. (1969). The diffusion of innovation among American states. *American Political Science Review*, *63*, 880–99.

Wayne, S.J. and Green, S.A. (1993). The effects of leader–member exchange on employee citizenship and impression management behavior. *Human Relations*, *46*, 1431–40.

Weber, M. (1958). *The Protestant Ethic and the Spirit of Capitalism*. New York: Scribner

Webler, T. and Tuler, S. (2000). Fairness and competence in citizen participation: Theoretical reflections from a case study. *Administration and Society*, *32*, 566–95.

Webster, F.E. Jr (1988). The rediscovery of the marketing concept. *Business Horizons*, *31* (3), 29–39.

Weeks, E.C. (2000). The practice of deliberative democracy: Results from four large-scale trials. *Public Administration Review*, *60*, 360–71.

Weiss, L. (Ed.) (2003). *States in the Global Economy: Bringing Domestic Institutions Back In*. Cambridge: Cambridge University Press.

Welch, E.W. (2005). Linking citizen satisfaction with e-government and trust in government. *Journal of Public Administration Research and Theory*, *15*, 371–91.

Wilenski, P. (1980). Efficiency or equity: Competing values in administrative reform. *Policy Studies Journal*, *9*, 1239–49.

Willbern, Y. (1984). Types and levels of public morality. *Public Administration Review*, *44*, 102–108.

Wilson, J.Q. (1987). *Bureaucracy*. New York: Basic Books.

Winkler, F. (1987). Consumerism in health care: Beyond the supermarket model. *Policy and Politics*, *15*, 1–8.

Witt, L.A., Andrews, M.C., and Kacmar, M. (2000). The role of participation in decision-making in the organizational politics–job satisfaction relationship. *Human Relations*, *53*, 341–58.

Woller, G.M. (1998). Toward a reconciliation of the bureaucratic and democratic ethos. *Administration and Society*, *30*, 85–109.

Yankelovich, D. (1991). *Coming to Public Judgment: Making a Democracy Work in a Complex World*. Syracuse, NY: Syracuse University Press.

Young, B.S., Worchel, S., and Woehr, D.J. (1998). Organizational commitment among public service employees. *Public Personnel Management*, *27*, 339–48.

Index

Abrahamson, E. 167
accountability 50–51, 53, 59–60, 217–18
active citizenship 70–72, 208–9
Adams, M. 15
AIDS policy 168–69
Aiken, M. 87
Almond, G.A. 56, 73, 88, 109, 118, 201, 205, 208
Argyris, C. 173
Aristotle 198
Aucoin, P. 21, 22
Avolio, B.J. 123, 131

Balk, W.K. 49, 59
Barber, B. 68, 73, 89, 96
Barker, E. 188
Barner, C. 89, 204
Baron, R.M. 110, 138, 139
Bass, B.M. 123, 131
Bentler, P.M. 127
Berelson, B.R. 208
Berman, E.M. 47, 59, 60, 74, 136, 163
Bernstein, P. 198
Berry, F.S. 166, 174
Block, P. 56
Bollen, K.A. 127
Bonett, D.G. 127
Borins, S. 54, 169, 170, 173, 176, 180, 182, 186
Bouckaert, G. 22, 47, 85, 98, 136, 166, 183
Box, R. 29, 105
Box, R.C. 67, 68, 70, 75, 80, 81, 82, 83–84, 117, 124, 129, 131, 151, 205
Bozeman, B. 49, 67, 142
Brady, H. 99, 204, 208
Brady, H.E. 88, 89, 136
Braithwaite, J. 191, 194
Brief, A.P. 68, 82
Brinton, M.H. 76

Bruce, R.A. 185
Brudney, J.L. 68, 72, 76
bureaucracy
    versus democracy 29–30
    meanings of 199–200
    roots of 154–55
bureaucracy-democracy interaction study (Israel)
    alternative model, direct effects 122f, 123–24
    causal implications, caution over 132
    citizens' responsibilities 132
    decision-making, participation in 123, 130, 131–32
    descriptive statistics and inter-correlations matrixes 99, 100, 125t, 126t, 127
    dual-source approach 147
    empirical longitudinal effort, implications of 146–47
    fully mediated model 122f, 123–24
    future endeavors 132–33
    goodness of fit indices 101, 102, 126t, 127–28
    Israeli culture, study confined to 133
    managerial quality, investment in 131
    mediating model 129
    models, non-equivalence of 132
    NPM-style reforms, calls for 129
    organizational data 125
    path coefficients and explained variance 102–3, 102t, 127t, 128–29
    perceived performance, as buffer 130
    pilot study 124–25
    representative bureaucracy 129
    satisfaction-trust relationship 130
    source bias/common method error 132
    spillover theory 121, 130
    theoretical model 121–23

variables, inter-correlations between
        99, 100
bureaucratic-democratic paradox
        black box interface 43–44, 43f, 93,
            197
        literature on 1–2
        reconciliation of 151–53
Buss, T.F. 42, 131–32, 204

Cabula, R.J. 50
Caiden, G. 61
Caiden, N. 61
Camdessus, M. 37–38
Campbell, A. 208
Carayannis, E.G. 176
Carlson, D.S. 57, 135
Carnis, I. 25, 26
Carter, N. 49, 58, 59
Charng, H.W. 75, 79, 200
Chi, K.S. 60, 129, 130, 208
citizens' committees 83
citizens' conferences 83
citizenship behavior
        democracy 67–68
        individual level 75–76
        macro-citizenship (MC3) 78–79
        meta-citizenship (MC4) 79
        micro-citizenship (MC1) 77–78
        midi-citizenship (MC2) 78
        multi-dimensional model of 80
        NPM 80–82
        participation 72–75
Citrin, J. 14, 15, 85, 86, 96, 98
civic society 205
Coble, R. 76
Cohen, A. 68, 75, 77, 140, 201, 202
collaboration
        citizenship types 201–3
        conflict management 31
collaboration, in public administration
        bureaucratic-democratic paradox
            151–53
        citizen passivity 151–52
        cross-sectoral collaboration 152
        freedom of voice 163
        future of 163–64
        governability 153–54, 158–59
        management science 162

political science 162
        as problematic 162–63
        public administration, types of
            154–55, 160–61
        as reform in progress 161
        responsiveness 151, 155–59
        sociology 162
        and strong nations 160–61
        Weberian legacy 162
        welfare state, and competition 152
Collin, S.O. 159
community involvement 73, 89, 109, 222
competition 152, 165
Conover, P.J. 75, 200
contingency theory 182
Cooper, T.L. 51, 55
corporatism 13–14
Cotton, J.L. 68
Coulson, A. 85
Craig, S.C. 89
creativity 50, 51, 53–54, 218
Crewe, I. 75, 200
Cropanzano, R. 142, 173
Crozier, M. 12
Customer Satisfaction Index 135

Dahl, R.A. 12, 107
Damanpour, F. 166, 172, 173, 174, 184,
        185
de Pouvourville, G. 167, 169, 182
decision-making, participation in
        authentic participation 87
        bureaucracy-democracy interaction
            study 123, 130, 131–32
        participation ladder 86–87
        perceived performance 86, 130
        political participation 130, 209
DeLeon, L. 51, 55, 135
democracy
        active citizenship 70–72
        versus bureaucracy 29–30
        citizens as clients 69–72
        community involvement 89
        discrimination 90–91
        exit, power of 69
        good citizenship 83–84
        good soldier syndrome 71, 200
        governability 39–40, 69–72, 82–83

Israeli, unique characteristics of
119–20
liberal values 29
loop model of 67
new models of 198
participation 86–87, 88, 91
political efficacy 89–90
public administration, decline of
70–71
representation 90–91
social contract 69–70
technology 204–5
trust 85–86, 91, 195, 196–97
values, enriching 197
voice, power of 69
see also citizenship behavior;
managerial quality, and
performance (study)
democratic participatory behavior (DPB)
88
Deshpande, R. 172, 173, 175, 186
Dess, G.G. 183, 185
Dienesch, R.M. 71
Dolowitz, D. 189
Drahos, P. 191, 194
Drory, A. 57, 142, 145
Drucker, P. 78, 130, 131
Duncombe, W.D. 72, 76
Dunham, R.B. 174
Dye, T. 12, 176

Earley, C.P. 78
Eisinger, R.M. 163
Elden, M. 198
Erber, R. 96
Erez, M. 56, 78, 137
Esman, M.J. 135
ethics
managerial quality 50, 51, 55–56
questionnaire 219
see also organizational politics study
Etzioni, A. 31, 71, 73, 89
Etzioni-Halevy, E. 9, 10, 11, 12, 13, 14
(9–14), 27
Evans, K.G. 174, 181

Fandt, P.M. 56, 173
Fanklin, B. 167

Farazmand, A. 176, 181, 182, 184
Farh, J. 123
Farley, J.U. 172, 175
Feltey, K.M. 48, 71, 76
Ferris, G.R. 56–57, 57, 135, 173
Finkel, S.E. 90
Finkelstein, N.D. 53
Finnemore, M. 192
Fleming, A. 168
Folger, R. 173
Fombrun, C. 65
Fomburn, C.J. 65
Fornell, C. 107
Fox, C.J. 17, 44, 67, 205
Frambach, R.T. 174
Frederickson, G.H. 31, 67, 68, 72, 79, 83,
205
Freeman, E.W. 62
Freeman, R.E. 198

Gaebler, T. 17, 19, 40, 49, 166, 180, 208
Galton problem 191
game theory 30
Gandz, J. 56
Garson, G.D. 20, 21, 22
Gawthrop, L.C. 51, 55, 104, 134, 136,
142, 145, 146
Giddens, A. 17, 40, 205
Gidron, B. 76, 159
Glaister, S. 159
global reforms, in public administration
administrative reforms 187
global village, strong nations in 194
innovation 176, 177f
public policy 54, 187–88, 193–94
see also policy transfer, and policy
diffusion
Goel, M.L. 88, 89, 136
Goldoff, A.C. 135
Golembiewski, R.T. 22, 23, 51, 54, 65,
67n1, 162, 169, 173, 180, 181,
198n, 199, 200, 202, 202f, 203,
204, 205
Gonzalez, E. 176
good citizenship 83–84
good soldier syndrome 71, 200
Goodsell, C.T. 199
Gopalakrishnan, S. 184, 185

governability
  bottom-up 30, 31–33
  bureaucracy 206
  citizenship-infused 82–83
  communal solidarism 31
  concept of 2–3
  democratic pressures 39–40, 42–43
  discontent, sources of 42–43
  economic growth 34–36, 34f, 35, 36f
  governance types 32–33, 33t
  governments, need to rule 206
  grass-roots-driven models 31–32
  instrument types 32t
  performance 29
  planned change 30
  players 32–33
  political transformations 41–42
  professionalism 207–8
  rational choice theory 30–31
  red tape, reducing 207
  responsiveness 158–59
  September 11 effect 153–54
  social/economic exchange theory 31
  socio-cultural transformations 40–41
  stress, curve model of 43
  technical transformations 42
  top-down 30–31
  welfare state, decline of 37–39
  world transformations 40
governance types 32–33, 33t
Gow, J.I. 185
Graham, J.W. 71, 73, 76, 80, 201, 202
Grandey, A. 175
Grant, N.K. 49, 50, 51, 59
Gray, V. 190
Green, S.A. 123
Grubbs, J.W. 159
Guo, K. 131–32

Haas, M.P. 191
Hage, J. 87
Halachmi, A. 47, 53, 109
Hall, A.P. 192
Harris, K.L. 57
Harrison, J.B. 198
Hart, D.K. 49, 50, 51, 59
Heater, D. 79, 199
Hegel, G.W.F. 9

Henry, G.T. 14, 49, 61
Hibbing, J.R. 14, 15, 105, 208
Hill, C.J. 117
Hirschman, A.O. 60, 78, 208
Hobbes, T. 69–70, 199
Hobby, G.L. 168
Holzer, M. 50, 51
Hood, C. 7, 20, 166, 176, 181, 184
Hulin, L.C. 78
Hunt, R.G. 202
Hurd, D. 73

image 64–66, 216
Immerwahr, S 62
Ingraham, P.W. 133, 134, 135, 142, 165,
    174, 180
innovation
  achieving 179, 182–83
  antecedents to 172–74
  bureaucratic experiences 168–69
  bureaucratic structure 173–74
  competition 165
  defining 167
  disciplinary origins of 178, 180–81
  elements of 185–86
  evaluating 179, 183
  globalization 176, 177f
  holistic 176
  idea *versus* process 167
  ideas, flow of 178, 182
  individual outcomes 174–75
  information management 172–73
  intra-organizational conflicts 173
  key beneficiaries of 178, 181
  meaning of 178, 180
  modernization 165–66
  moral justifications for 179, 183–84
  need for 178, 180
  and NPM 166, 176, 180, 181, 183, 184
  organizational outcomes 175
  players 179, 182
  primary goals of 178, 181
  problems of in public sector 169–70
  sociopolitical firewall 175–76
  system-based approach 166, 170–76
  top public management 174
Irvin, R.A. 86, 87, 106, 107

Jacobson, R. 175
Jacoby, W. 189, 191, 193
Janoski, T. 76
Jaworski, B.J. 172, 173, 174, 186
John, D. 160
Jordan, A. 31–32
Joyce, M.S. 80

Kaase, M. 88
Kacmar, K.M. 56–57, 135, 173
Kaemmerer, W.F. 186
Kahn, L.M. 50
Kahn, R.L. 71, 74
Kapoon, D. 133, 173
Katz, D. 71, 74
Keller, R.T. 74
Kelly, J.M. 14, 61
Kelly, M.R. 49, 129, 134, 135, 144
Kenny, D.A. 110, 116, 138, 139
Kimberly, J.R. 54, 167, 169, 182
King, C. 12, 14, 15, 48, 71, 73, 75, 76, 84,
    86, 87, 107, 124, 131, 164, 180,
    182, 186, 205
King, D.C. 105, 208
Kipnis, D. 56, 137, 173
Koch, J. 50
Kohli, A.K. 172, 173, 174, 186
Konovsky, M. 75, 201
Kraemer, K. 67
Kramer, R.M. 76, 84, 159, 164
Kuhn, T.S. 168

Lane, R. 15, 52
Latham, G.L. 123
Lau, R.R. 96
Lazarsfeld, P.F. 208
leadership 50, 51–53, 123, 217
Lennon, M.J. 15
Levi-Faur, D. 181, 187n, 190t
Lewin, K. 57, 65, 136, 158
Lipski, M. 76
Listhoug, O. 14, 15
Locke, J. 199
Luhmann, N. 85
Lui, T.T. 51, 55
Luks, S. 14
Lum, L. 74
Lumpkin, G.T. 183, 185

Lynn, L.E. 21, 24, 67, 70, 155, 181

Maastricht Treaty 39
Machiavelli, N. 199
MacKenzie, S.B. 68, 75, 82, 84, 201
Majone, G. 188–89
managerial quality, and performance
    accountability 50–51, 53
    citizens' perspective 49
    communication channels 57–58
    creativity 50, 51, 53–54
    ethics 50, 51, 55–56
    human resource management approach
        50
    image 64–66
    innovation 50, 51, 53–54
    leadership 50, 51–53
    managerial quality 50–51
    NPM, and Performance Indicators 47,
        49, 58–62
    operative measurement 51
    organizational politics, perceptions of
        56–57
    perceptual approach 66
    performance indicators 48
    political economy approach 48
    professionalism 50, 51–53
    public opinion 48–49
    public *versus* private sector
        performance 47–48
    reputation 64–66
    stress 57–58
    transparency 50–51, 53
managerial quality, and performance
    (study)
    citizen participation 106–8
    citizenry principles 118
    community involvement 109
    control variables used 109
    cozy chair effect 118–19
    democratic participatory behavior
        117–18
    demographic variables 116–17
    Israeli democracy, unique
        characteristics of 119–20
    managerial quality, and participation
        107
    methods and data 94–95

monopolistic government services 107
multiple hierarchical regression
    analyses 110, 113, 114–16
NMP approach 108, 109, 119
political participation 109
public sector performance 108
questionnaire 94–95
research variables 95, 95t, 110, 111,
    112, 118
response rate 94
spillover theory 118
trust 109
marketplace, nations as 8f, 9, 25–27
Marsh, A. 88
Marsh, D. 189, 191, 193
Marshall, D. 83
Marshall, G.S. 29, 105
Marshall, T.H. 72, 118, 205
Marx, K. 9
Marxist theory 9–10
Mattei, F. 89
McKevitt, D. 75
McPhee, W.N. 208
McPherson, J.M. 76
Medsker, G.J. 127
Meseguer, C. 192
Meyer, J.W. 190
Michael, H. 76
Michels, R. 9
Milbrath, L.W. 73, 88, 89, 136, 208
Miles, R.E. 65, 174
Miller, A.H. 14, 15
Miller, H.T. 17, 44, 67, 205
Miller, W.E. 208
Mintzberg, H. 56
Mises, L. 25, 26–27, 31
Mishler, W. 15
Mizrahi, S. 106n, 107, 121, 121n, 129, 147
Monroe, K.R. 75, 79, 200
Montesquieu, C.-L. 73, 199
Moon, M.J. 174
Moorman, R.H. 123
morality *see* ethics
Morrison, E.W. 68, 77, 82
Mosa, G. 9
Mosher, F. 106, 108, 117, 121, 129
Motowidlo, S.J. 68, 82
Muczyk, J.P. 173

Murray, V.V. 56
Muste, C. 85, 86, 96, 98
Muzzio, D. 62

Nagel, J.H. 88
Nalbandian, J. 134, 140, 160
Narver, J.C. 172, 173, 175, 180
nation building
    authority, three types of 11
    concept of 5–6, 7–8
    corporatist view 13–14
    elite groups 9, 10, 12–13
    governments, mistrust in 14–17
    'iron rule of oligarchy' 10–11
    marketplace, nations as 8f, 9, 25–27
    Marxist theory 9–10
    organizations, nations as 8f, 9
    pluralistic view 11–14
    'science' of nations 27–28
    socio-political disciplines, nations as
        8f, 9–16
    technocratic view 12–13
nation-state, future of 193–94
nations, state of modern 5–6
Near, J.P. 68, 202
New Public Management (NPM)
    accuracy, testing for 157–58
    active citizenship 70–72
    administration *versus* management
        18–19, 21
    citizenship behavior 67–68, 84
    collaboration 158
    core principles of 20
    critique of 22–23
    definitions of 18, 20, 155
    democracy 84
    doctrinal components of 20
    governability 29, 69–72
    influence of 17–18
    innovation 166, 176, 180, 181, 183,
        184
    organizational politics 134–35
    popularity of 20–21
    reforms, need for 21–22
    responsiveness 151, 155–59
    satisfaction and trust, causality study
        105
    theoretical foundations 18–19

what makes it 'new' 20–24
see also Performance Indicators
Nie, N.H. 73, 88
Niehoff, B.P. 123
Niemi, R.G. 89, 135, 136
Nigro, L.G. 55
Nilakanta, S. 184
Niskanen, W.N. 25–26, 31
NPM *see* New Public Management
Nye, J.S. 14, 15, 96, 99, 105, 208
Nyhan, R.C. 59, 60

O'Connell, B. 76
Ohame, K. 193
Oliver, D. 79, 199
Organ, D.W. 68, 71, 74, 75, 77, 82, 123, 200, 201, 202
Organizational Citizenship Behavior (OCB) 68, 71, 75, 200–202
organizational politics study
    causal implications, caution over 145
    citizens' perceptions 134–35, 135, 136, 140
    citizens' satisfaction 142
    cognitive *versus* behavioral approach 136–37
    core variables, change over time 137, 140, 144f
    democratic system, attitudes towards 135–36
    ethical administration, roadmap to 144–45
    interdisciplinary perspective 140
    multiple regression analyses 138, 142t
    NPM reforms, and democratic polity 134–35
    organizational change 133–34
    relationships, direct and indirect 135
    research variables correlation matrix 137–38, 141
    revised model, path coefficients and effect sizes 140, 143f, 144
    satisfaction and trust, mediating effect of 138–39, 143t
    source bias/common method error 145
    spillover effect 133
    study limitations 145
    theoretical model 135–37

trust, in government 136
variables, quality of 145
voice orientations 136, 138, 142, 142t, 144
Osborne, D. 17, 19, 40, 49, 166, 180, 208
Osterman, P. 107
Ostrom, E. 30, 81
Overman, E.S. 20, 21, 22

Pablo, A.L. 185
Palfrey, C. 49, 59, 60, 61, 64, 156, 157
Parry, K. 123, 131
participation, of citizens
    civic virtue 73
    community involvement 73
    freedom and 'general will' 73
    improved commitment/performance 74
    national/communal arenas 72–73
    organizational arena 72, 73–75
    see also decision-making, participation in
passive citizen concept 39, 151–52
Pateman, C. 68, 74, 107, 198
Peled, A. 171, 181, 185
Pelham, A.M. 175
perception of organization politics scale (POPS) 135
performance *see* managerial quality, and performance
Performance Indicators (PIs) 183
    accountability 59–60, 60
    attitudinal-behavioral approach 59
    citizens' satisfaction, measuring 60, 61, 62–63
    economic approach 59
    internal performance measures 59
    outcome measurability 60
    performance-based culture 24
    public opinion 156–57
    public sector 58–59, 60, 61–62
    responsiveness, measuring 60–61, 63–64
    voice, option of 60
Perry, J.L. 67
Peters, G. 33, 117, 191
Peterson, S.A. 56, 68, 78, 80, 118, 121, 133, 136, 202

Pfeffer, J. 56
Pharr, S.J. 14, 15
Pierce, J.L. 174
Pierre, J. 130
Piliavin, J.A. 75, 79, 200
Podsakoff, P.M. 68, 75, 82, 84, 123, 201
Poister, T.H. 14, 49, 61
policy transfer, and policy diffusion
    convergence theories 193
    global policy networks 192
    learning *versus* emulation 192–93
    paradigm of diffusion, advantages of
        190–91
    paradigms 189–90
    policy diffusion, defining 189, 190t
    policy transfers, defining 189, 190t,
        191–92
    rationality, and process of change
        192–93
    state interests 192
    structural *versus* contagious causes
        191
Pollitt, C. 22, 49, 58, 62, 68, 70, 72, 81,
        109, 157, 166, 176, 180, 183, 208
Popper, K.R. 187
Porter, L.W. 131
Protestant Ethic 152
public administration
    decline of 70–71
    discourse theory of 205
    types of 154–55
public choice theory 25
Public-Private Partnerships (PPPs) 183
Putnam, R. 68, 73, 86, 107

questionnaire
    accountability 217–18
    business orientation 219–20
    citizens' satisfaction 212
    communication channels 220
    community involvement 222
    creativity 218
    image 216
    innovation 218
    leadership 217
    organizational politics 215–16
    political efficacy 220–21
    political participation 221

    professionalism 217
    reputation 216
    responsiveness 218
    social orientation 219
    stress 216–17
    transparency 217–18
    trust 213, 214–15

Rabin, J. 50, 51
Rainey, H. 19, 70
Ranson, R. 58, 60, 61, 63, 156
rational choice theory 25
Redburn, F. 131–32
Reed, B.J. 29, 105
Reinmann, B.C. 173
reputation 64–66, 216
responsiveness
    measuring 60–61, 63–64
    NPM 151, 155–59
    questionnaire 218
Rhodes, R.A.W. 64, 157, 191
Rice, R.W. 202
Richardson, W.D. 51, 55, 197, 200
Ridder, H.G. 117
Rim, Y. 56, 137
Rimmerman, C.A. 68, 74, 82, 117
Robbins, M.D. 86
Rogers, E.M. 166, 167, 168, 169, 171,
        173, 176, 181, 183, 189, 190
Romm, T. 145
Rose, G.M. 174, 186
Rose, L. 107, 192
Rose, R. 15
Rosenfeld, R. 185
Rosenwien, R.E. 89, 204
Roth, P.L. 172, 185
Rotolo, T. 76
Rourke, F.E. 12, 61, 63, 156, 160
Rousseau, J.B. 73, 199
Ruhil, A.V.S. 144
Ruscio, K.P. 96, 98
Russ, G.S. 56, 173
Ryan, K. 201

satisfaction and trust, causality study
    administrative performance 96–98
    causality 103–6

citizens' satisfaction, measuring 60, 61, 62–63
complexity 104–5
managerial quality/administrative performance/trust, relationships among 97–98f
midrange effects 98f, 99, 101–3
NPM approach 105
organizational politics 138–39, 143t
performance leads to trust 97f, 99, 101–3
questionnaire 212
trust, as psycho-political concept 96
trust leads to performance 97f, 98–99, 101–3
Schachter, H.L. 81
Schall, E. 51
Schein, E.H. 162, 176, 182
Schillewaert, N. 174
Schlozeman, K.L. 99, 204, 208
Schmidt, S.M. 56
Schnake, M. 123
Schneider, A.L. 159
Scott, S.G. 185
Searing, D.D. 75, 200
Selnes, F. 174, 175, 182
Senge, P.M. 173
September 11 effect 153–54
Servo, J.C. 185
Shanks, J.M. 208
Shanley, M. 65
Shavinina, L.V. 176, 180
Shoham, A. 174, 186
Siegel, S.M. 186
Simonsen, W. 86
Sitkin, R.B. 185
Skarlicki, D.P. 123
Slater, S.F. 172, 173, 175, 180
Sloan, S. 174
Smith, C.A. 68
Smith, J.N. 193
Smith, P. 49, 58, 59, 60, 81, 158
Smith, S.R. 76
Sobel, R. 68, 73, 78, 80, 89, 118, 121, 130, 133, 202
social choice theory 159
Staats, E.B. 50, 51
Stansbury, J. 86, 87, 106, 107

Stewart, J. 58, 60, 61, 63, 156
Stewart, W.H. 172, 185
Stipak, B. 14, 61, 62
Stivers, C. 14, 15, 63, 73, 75, 84, 107, 124, 134, 145, 156, 160, 164, 205
Stone, D. 191, 192
Strang, D. 191
Strange, S. 193
Structured Equation Modeling (SEM) 93, 132, 147
Subramanian, A. 184
Susel, B.O. 48, 71, 76
Suzuki, P.T. 51, 55
Swindell, D. 14, 61
system-based approach 166, 170–76

Tarde, G. 193
technology, and democracy 204–5
Terry, L.D. 23, 129, 130, 170, 176, 180
Theiss-Morse, E. 14, 15, 105, 208
third sector 74, 76, 80
Thomas, J.C. 86, 130
Thomas, P. 49, 59, 60, 61, 64, 157
Thompson, A.A. 48, 65, 104, 117, 119, 121, 145, 147, 159, 160
Thompson, D. 208
Thompson, J.R. 133, 134, 135, 142, 165, 174, 180
transparency 50–51, 53, 217–18
trust
    administrative performance 96–98
    definitions of 85–86
    democracy 85–86, 91, 195, 196–97
    governmental institutions 14–16
    managerial quality 109
    measurement of 85, 86
    micro-level of 85
    psycho-political concept 96
    questionnaire 213, 214–15
    see also satisfaction and trust, causality study
Tuler, S. 135

Ulbig, S.G. 104, 106, 130

Van de Walle, S. 85, 98, 136, 196
Van Dyne, L. 71, 73
Van Ryzin, G.G. 62, 135, 136, 137, 142

Van Waarden, F. 191
Vardi, Y. 77
Verba, S. 56, 73, 88, 99, 109, 118, 135,
    136, 201, 204, 205, 208
Vigoda, E. 14, 15, 22, 23, 29, 48, 49, 50,
    51, 54, 60, 67n1, 68, 75, 84, 85, 96,
    105, 106, 118, 124, 133, 135, 136,
    145, 151, 151n, 156, 157, 158, 162,
    163, 169, 173, 180, 181, 188, 200,
    201, 202, 205
Vigoda-Gadot, E. 31, 54, 57, 77, 85, 96n1,
    104, 106n, 106n2, 121, 121n, 129,
    133n, 135, 140, 147, 151n, 165n,
    173, 176, 181, 183, 187n, 190t,
    198n, 202f, 203, 204
voluntary and not-for-profit organizations
    (VNPOs) 165, 183
voluntary groups, coordination of 83
Vroom, V.H. 130, 131, 158

Waldo, D. 79, 104, 106, 108, 117, 121,
    129, 146
Walker, J. 190
Wayne, S.J. 123
Weber, M. 9, 152, 162
Webler, T. 135
Webster, F.E. 172, 174, 175

Weeks, E.C. 86
Welch, E.W. 136
welfare state, decline of
    demographic factors 37
    globalization 37–38
    public spending levels 38–39
West, J.P. 136
Wiener, Y. 77
Wilenski, P. 51, 55, 135
Willbern, Y. 135
Wilson, D.T. 175
Wilson, J. 76
Wilson, W. 79, 197, 200
Winkler, F. 49, 59, 61, 64, 156
Witt, L.A. 135
Woehr, D.J. 74
Woller, G.M. 108, 121
Worchel, S. 74

Yankelovich, D. 117
Young, B.S. 74
Yuval, F. 15, 85, 96n1, 104, 124, 129, 136

Zaltman, G. 173, 186
Zelikow, P.D. 96, 105, 208